DEVELOPING LEARNER AUTONOMY THROUGH TASKS

Andrzej Cirocki

DEVELOPING LEARNER AUTONOMY

THROUGH TASKS

THEORY, RESEARCH, PRACTICE

Copyright © 2016 Andrzej Cirocki

The right of Andrzej Cirocki to be identified as the author of this work has been asserted in accordance with sections 77 and 78 of the Copyright, Designs and Patents Act 1988.

Published in the United Kingdom by LinguaBooks

ISBN: 978-1-911369-01-1

A CIP catalogue record for this book is available from the British Library.

Proofreaders: Michael Butler, David Jay
Cover illustration copyright © 2016 David Almeida
Cover and task graphic design by David Almeida, SD Studio

Every effort has been made to trace the holders of intellectual property rights in respect of the content of this publication but the publishers will be pleased to hear from any copyright holder whom we have been unable to contact. If notified, the publisher will attempt to rectify any errors or omissions at the earliest opportunity.

All rights reserved, including the rights of translation into any foreign language. No part of this publication may be reproduced, stored in a retrieval system or transmitted, in any form or by any means, electronic, mechanical, photocopying, recording or otherwise, without the prior permission of the publisher.

This book is sold subject to the condition that it shall not, by way of trade or otherwise, be lent, re-sold, hired out or otherwise circulated without the publisher's prior consent in any form of binding or cover other than that in which it is published and without a similar condition including this condition being imposed on the subsequent purchaser.

LinguaBooks
The Elsie Whiteley Innovation Centre
Hopwood Lane
Halifax
West Yorkshire
HX1 5ER
United Kingdom

www.linguabooks.com

An imprint of
LinguaServe GbR
Zerrennerstr. 26
75172 Pforzheim
Germany

www.linguaserve.eu

I dedicate this book to two young pals
Dawid and Samuel
for the great deal of laughter and joy they bring

ACKNOWLEDGEMENTS

I owe a debt of gratitude to Prof. Dr. Wolfgang Hallet, Prof. Dr. Michael Legutke, Prof. John McRae and Prof. Teresa Siek-Piskozub, whose valuable advice in the course of writing this book, as well as detailed and constructive comments on the completed manuscript, helped me to make considerable improvements and determine its final form.

I would like to thank the research participants, both the teachers and the students from Polish secondary schools, for their participation in the mixed-methods study and for sharing their stories and experiences.

Also, I am very grateful to Cambridge University Press for giving me permission to use two pieces of copyright material. The first is adapted from Section 17.3 Features of access-self materials (pp. 417-418) in Chapter 17 "Access-self materials" of *Materials Development in Language Teaching*, edited by Brian Tomlinson and published in 2011. The second is Table 1 on page 24 of the *Common European Framework of Reference for Languages: Learning, Teaching, Assessment* originally published by the Council of Europe in 2001.

Finally, special thanks go to Michael Butler and David Jay, who proofread the final draft.

Any errors in this book are my own. I also bear full responsibility for its central argument and for any factual mistakes that may be found.

TABLE OF CONTENTS

List of Figures 10
List of Tables 11

Preface 13

CHAPTER ONE
FIRST THINGS FIRST 17

CHAPTER TWO
FOSTERING LEARNER AUTONOMY IN THE EFL CLASSROOM 26
2.1 Defining Learner Autonomy and the Autonomous Learner 27
2.2 Learner Autonomy in Language Education: The Roots 31
    2.2.1 Psychological Origins of Learner Autonomy 34
        2.2.1.1 The Zone of Proximal Development 35
        2.2.1.2 Interaction and Meaning Negotiation 37
        2.2.1.3 Mediation and Scaffolding 40
        2.2.1.4 Collaboration and Problem-solving 43
    2.2.2 Educational Roots of Learner Autonomy 45
    2.2.3 Learner Autonomy in Political Philosophy 46
    2.2.4 Autonomy as a Language Learning Concept 48
2.3 Approaches to Developing Learner Autonomy 49
    2.3.1 The Learner-related Approach 51
    2.3.2 The Classroom-related Approach 55
        2.3.2.1 Planning Classroom Learning 55
        2.3.2.2 Assessing Classroom Learning 58
    2.3.3 The Resource-related Approach 62
        2.3.3.1 Self-access Learning Centres 63
        2.3.3.2 Self-access Materials 65
    2.3.4 The Technology-related Approach 71
2.4 Conclusion 76

CHAPTER THREE
MATERIALS AND PEDAGOGICAL TASKS FOR DEVELOPING LEARNER AUTONOMY 78
3.1 Selecting Texts for Facilitating Learner Autonomy 80
    3.1.1 Criteria for Text Selection 84
        3.1.1.1 Connectivity 84
        3.1.1.2 Suitability of Language 86
        3.1.1.3 Suitability of Content 91
        3.1.1.4 Suitability for Personalisation 94
        3.1.1.5 Exploitability 96
        3.1.1.6 Variety 100
3.2 Pedagogical Tasks for Developing Learner Autonomy 103

3.2.1 Task Authenticity 109
　　　3.2.2 Task Complexity 113
　　　3.2.3 Task Purposefulness 115
3.3 Learner Autonomy in EFL Course Books 116
　　　3.3.1 Turning Course Book Activities into Learner Autonomy Tasks 122
3.4 Conclusion 124

CHAPTER FOUR
LEARNER AUTONOMY IN THE POLISH EFL CONTEXT:
A MIXED-METHODS STUDY 125

4.1 Background to the Study 126
4.2 Research Objectives 128
4.3 Why Combine Quantitative and Qualitative Methods? 130
4.4 Pilot Study 133
4.5 Learner Autonomy in the Secondary School EFL Classroom: The Study ... 138
　　　4.5.1 Participants and Time Allocation 139
　　　4.5.2 Research Tools and Procedures 140
　　　　　4.5.2.1 The Questionnaires 141
　　　　　4.5.2.2 The Journals 142
　　　4.5.3 Data Analysis 144
　　　4.5.4 Ethical Considerations 146
　　　4.5.5 Limitations of the Study 146
4.6 Conclusion 147

CHAPTER FIVE
PRESENTATION OF THE RESEARCH DATA 148

5.1 Learner Autonomy in the EFL Classroom: Inquiry 1 148
　　　5.1.1 Importance of Developing Learner Autonomy 149
　　　5.1.2 Undertaking Learner Autonomy Development 152
　　　5.1.3 Teacher Involvement in Task Development 165
　　　5.1.4 Obstacles to the Successful Development of Learner Autonomy 169
5.2 Learner Autonomy in the EFL Classroom: Inquiry 2 171
　　　5.2.1 Importance of Developing Learner Autonomy 171
　　　5.2.2 Learning Resources and Learner Autonomy Development ... 172
　　　5.2.3 Obstacles to the Successful Development of Learner Autonomy 182
5.3 Conclusion 186

CHAPTER SIX
DISCUSSION OF THE RESEARCH FINDINGS 187

6.1 Importance and Sustainability of Developing Learner Autonomy 187
6.2 Ways of Fostering Learner Autonomy 190
6.3 Involvement of Teachers in Task Development 194
6.4 Obstacles to the Effective Development of Learner Autonomy 198
6.5 Conclusion 205

CHAPTER SEVEN
DESIGNING PEDAGOGICAL TASKS FOR LEARNER AUTONOMY 206

7.1 Designing Pedagogical Tasks: The Model 207
    7.1.1 Reflecting on Past and Present Tasks and Thinking about Future Tasks 211
    7.1.2 Designing Tasks 212
        7.1.2.1 Goals 213
        7.1.2.2 Input 215
        7.1.2.3 Procedures 221
        7.1.2.4 Teacher Roles 222
        7.1.2.5 Classroom Setting 224
        7.1.2.6 Feedback 227
    7.1.3 Piloting Tasks 228
    7.1.4 Revising Tasks 229
    7.1.5 Implementing Tasks and Monitoring their Use and Impact 230
7.2 Final Remarks on the Model 231
7.3 A Bank of Tasks for Fostering Learner Autonomy 234

CHAPTER EIGHT
CONCLUSION, IMPLICATIONS AND FUTURE RESEARCH 245

8.1 Implications for Teacher Education and Materials Writing 248
    8.1.1 Implications for Teacher Education 248
    8.1.2 Implications for Materials Writers 250
8.2 Future Research 251

REFERENCES 253

APPENDIX A 300
APPENDIX B 315
APPENDIX C 317
APPENDIX D 324

Subject Index 325

LIST OF FIGURES

1. Features of access-self materials (adapted from Tomlinson, 2011a, pp. 417-418) 70
2. Common reference levels: Global scale (Council of Europe, 2001, p. 24) 90
3. What's bothering you?: An example of a course book activity 122
4. What's bothering you?: An example of a course book task 124
5. The teacher population: Age, gender, qualifications and employment status 139
6. The student population: Gender and Matura examination preferences 140
7. The importance of developing learner autonomy 149
8. The frequency of fostering learner autonomy 151
9. Readiness of teachers to develop learner autonomy in their teaching practice.... 151
10. The methods and techniques teachers employ to foster learner autonomy.......... 153
11. The teaching resources EFL instructors use to foster learner autonomy 154
12. The criteria teachers use to choose the Year One course book 156
13. The criteria teachers use to choose the Year Three course book.......................... 157
14. The criteria teachers use to choose Year One and Year Three course books........ 158
15. The effectiveness of Year One course books in promoting learner autonomy 160
16. The effectiveness of Year Three course books in promoting learner autonomy 164
17. The frequency of designing pedagogical tasks by teachers 165
18. The frequency of designing learner autonomy tasks by teachers 166
19. Learner autonomy tasks that should be included in course books....................... 168
20. Possible problems that prevent teachers from fostering learner autonomy 170
21. The importance of developing learner autonomy 172
22. Student satisfaction with the number of learner autonomy tasks received in the classroom 173
23. The promotion of learner autonomy by Year One course books: A student perspective 174
24. The promotion of learner autonomy by Year Three course books: A student perspective 177
25. The frequency of receiving non-course-book-based tasks 180
26. The contribution of non-course-book-based tasks to learner autonomy 181
27. Issues that may prevent the fostering of learner autonomy 183
28. Common responses about problems that prevent the fostering of learner autonomy 185
29. Developing pedagogical tasks for learner autonomy 208
30. Task instruction 218
31. Task stimulus material 219
32. Task table with pre-defined categories 219
33. Newsletter templates 220
34. Task A: Foreign language listening questionnaire 233

LIST OF TABLES

1. Research questions for Inquiry 1 and Inquiry 2 .... **128**
2. Pilot study data gathering **134**
3. The importance of developing learner autonomy **149**
4. The frequency of fostering learner autonomy **150**
5. Readiness of teachers to develop learner autonomy in their teaching practice **151**
6. The methods and techniques teachers employ to foster learner autonomy **152**
7. The teaching resources EFL instructors use to foster learner autonomy **154**
8. The criteria teachers use to choose the Year One course book **155**
9. The criteria teachers use to choose the Year Three course book **157**
10. The frequency of designing pedagogical tasks by teachers **165**
11. The frequency of designing learner autonomy tasks by teachers **166**
12. Learner autonomy tasks that should be included in course books **167**
13. Possible problems that prevent teachers from fostering learner autonomy **169**
14. The importance of developing learner autonomy **172**
15. Student satisfaction with the number of learner autonomy tasks received in the classroom **173**
16. The frequency of receiving non-course-book-based tasks **180**
17. The contribution of non-course-book-based tasks to learner autonomy **180**
18. Issues that may prevent the fostering of learner autonomy **182**
19. Common responses about problems that prevent the fostering of learner autonomy **185**

PREFACE

This book reflects my personal interest in the following two aspects of foreign language pedagogy: *learner autonomy* and *materials development*. Let me start off with learner autonomy, in which I have been keenly interested since the 1990s, when my teaching career began. My teaching has always aimed at empowering learners via innovative ways. I also try to encourage students to assume responsibility for their own learning. Yet my first steps in fostering learner autonomy were rather complicated.

Since I have always been a passionate teacher, I decided to take my first students on a learning journey based on innovative teaching methodology. I designed a four-year language pathway for thirty students in one of the secondary schools in Poland. I was their EFL teacher and also their head teacher. The students were divided into two groups and attended three hours (in Year One), four hours (in Year Two and Year Three) and five hours (in Year Four) of English a week. The course was based on the weak version of communicative language teaching. It gave learners plenty of occasions to use their target language for communicative purposes. All the classes were very interactive and engaging. The classes also required the students to work harder than the norm. The students worked in pairs and groups, were involved in both in-class and out-of-class projects, used computer technology for presentations, established their own reading club, staged *Macbeth* and took part in a one-semester extensive reading programme. Rarely did other students from this school and neighbouring schools have such opportunities.

Strangely enough, I soon realised that there was a gulf between the theory I learnt in a teacher training college and classroom practice. I was trained to incorporate interesting strategies and cutting-edge methodology into my teaching. However, I quickly learnt that the Polish system was not ready for such a drastic change, at least not in the area where I lived. For example, I was summoned to the Headmaster's office when I used communicative tasks and group work in the classroom. In his office, I was told to keep discipline during a lesson; classrooms were supposed to be quiet. Noise in the class indicated a lack of learning. Apart from communicative activities, I also involved my students in an extensive reading programme. They read short stories in the target language and later talked about them in the class discussion club. The students selected the texts they wanted to read and they decided which parts of the books to discuss with their classmates. Some of them wrote summaries of the texts, which I later analysed in the student reading portfolios. Again, the discussion club was quickly criticised. The idea of students selecting their own texts was also disapproved of by other teachers in the school and the students' parents. The common belief was that it was the teacher, not the students, that knew best what students needed and what they should do to succeed. Likewise, staging *Macbeth* was not enthusiastically welcomed in the school, either. Students were expected to learn English from course books. It was serious study that counted, not fun.

Despite these difficulties, I persisted with my plan. I felt my students found my teaching enjoyable. Also, I quickly saw the fruits of my work. On a few occasions, the students mentioned I was different from other teachers, which appealed to them. They liked that I regularly negotiated the teaching-learning process with them. The students had their say in the classroom. We were partners and made many decisions together. What is more, the target language was always used in the classroom, which provided the students with plenty of opportunity to use English in meaningful communication.

Then came the day of the Matura examination (equivalent to UK A-levels or the German Abitur) results. It turned out that all the students had passed the examination and achieved very high grades. The grades in the group concerned were much higher than in the other classes. Everyone was happy, including the parents and the Headmaster, who wished to continue this pathway in the new school year. "The time for change in this school has finally come", I thought. The second rewarding day came a month and a half later when I found out that a considerable number of my students had passed their entrance examinations to leading universities in Poland. Thirty percent of the students from my class became undergraduates in Teaching English as a Foreign Language, which was an impressive achievement for a small town secondary school.

I frequently implemented my own tasks in the classroom. This required that I either adapted various materials or created new tasks. The purpose was to engage students in their, not always easy, experiences with English as a foreign language. Initially, the process of designing engaging and useful tasks was difficult and time-consuming, but my enthusiasm for teaching would successfully overcome these obstacles. With time, I became increasingly satisfied with the outcomes and decided to share the tasks with my colleagues. The publication of some of the tasks turned out to be a major incentive for focusing on designing instructional materials on a larger scale. That is how my second research interest developed.

When I finished teaching at the secondary level in Poland, I went to the UK for some time. I met Marie McCullagh – Senior Lecturer in Professional Communication and Applied Linguistics at the University of Portsmouth. Her passion for materials design turned out to be highly infectious and I attended a number of her sessions on materials development. It was Marie that drew my attention to the nitty-gritty of creating, adapting and evaluating classroom materials.

The readings she recommended ideally supplemented her sessions. Many of these books and articles were written by Brian Tomlinson, Alan Maley or David Nunan. Their writings, as well as their conference speeches, heavily influenced my approach to materials development. This initial interest in materials design soon became one of my main research areas.

This volume is informed by my twenty years of teaching experience, thorough reading in the rapidly growing field of Applied Linguistics and my own empirical research in the area of foreign language pedagogy. I also want to stress that this volume would not have come to fruition had it not been for the effort, time, expertise and constructive feedback from Prof. Dr. Wolfgang Hallet, Prof. Dr. Michael Legutke, Prof. John McRae and Prof. Teresa Siek-Piskozub. I cannot thank them enough. At the same time, I assume full responsibility for the content of the book. May the reader not only enjoy the volume, but also benefit from it.

Andrzej Cirocki

CHAPTER ONE

FIRST THINGS FIRST

The purpose of this introductory chapter is to lay the ground for the book as a whole. In this chapter, relevant background information on learner autonomy, its place and role in modern language education and applied linguistic research are provided. Before delving into a detailed discussion on the fostering of learner autonomy and the designing of high-quality tasks, it is essential that the reader be familiar with the structure of the book, what content individual chapters contain and why the chapters follow this particular order.

It is becoming increasingly difficult these days to ignore the issue of learner autonomy in language pedagogy. There are two major reasons behind this. On the one hand, this concept has been part of seminal language education documents issued by the Council of Europe since the 1980s. Thus, learner autonomy is at the heart of successful EFL (English as a Foreign Language) instruction. The debate about the place and role of learner autonomy in language education began with *Autonomy and Foreign Language Learning*, published by Holec in 1981. More recently, however, the publications by O'Rourke and Carson (2010), Benson (2011), Irie and Stewart (2012) and Benson and Cooker (2013) have contributed to our deeper understanding of the concept at issue not only in the area of foreign language instruction, but also language curriculum and language policy. The other reason the issue of learner autonomy cannot be ignored is directly linked to the psychological, educational and philosophical roots of learner autonomy. All these factors contribute to the inherent complexity of this notion. It is the multidimensionality of learner autonomy that captures researchers' attention, and consequently lends itself to numerous empirical investigations and diverse interpretations.

Unfortunately, this complexity is more often than not a cause of misconceptions about learner autonomy (e.g. Martinez, 2008; Schwienhorst, 2011; Smith, 2003). For example, teachers tend to equate learner autonomy with self-instruction. This, however, is an erroneous statement. Self-instruction is defined as a learner's ability to plan, organise, direct and assess their learning experiences without teacher intervention. In learner autonomy development, as this volume will further show, teachers play a major role. They are responsible for, among other things, offering adequate support and guidance to learners at an appropriate time. Occasionally, learner autonomy is perceived as something teachers provide for their learners. The truth is that teachers cannot provide learner autonomy for their students because the concept in question is a referent of cognitive ability. Another misconception about learner autonomy is that it is related to a person as an individual, as opposed to a person as a social being. It is Lantolf (2008) that effectively tackles the concept of the individual from a social constructivist perspective. According to him, individuals are "formed on the basis of their relations with other human beings and on culturally constructed artefacts, including language" (Lantolf, 2008, p. 215). Besides, Lantolf (2008, p. 215) adds that "the source of the individual is situated not in biological genes but in the sociocultural world created by objective purposive activity" (Lantolf, 2008, p. 215). Individuals are not only brought into being through socialisation, but they cannot exist independently of it, either.

It is important to point out that the notion of learner autonomy has evolved in the past twenty five years. The definitions of learner autonomy that are available now are much more complex than those put forward at the beginning of the 1980s. Today, learner autonomy is more often than not conceptualised as a capacity for decision-making, choices, negotiation, control over the learning content, planning, assessment, independent action as well as critical reflection and analysis. In other words, the definition of learner autonomy encompasses three important levels of learning. These are: (1) learning management; (2) social, cognitive and affective processes and (3) the learning content. More specifically, developing learner autonomy requires both personal qualities and skills. The former are related to confidence, motivation and the ability to take the initiative in the learning process. The latter consist of various academic, intellectual and (inter)personal skills. Given this evidence, it can be inferred that the enhancement of learner autonomy on the part of learners is tied to the concept of learner development. As such, learner autonomy development can be characterised as a cognitive, affective and social development through which students increase both their awareness of themselves as foreign language learners and their readiness and capability of regulating their own learning in the social environment of the classroom. As students develop, they learn to handle unanticipated contingencies beyond the school walls.

Recent developments in the fields of Education and Applied Linguistics have led to an even greater interest in learner autonomy. It has become the focal point in educational policies around the globe (e.g. Benson, 2011; Benson & Cooker, 2013; O'Rourke & Carson, 2010). This strong interest also results from the fact that autonomy is central to lifelong learning and employability notions. The popularity of learner autonomy is well reflected in the numerous empirical studies and research projects conducted in different settings, including Canada, China, Germany, Hong Kong, New Zealand, Poland, Singapore and the USA. For example, Morita (2004) and Hawkins (2005) examined the construction of learner identities in the classroom community of practice. Gao (2007), in her case study, focused on how English learners contributed to the formation of the learning community. Pawlak (2008) measured the extent to which Polish secondary school students were autonomous learners. Hellerman (2008) probed how language learners engaged in paired teacher-assigned in-class tasks. Close attention was paid to how learners negotiated their participation in the classroom. Active learner participation and learner responsibility were also analysed by Kaupmann (2012). Chiu (2012) looked into the development of autonomous learning skills in reading and writing in an independent language learning centre. Kehrwald (2013), in turn, explored learner autonomy via her learners' beliefs about language learning.

Studies in learner autonomy have been carried out in a large number of areas and in a wealth of contexts. The reader, therefore, may raise questions about this volume's novelty and contribution to the field. These questions are completely justified. It must be clarified that this book takes into account the long tradition of the concept of learner autonomy in language education. It has been observed that in the past thirty years, the concept in question has been frequently portrayed as a theoretical notion with broad pedagogical implications. The purpose of this volume, however, is to ascertain whether learner autonomy indeed happens in the language classroom. In other words, this volume aspires to discover to what extent the notion of learner autonomy underlies teachers' and students' thinking and beliefs, teachers' instructional methods and approaches, the pedagogical tasks teachers use or design and the teaching practice of these teachers in general. Since very little attention has so far been paid to the link between learner autonomy development and pedagogical tasks, this area was selected as the subject matter for the present volume. It should also be accentuated that although numerous references are made to the Polish educational context, the material in this book is equally suitable for other contexts where learner autonomy exists in theory, but not yet in practice, such as all the former Eastern Block countries in Europe, as well as many Asian countries.

The focal point is addressed by discussing a number of issues involved in the design of learner autonomy tasks. For example, some of these issues are related to presenting characteristic features of complex tasks. Other issues deal with selecting suitable textual material to be the basis for learner autonomy tasks. The ensuing presentation and analysis of a mixed-methods study data, in turn, aims to reveal the current state of learner autonomy development in secondary school EFL classroms in Poland. More specifically, the study was conducted in four provinces and involved both teachers and students. The research questions posed in the study seek to ascertain whether teachers promote learner autonomy in their teaching practice, and if so, what methods and resources they employ to attain this goal. The study aims to find out whether or not teachers develop pedagogical tasks to help their students to become independent learners. It also investigates possible problems that impede the cultivation of learner autonomy.

As such, the current study expands on the theory and findings relating to learner autonomy within the field of Applied Linguistics. This project is original in the fact that it marries the two previously mentioned concepts: learner autonomy and pedagogical tasks. It is also hoped that the present study will serve as a springboard for similar studies, or replications of the current one, in other teaching contexts. Findings from different contexts can be compared and changes can be recommended so that optimal learning and successful language provision are promoted.

Returning to the project's research questions, it seems fitting to provide some expected answers. Considering the fact that modern language pedagogy has been embedded in Polish language curricula at all levels, the promotion of learner autonomy is expected to thrive in the classroom. Language teachers are believed to regularly create situations for fostering learner autonomy when using authentic texts, computer technology, collaborative learning and integrating meaningful tasks they designed themselves, to name a few. Course books are not considered to be the only available resource used.

Two problems can also be anticipated. For example, the examination--orientated instruction at the secondary level may be one of the serious impediments to effective learner autonomy development. Another issue may be related to a common procedure employed in many countries nowadays, namely minimising teacher education courses in terms of study contact hours as part of the government's savings strategy. In other words, insufficient knowledge of developing learner autonomy on the part of teachers may also be a source of dissatisfaction among research participants, both language instructors and students.

The overall structure of this book is made up of eight chapters. Before providing a brief description of these chapters, it is necessary to explain the adopted framework for the literature review in which the concept of learner autonomy has been immersed. The discussion in this volume is rooted in the philosophy of social constructivism. This philosophy promotes learner initiative, social interaction, self-reflection and learner collaboration as a way to learn new concepts, to name a few. All these tenets are closely related to the concept of learner autonomy. By force of circumstances, there is an emphasis on the constructivist origins of learner autonomy.

It should also be pointed out that constructivist learning environments underscore the role of meaningful context in language pedagogy. Constructivist classrooms promote tasks which involve both problem-solving and meaningful language use. With this in mind, the deliberation on developing learner autonomy is followed by a discussion concerning instructional materials and pedagogical tasks. Teachers must know which texts to select for designing holistic, complex and challenging learner autonomy tasks.

More specifically, the development of learner autonomy is the purpose of Chapter Two. This chapter begins with a definition of learner autonomy and a profile of an autonomous learner. Then, psychological, educational and philosophical roots of learner autonomy are introduced. The discussion favours the psychological origins of learner autonomy. For this reason, various tenets of social constructivism are included. These tenets lay the foundations for the subsequent discussion in the book. Chapter Two concludes by reviewing four approaches to the successful development of learner autonomy in the language classroom. The first approach is the learner-related approach. It seeks to combine language instruction with strategy training to help students to learn and think about their learning. The second approach is classroom-related. Language learners are seen as "developing practitioners of learning" (Allwright & Hanks, 2009, p. 2). This approach focuses on involving learners in curriculum negotiation, planning classroom learning and evaluation of learning outcomes. The last two approaches are resource- and technology-related. As their names suggest, the former promotes the development of learner autonomy through self-access centres, whereas the latter makes use of various educational technologies. In fact, these two approaches have much in common and could be discussed under the heading of a resource-related approach to fostering learner autonomy. However, because of the heavy emphasis on new technologies in the enhancement of learner autonomy, these two approaches are examined separately.

The discussion in Chapter Two reveals the various intricacies of learner autonomy. This chapter also emphasises that these intricacies need to be properly addressed in classroom practice for successful cultivation of the concept in question. For example, one of the central issues in the discussion is the need for appropriate materials and tasks. For this reason, Chapter Three inspects various text selection criteria and pedagogical task specifications for successful learner autonomy development. The initial discussion revolves around six text selection criteria. These are: connectivity, suitability of language, suitability of content, suitability for personalisation, exploitability and variety. The overview of these criteria additionally highlights the usefulness and need for multimodal texts in language pedagogy. Subsequently, pedagogical tasks and their features (e.g. authenticity, complexity, purposefulness) are discussed with regard to learner autonomy development.

The literature review shows that learner autonomy should be promoted in the classroom through a range of approaches. To check whether theory is reflected in practice, a research project was designed and conducted in the Polish secondary school EFL classroom. Chapter Four focuses on the research methodology employed in this project. First, this chapter provides a rationale for a mixed-methods study. A presentation of the pilot study, its aims and its outcomes are given. The subsequent sections in this chapter describe the research population, research tools, data analysis procedures, limitations of the study and ethical considerations.

The purpose of Chapter Five is to present the research data. The analysis of the gathered data is divided into two parts. The first part presents the data collected from teachers, whereas the second part deals with the data gathered from students. All the data acquired in this project were analysed both quantitatively and qualitatively, and consequently, presented either in bar graphs or in text form.

Chapter Six is devoted to the discussion and review of the research findings in relation to a wider context. Links are made to the literature review and the eight research questions posed in Chapter Four.

The discussion so far discloses a number of observations. The most interesting ones are that: learner autonomy is of interest to language educators, educational researchers, classroom practitioners and students; modern ELT materials do not sufficiently promote learner autonomy; complex learner autonomy tasks are in great demand and in-service EFL teachers do not engage in designing pedagogical tasks for their students. To address these issues, a model for developing pedagogical tasks for learner autonomy must be proposed. It is vital that teachers be familiar with the processes involved in task design. The model is the subject matter of Chapter Seven. Knowing the procedure, teachers will be able to design their own tasks and supplement course books. A collection of learner autonomy tasks is also displayed in Chapter Seven. The purpose of the exemplary tasks is to show teachers what tasks they could use in their own teaching practice to effectively promote learner autonomy. The design of these tasks has been underpinned by recent findings from applied linguistic research as well as the various tenets of social constructivism discussed in Chapter Two.

The final chapter, Chapter Eight, offers concluding remarks, various implications for teacher education and materials development and directions for future research. The aim is to enrich the system of language education in Poland, and possibly, in all the other contexts in which the fostering of learner autonomy is still not working. Future research should be directed at other aspects which can contribute to a more effective cultivation of learner autonomy.

To conclude, it should be emphasised that the various approaches to fostering learner autonomy suggested in this volume have been strongly influenced by what is referred to as self-directed learning. In language pedagogy, self-directed learning is defined as the type of learning that is directed by learners themselves. Learner self-direction is related to the individual features that lead to assuming responsibility for personal learning. More precisely, in order for self-directed learning to take place, learners must acquire autonomy and learn to act independently. As a result, learner autonomy and autonomous learning must be regarded as subsets of learner self-directedness and self-directed learning. It is necessary that the reader is aware of the difference between autonomous learning and self-directed learning. These two concepts are not the same and must not be used interchangeably. Unfortunately, as the literature shows, the terms *are* often used interchangeably.

To prevent another possible confusion in terminology, it is very important to distinguish between *instructional materials* and *tasks*. In this volume, materials are understood as anything (e.g. textbooks, CDs, videos, newspapers, graded readers) that can be used in the teaching-learning process to help learners with the target language. Tasks, by contrast, are in- and out-of-class activities that require learners to use the target language to attain specific objectives.

CHAPTER TWO

FOSTERING LEARNER AUTONOMY IN THE EFL CLASSROOM

Learner autonomy has been a pedagogical goal in foreign language classrooms for a number of years. Numerous educational documents and pedagogical literature (e.g. Benson, 2011; Council of Europe, 2001; Schwienhorst, 2008; Thomas & Reinders, 2010) invariably stress its significance by clarifying that on no account is learner autonomy an add-on competence that students should master, either in or out of the classroom. On the contrary, it is firmly stated that learner autonomy is an integral part of the teaching-learning process. The critical importance of fostering learners' autonomous behaviour lies in the fact that it assists learners in developing tools for critical reflection, supports lifelong learning and prepares language learners for successful communication in international settings. Hence, the cultivation of learner autonomy in a foreign language classroom cannot be limited to merely developing it in learning as such. The cultivation of learner autonomy must also refer to fostering learner autonomy in language use.

Since the following chapters will centre on the construct of task development for learner autonomy in the EFL classroom and will present a learner autonomy mixed-methods study, it is vital that teachers know what features the umbrella term of *autonomy* conceals, how these features are reflected in the profile of an autonomous learner, as well as how the features should be challenged in classroom teaching. Consequently, the discussion in Chapter Two will first concentrate on the definitions of autonomy delivered by language educators, practitioners and learners.

Then, characteristic features of autonomous learners will be displayed. To better understand the notion of learner autonomy in the context of language education, the history of this concept will also be presented. The historical overview will emphasise the social constructivist position which is a dominant feature of all further discussion in this book. The chapter will close with an overview of various approaches and materials for developing learner autonomy.

2.1 DEFINING LEARNER AUTONOMY AND THE AUTONOMOUS LEARNER

The notion of *learner autonomy* entered the domain of mainstream EFL instruction with Holec (1981), who defined it as the learner's capability of assuming responsibility for their own learning. This, in turn, means assuming the rationality for such aspects of the learning process as goal setting; selecting course content, as well as appropriate methods, techniques and strategies; monitoring the learning process and appraising all that has been learnt. Following Holec's line of reasoning, it can be concluded that autonomous learners are capable of controlling their own learning. In this vein, all the crucial decisions relating to both the management and organisation of this process are made solely by the learner (see 2.3.2).

The above definition describes the learning process as one in which independent learners are expected to exercise control. However, autonomy does not primarily focus on how learning is organised. Quite the contrary, learners take control over various cognitive processes which play a significant part in the efficient and productive self-management of learning. For instance, Little (1991, p. 4) points out that:

> (...) autonomy is a capacity – for detachment, critical reflection, decision-making, and independent action. It presupposes, but also entails, that the learner will develop a particular kind of psychological relation to the process and content of his learning. The capacity for autonomy will be displayed both in the way the learner learns and in the way he or she transfers what has been learned to wider contexts.

Little's definition seems of vital importance as it adds an essential psychological dimension. This element is more often than not absent in other definitions of autonomy. The focus on psychological aspects is also seen in the writings of Kenny (1993) and Peters (1998). In more detail, learner autonomy is perceived as an opportunity to become a person (Kenny, 1993) as well as in terms of metacognition, where learners not only verify, but also think deeply about the cognitive strategies they employ while learning (Cohen, 2008, 2011; Oxford, 2008, 2011; Peters, 1998; Vandergrift, 2008). Apart from the purely psychological dimension, a socio-psychological view of learner autonomy can be distinguished. The latter position, with the exception of the aspects mentioned above, stresses that autonomous learners actively contribute to the social processes of learning (Kehrwald, 2013; Lamb, 2013; Trebbi, 1990).

Another observation that can be made about the above views on learner autonomy is that they all share the same fundamental element. Autonomous learners ought to possess the freedom and volition to set their own objectives if the learning process is to be equated with genuine self--direction (Benson, 2001, 2011; Deci & Flaste, 1996). This is also in agreement with earlier discussions where autonomy was examined in a political framework (see 2.2.3) and regarded as an acknowledgement of the rights of learners in educational structures (Benson, 1997).

Having presented how language educators view learner autonomy, it is time to see how this construct is perceived by EFL practitioners. To a large extent, the theories and research of the former have influenced language teacher cognitions, that is, "what teachers think, know, believe and do" (Borg, 2003, p. 81). Taking part in various teacher development courses as a teacher-trainee and a teacher-trainer, I have observed that practitioners generally view learner autonomy in two ways. They see it first as a way to be willingly, creatively, strategically and reflectively involved in the process of learning both in and out of the classroom. They see it secondly as a way to make independent decisions and control the entire process of study so as to bring positive results. For instance, some colleagues have defined learner autonomy in the following way:

> *Learner autonomy is a capacity to individually make decisions about the learning process. Such decisions affect both the inside and outside classroom actions of students (Teacher 1, Denmark).*

> Learner autonomy is related to learners' ability to be responsible, reflective and strategic about their learning of English as a foreign language. Put simply, language learners successfully manage their learning experience and learn to think for themselves so as to be capable of constructing the reality round them (Teacher 2, Germany).
>
> Learner autonomy, apart from requiring one to be responsible for one's own ability to study English, includes self-discipline, confidence and persistence (Teacher 3, Sweden).

With teachers' perspectives on learner autonomy defined, it seems natural and proper to ask how learners view the concept in question. Being actively involved in teaching English as a foreign language to adults, I have so far had several opportunities to ask my international students to define what learner autonomy means to them. Some definitions are listed below.

> Learner autonomy involves making general decisions about English language learning, so I should be involved in making decisions about what I want to learn, what materials I will be using and how I will be assessed during the language course (Student 1, Austria).
>
> Learner autonomy means that students are in charge of their learning. They decide what and how to learn because they know their own motivations for learning English. Therefore, students should be allowed to apply different methods and then decide what worked and what did not, in order to avoid repeating the same mistakes (Student 2, Switzerland).
>
> Learner autonomy is equivalent to independent work. Also, learner autonomy is related to employing different techniques while learning and having a clear plan for achieving some aims. Autonomy makes me the manager of my own learning and allows me to assess my target language performance without routine class tests (Student 3, Norway).

The preceding discussion reveals the eclectic quality of the concept of learner autonomy in which various psychological, educational, social, cultural and situational factors play a role. In consequence, building a profile of the autonomous language learner is a complex task. The definitions presented above clearly reveal the characteristic features of the autonomous learner. Considering that the subject matter of this book is immersed in the philosophy of social constructivism (see 2.2), the profile of the autonomous learner combines the perspective of the learner, the perspective of the language classroom as well as the perspective of the wider social context in which learners operate. As a result, autonomous learners:

- have an intrinsically-motivated approach to learning the target language, which they regard as a means of communication;

- make cogent decisions and assume responsibility for their own learning;
- set individual and realistic targets for themselves as well as regulate their behaviour with regard to previously formulated goals;
- negotiate the syllabus, thus making decisions on course content, materials and course assessment;
- estimate personal strengths and weaknesses and choose their own learning tasks with reference to previously set objectives;
- identify what has already been discussed in the classroom as well as know when, how and why they learn new information and what available resources to resort to in order to be successful in foreign language learning;
- are able and willing to adapt to new learning contexts;
- select and implement appropriate strategies in order not only to fully make use of the environment they find themselves in, but also to be able to negotiate between their own wants and the needs of other members of the classroom culture;
- manage their foreign language learning experience, systematically monitor their progress and critically evaluate learning outcomes;
- are fully involved in collaborative practices, seeking guidance from peers and language teachers alike, if need be; and
- reflect on their learning experiences so that they can decide on what to do next.

As outlined above, many different features come together under the umbrella of *learner autonomy*, at the same time making teachers aware that defining autonomy from the perspective of learning must also be taken into consideration when promoting autonomous behaviour in the classroom. Furthermore, apart from their intrinsic value, all these definitions constitute solid foundations for the assumption that exercising responsibility for the learning process reshapes not only the interrelation between learners and existing knowledge, but also the way in which knowledge is constructed and developed in the classroom. As the literature reveals (e.g. Johnson, 2013; Komorowska, 2002a; Legutke, 1999; Rüschoff & Wolff, 1998; Siek-Piskozub, 2004, 2006; Ur, 2012; Wolff,

1999), learners construct their own view of the surrounding reality by reflecting on their individual experiences (see 2.3.2.2). Hence, it is recommended that instructors no longer regard teaching as a process of learning production, but as learning facilitation (Capel, Leask, & Turner, 2013; Johnson, 2013; Komorowska, 2002a; Legutke, 1999; Rüschoff & Wolff, 1998; Siek-Piskozub, 2004, 2006; Ur, 2012; Wolff, 1999). What is more, it is vital that learning be considered both an active and constructive endeavour through which learners change the facts offered to them into acquired knowledge in a skilful and effective fashion. These issues are discussed in detail in the sections to come.

2.2 LEARNER AUTONOMY IN LANGUAGE EDUCATION: THE ROOTS

As the preceding discussion reveals, the introduction of the concept of learner autonomy into language pedagogy is mainly ascribed to Holec (see 2.1). However, despite his considerable input, there were several other factors that made an indisputable contribution to the emergence and spread of the concept of learner autonomy at the end of the 1960s. For instance, the intense debate about autonomy came into being as a reaction against *behaviourism*, a theory which promoted learning through habit formation (Skinner, 1957). Contrary to its promise, behaviourism failed to elucidate the development of human language. Learner autonomy was also encouraged by the development of alternative currents of thought in education, philosophy, psychology (e.g. humanistic psychology or cognitive psychology) and linguistics (e.g. sociolinguistics), all of which highlighted the important role and active participation of the learner in the educational process. Additionally, technological advancements (e.g. TV, video-recorders, the computer, laptops, tablets) provided a large array of tools for the implementation of independent learning and self-attainment. Finally, different aims of learning as well as various learning styles of learners (see 3.1.1.4) required flexible language courses with varying degrees of learner-centeredness and autonomy.

It is notable that learner autonomy encompasses the philosophy of *constructivism* – a psychological construct and a contemporary philosophical viewpoint in education. This philosophy is generally defined as a theory of knowledge and learning which delineates precisely what knowing is and how humans come to know. It is also characterised as an educational philosophy within the larger category of philosophies described under *rationalism*. In turn, it is rationalism that holds reason as the primary source of information and reality as being constructed rather than discovered. Constructivism originated as a theory of learning which emphasises that reality is construed by the learner in the course of the learning process. Constructivism can more broadly be considered a theory of both personal and scientific knowledge, as well as a theory of teaching.

In the educational context of foreign language teaching, constructivism is illustrated in several ways. Firstly, it perceives human beings as active acquirers of knowledge (Capel, Leask, & Turner, 2013; Howe & Berv, 2000; Jennex, 2011; Rüschoff, 1999; Siek-Piskozub, 2004, 2006; Wendt, 2000). This active acquisition results from the fact that the function of cognition is adjustable and assists in the formation of the experiential world. Consequently, cognising subjects do not find truth but construct feasible accounts of their life experiences. Secondly, learning is regarded as a developmental and recursive process where active learners come into interaction with both physical and social realities (see 2.2.1.2). Finally, individuals engage in building personal views of the surrounding world by ruminating on their own experiences (Jonassen, 1991; Wąsik, 2006). Hence, it can be concluded that all cognising subjects create individual mental models when pursuing ways to read the world.

Additionally, the definitions presented above make it clear that constructivism is applied to two quite dissimilar concepts, namely: *social constructionism* and *psychological constructivism*. The former, established by the Edinburgh School of sociologists, maintains that knowledge is governed by sociological agents, including human interests or religion (Phillips, 2000). Accordingly, knowledge can be entirely elucidated in terms of sociology. However, not all supporters of social constructionism faithfully follow this strong position. In the past few decades, various schools of thought in the domain of social constructionism have emerged. For instance, *progressive constructivism* assumes that knowledge is only partially generated out of social relations. *Endogenous constructivism* posits that learners' knowledge construction and development stem from their exploration of and interaction with the external world. Finally, *exogenous constructivism* assumes that knowledge is the result of environmental interactions and a reorganisation of structures occurring in the external reality.

At the other end of the continuum lies psychological constructivism, a radical version of which is practised by von Glasersfeld. His numerous writings clarify two things. Firstly, knowledge resides in the heads of thinking subjects. Secondly, people construct what they know on the grounds of their individual experience.

The radical faction is countered by psychologists who consider the process of knowledge creation to be socially orientated (Phillips, 2000). The latter group affirms that knowledge is something humans, as social beings, do together on a regular basis. Thus, objective reality is produced by processes of social construction. Furthermore, since knowledge is socially generated, it varies across cultures because different groups hold different beliefs and attitudes towards human development. In addition, psychologists such as Vygotsky (1978), Luria (1979) as well as Feuerstein, Rand, Hoffman and Miller (1980) emphasise the role of language in modelling people's construction of knowledge and define language as a social phenomenon. It is clear therefore that it is through the medium of language that more knowledgeable others affect the way less experienced individuals come to understand. It should also be clarified that it is thanks to this latter group of psychologists that psychological constructivism is frequently termed *social constructivism*. It is this concept which underpins the argument in the present volume.

As can be seen, the idea of learner autonomy is not primarily a language learning concept. It has its roots in the psychology of learning as well as the educational reform and the political philosophy of the 20th century. The ensuing discussion will focus first on the psychological origins of learner autonomy. More specifically, there will be considerable emphasis placed on the framework of social constructivism, whose tenets are directly linked to the notion of learner autonomy – the subject matter of this book. Then, the educational and philosophical roots of autonomy follow. Finally, the focus will turn to autonomy as a learning concept.

2.2.1 PSYCHOLOGICAL ORIGINS OF LEARNER AUTONOMY

The notion of learner autonomy can be found in different psychological theories. For instance, autonomous learning was first discussed in Erickson's *Theory of Psychosocial Development*. Erickson's proposal makes references to Freud, but Erikson, in contrast to Freud, perceives children as active and inquisitive beings whose intention is to accommodate to their social realities. Erikson (1963) also gives far more prominence to the role of cultural influences in human development than Freud, distinguishing eight developmental stages in the theory, the second of which is the most relevant for the purposes of this discussion. This second stage, *autonomy vs. shame and doubt*, concentrates on the first three years of a child's life when they learn to control their bodily functions. At this stage, children develop a sense of personal control and independence from their carers, which guarantees them a sense of security and confidence. However, those who are not successful in experiences with autonomy feel shame and doubt (Erikson, 1963).

Another push towards learner autonomy can be traced in Rogers' *Experiential Learning Theory*, which promotes holistic development (see 2.3.3.2), where the process of learning involves learners both intellectually and psychologically (Rogers, 1969). In other words, learning is defined as a dynamic process of knowledge construction in which learners and teachers have different roles to play (McGrath, 2013; Müller-Hartmann & Schocker-von-Ditfurth, 2011; Renandya, 2012; Willis & Willis, 2007). As a result, learners are in charge of their own learning, whilst teachers are obliged to create active, student-centred, as well as personal, change- and growth-promoting learning environments.

Vygotsky's *Developmental Psychology* has also made a profound impact on the theory of autonomy in language learning. Inasmuch as this book centres on the constructs of learner autonomy development (see 2.3) and task design for learner autonomy (see 7.1) in the EFL classroom, the following examination is narrowed down to psychological notions that underpin the concept and successful facilitation of learner autonomy. The discussion of these ideas is intended to indicate salient aspects which will be taken into account while designing tasks for learner autonomy cultivation examined in Chapter Seven. The key notions to be discussed are: the zone of proximal development, interaction, meaning negotiation, mediation, scaffolding, collaboration and problem-solving. They are discussed in four sections below.

2.2.1.1 THE ZONE OF PROXIMAL DEVELOPMENT

Vygotsky's sociocultural theory highlights that instruction should occur in the *zone of proximal development* (ZPD), which is defined as:

> the distance between the actual development level as determined by independent problem solving and the level of potential development as determined through problem solving under adult guidance or in collaboration with more capable peers (Vygotsky, 1978, p. 86).

As this definition reveals, people in the ZPD are involved in construing meaning through socially-mediated interaction, whereby experts come into social interaction (see 2.2.1.2) with novices to assist them in both language learning and cognitive development. More precisely, novices are engaged in the transformation of what experts offer them (Lantolf, 2000). This transformation process is based on imitation, where novices are regarded as complex, culturally bound, communicative beings, not mere reproducers (Newman & Holzman, 1993). The marriage of imitation and collaboration (see 2.2.1.4) in the ZPD constitutes nothing less than a "source of all the specifically human characteristics of development" (Vygotsky, 1987, p. 210).

Considering the fact that this discussion concerns EFL instruction, the ZPD, by analogy, can be defined as the distance between the actual development level of learners as determined by independent performance in the target language and the level of potential development as determined through language generated with other class participants in a collaborative undertaking. Additionally, it should be noted that the ZPD, when transferred to classroom learning, is not the classroom itself, as is often believed, but the purposeful tasks occurring in it (see 3.2.3). In other words, it is collaborative problem-solving tasks that set up the ZPD for the participants of a class culture. The foregoing observation is rooted in Vygotsky's position that:

> an essential feature of learning is that it creates the zone of proximal development; that is, learning awakens a variety of internal developmental processes that are able to operate only when the child is interacting with people in his environment and in cooperation with his peers (Vygotsky, 19878, p. 90).

Consequently, learning occurs in relevant and meaningful tasks (see 3.2.1) since these enable novices and experts to construct products with their own intrinsic values (Goodman, Bird, & Goodman, 1991; Wells, 1994). In successful learning tasks, individual students' answers to classroom questions tend to result from prior knowledge and experience. These responses, however, are likely to draw other classmates to their ZPD. Therefore, it is necessary that tasks be open-ended, modifiable, multi-sensory and action- and whole-person-orientated, simultaneously enabling learners to structure and coordinate acts of knowledge creation (Jonassen, 1994; Liebenhoff, 2004; Müller-Hartmann & Schocker-v. Ditfurth, 2011; Rüschoff, 1999; Waschk, 2004; Wolf, 2002a). In general, it is advisable that learning tasks are planned in such a way so as to embrace both students' current level of language competence (see 3.1.1.2) and what they can learn with the help of others. In this vein, every lesson serves as a store of affordances and limitations to the learning process which takes place in the ZPD.

The present discussion challenges the perception of the ZPD as a physical space. It is, by contrast, a symbolic space in which learners become communicators within the social practices provided in the classroom (Lantolf, 2000). Thus, the ZPD, created in tasks, supplies environments in which class participants both teach and learn from one another, and where individual students' meanings confront social meanings.

It should be evident from all of the foregoing that the process of learning in the ZPD entails at least four types of transformation. These relate to: cognitive structures through which people make sense of information, learners' potential for future performance, tools and practices that mediate classroom tasks and the social context in which these activities are attended to. The ZPD additionally necessitates intense involvement from class participants and affective quality of interaction. The latter guarantees effective learning, based on trust, respect and integrity. Hence, the process of learning in the ZPD contributes not only to the development of skills, knowledge and learner independence, but also shapes learner identity and learner beliefs about the learning-teaching process (McKay, 2006).

The ZPD carries meaningful information for current language pedagogy and materials development. It is not a phenomenon that pre-exists in the language classroom nor is it the teacher's duty to find it. Conversely, the ZPD is a space for social interaction, which links learning with development. In this sense, the ZPD is constructed through action and social interaction and functions as part of the micro-culture of the language classroom. As a result, the process of teaching must not be confined only to delivering a standardised curriculum and evaluating its effectiveness. Teachers as well as curriculum and materials developers must be aware that learning is a complex process of internalising social experience. What is required then is high-quality tasks (see 3.2) and a distinctive teaching style which will bridge the gap between learners' current skill level and their potential level. A model for designing such tasks and examples of such tasks are the focus of Chapter Seven.

2.2.1.2 INTERACTION AND MEANING NEGOTIATION

According to sociocultural theories of learning (Gass, 1997; Lantolf, 2000; Lantolf & Thorne, 2006; Swain, Kinnear, & Steinman, 2015; van Lier, 1996), social environment plays a crucial role in the individual's intellectual development. Human beings develop differently in diverse sociocultural contexts and not only apply various mental abilities to solving problems (see 2.2.1.4), but also interpret their surrounding reality by relying upon the requirements and value systems of their own cultures (Vygotsky, 1978). Hence, human cognition is inherently sociocultural and determined by language, just one of the tools for intellectual adaptation individuals inherit from their culture. To be more precise, language is a sign system which children first learn in order to communicate with people in their culture; later, in becoming a mental process, it assists in the organisation of human thought (Vygotsky, 1978).

As can be seen, cognitive development co-occurs with linguistic and social development, all existing in a particular sociocultural context. Furthermore, attention, memory and consciousness stem from human social life and are constructed through interaction between children and other people in the course of development (see 2.2.1.1). Consequently, both social interaction and language must be regarded as vital elements in the construction of human knowledge (Pritchard & Woollard, 2013; Rüschoff & Wolff, 1998), since it is through social interaction that children construct meaning by comprehending the speech of others (Vygotsky, 1978). Language, on the other hand, unable to develop fully without instruction and interaction with more competent elders, is perceived to enable children to actively participate in the intellectual life of the surrounding community.

The concept of interaction can be analysed from two different perspectives, both of which are important for successful language learning. For instance, *intrapersonal interaction*, regarded as a reflective process, occurs in learners' minds and involves deep cognitive processing of input which, through internalisation and understanding, results in knowledge creation (Berg, 1999; Ellis, 1999). Internalisation, in turn, should be understood as a dynamic process through which learners' target language changes into both an interactive and cognitive resource for themselves. *Interpersonal interaction*, in contrast, applies to reciprocal events, and thus subsumes all types of contact between humans. It additionally deals with message (both verbal and non-verbal) transaction, leading to shared meaning creation and maintenance.

These shared meanings are the final outcomes of interpersonal negotiation and mutual understanding and are essential for human beings, as culturally organised existence is based on them. So is it dependent on mutual modes of discourse for negotiating distinctness in both meaning and interpretation (Bruner, 1990). It must therefore be recognised that meanings exist only in a world of shared understandings, thus making human nature dependent on culture.

There are three types of negotiation: *personal*, *interactive* and *procedural* (Breen & Littlejohn, 2000). The first one is a psychological process. It arises in two situations: when human beings search for understanding and when they make efforts to be understood by others. Interactive negotiation deals with circumstances in which people use language to show their understanding or lack of understanding of received input (see 7.1.2.2). It is interactive negotiation that stimulates the development of learner interlanguage discussed in this section below. Finally, procedural negotiation is used to reach agreements or solve problems (see 2.1.1.4). Interactive negotiation and procedural negotiation focus on sharing and disclosing meaning (Breen & Littlejohn, 2000).

Interpersonal interactions are valuable in the language classroom. Their aims are twofold: classroom conversations socialise learners into target language learning in pragmatically rich environments and provide opportunities for learners to experience how target language is employed in the social reality beyond the classroom (Donato, 2000). As a result, classroom interactions have been extensively researched and analysed from different angles (Gass & Varonis, 1985; Hellerman, 2008; Kötter, 2002, 2003; Krashen, 1980, 1989; Lantolf & Aljaafreh, 1995; Long, 1981, 1996; Pawlak, 2004; Pica, 1988, 1994; Schmidt, 1990, 1994). Careful analysis of the thirty-year-old second language acquisition (SLA) research reveals that conversational interaction lays a solid basis for the development of learner interlanguage. Interactional adjustments triggered by negotiation are reported to link input, internal learner capacities, selective attention and output (Long, 1996). It should also be noted that it is the element of negotiation that plays a crucial role since it not only helps learners to learn by clarifying unknown items, but also facilitates language development by making input understandable without simplifying it, by breaking it into smaller digestible pieces and providing support within which learners can produce increasingly complex utterances (Long, 1996).

It must be stressed that the production stage is extremely important from the point of view of successful language acquisition. Following Swain's *Output Hypothesis*, comprehensible input, which is provided, for example, by modified conversations, is not sufficient for acquisition to take place. Comprehensible input alone does not offer learners high enough levels of grammatical and sociolinguistic competence. More specifically, language learners may comprehend input by employing semantic processing only, without paying close attention to the linguistic form, which is impossible at the production stage. When language learners produce texts, they must activate syntactic processing, which means they must pay attention to grammar (Swain, 1995).

Skehan (1998, pp. 16–18) fully agrees with Swain on this point. Additionally, he provides five other roles production plays which are related to the two notions discussed in this section. These five roles are: generating better input, testing hypotheses, developing automaticity, developing discourse skills and developing a personal voice.

As can be seen, interaction and meaning negotiation appear to be facilitative and essential for foreign language acquisition. For this reason, both of them are a key element of modern language courses. As will be shown later, interaction and meaning negotiation are also a vital element of the complex tasks for developing learner autonomy (see 3.2.1). In the classroom context, social interaction is especially valued because it activates learners' higher mental functions such as reasoning, comprehension and critical thinking, thus facilitating efficient language learning. It also provides learners with opportunities to negotiate meaning, which substantially contributes to input comprehensibility (Pica, 1988, 1994; Sarré, 2011). Finally, interaction and negotiation of meaning enable learners to modify their output to make themselves understood (Swain, 1985).

2.2.1.3 MEDIATION AND SCAFFOLDING

As the preceding discussion has shown, learning is a socially-mediated process. The notion of *mediation*, directly linked with Vygotsky's use of tools and symbolic language in particular, stresses that human learning is shaped or, in other words, mediated by more knowledgeable others (Feurstein, Klein, & Tannenbaum, 1991; Feurstein, Rand, Hoffman, & Miller, 1980; Lantolf, 2000; Vygotsky, 1978). These mediating others, whether parents, teachers or peers, are responsible for the choice, organisation and provision of appropriate stimuli for children in order to successfully promote learning. These significant others also shape children's incipient, though not always successful, responses to stimuli in order to first prompt more suitable responses and second to make it clear why certain responses are better in particular contexts than others.

However, the notion of mediation must not be confused with the concept of *reciprocity* (see Feuerstein, Rand, & Rynders, 1988). The former is related to assisting learners to possess appropriate knowledge and competencies vital for further learning and meeting the new demands of a changing world. In other words, successful mediation results in learner autonomy, which allows learners not only to be in charge of their learning, but also makes them independent thinkers and strategic problem solvers (see 2.2.1.4). This latter, referring to the concept of *scaffolding* in Vygotsky's theory, stresses the significance of learners sharing the intent of mediators. Accordingly, learners, perceived as active participants in the mediation process, comply with what should be done and why.

What then is scaffolding? The notion refers to "a protective umbrella of explanations, interpretations, and clarifications (...) provided at the right moment by adults" (Mason, 1992, p. 216). It is therefore vital that scaffolding be perceived as an external supportive environment for the process of learning, and should be related to cognitive, emotional, physical or social help. Following Bruner's (1978) and Cazden's (1983) research, the concept of scaffolding has become more complex. In fact, two types of scaffolding can be distinguished: *vertical scaffolding* and *game-like routines* or *sequential scaffolding*. The former occurs when more expert others gradually require more information (e.g. by asking questions) from less experienced individuals, while sustaining their focus on a particular task. The latter, as the name suggests, is found in children's games and is related to structured interactions in which more knowledgeable others give less experienced individuals clues to the next stage in the process (see 2.2.1.1).

Scaffolding, also known as *assisted performance, collaborative dialogue* or *instructional conversation*, is frequently thought to be created via the guidance, modelling and feedback learners receive while mastering new skills (Ellis, 2003; Gibbons, 2015; Hutz & Kolb, 2007; Poole & Patthey-Chaves, 1994; Schmid-Schönbein, 2005; Tharp & Gallimore, 1991; Wood, Bruner, & Ross, 1976). However, it should be emphasised that scaffolding may also involve graphic organisers, supplementary materials, classroom routines or cue lists. Accordingly, assisted performance can take the form of: boosting learners' interest and curiosity in classroom tasks, explaining task purposes and providing clear directions, simplifying roles of learners in tasks or referring learners to worthy sources, maintaining pursuit of the goal, marking critical features and discrepancies between completed tasks and ideal end products, handling learner frustrations and anxiety during problem-solving or displaying solutions to learners. In this way, assisted performance is a valuable process which enables learners not only to manage tasks they are not currently capable of completing individually, but also brings them nearer to a state of competence which will finally allow them to accomplish such undertakings with no external help.

The importance of scaffolding and mediation in the language classroom has also been reported in solid research. For instance, some studies have drawn attention to the fact that scaffolding leads to more effective and productive work as well as communication in the classroom (Kaptelinin & Cole, 2001; Savery, 1998). Others show that scaffolding stimulates learner interest as well as motivation and responsibility for learning (Guzdial & Turns, 2000; Roehler & Cantlon, 1997). Finally, research on classroom mediation reports increased learner cooperation (Johnson & Johnson, 1996) and learner responsibility for their own behaviour (Thompson, 1996).

The picture that emerges from the present discussion is that mediation overlaps and supplements scaffolding. Both processes are essential in the classroom as they foster learning and affect learners' cognitive, emotional and social development. For this reason, it is advisable that teachers and classroom tasks both encourage learners to reflect on what is known and how the stored knowledge connects to new items (see 3.1.1.1). Also, it is desirable that students are provided with numerous opportunities to independently or collaboratively explore ideas and construct meaning as well as search for positive ways to meet their own wants and needs (see 7.1.2). Such opportunities are granted by learner autonomy tasks (see 7.3). Detailed guidelines with regard to the process of designing such tasks will be presented in the later part of this volume (see 7.1). Finally, it is highly recommended that classroom mediation be actively promoted to produce more attentive, eager and collaborative learners.

2.2.1.4 COLLABORATION AND PROBLEM-SOLVING

Vygotsky's concept of the ZPD (see 2.2.1.1) promotes not only social interaction (see 2.2.1.2), but also collaboration. Vygotsky affirmed that learning should take place "through problem-solving under adult guidance, or in collaboration with more capable peers" (Vygotsky, 1978, p. 86). Hence, pedagogies grounded in Vygotskyan frameworks regard both cooperation and collaboration as permanent components of effective teaching. In this kind of instruction, language teachers act as experts and learners act as apprentices. The collaboration between them invariably entails successful use of the target language and problem-solving. As will be seen later, all these features will also be included in learner autonomy tasks (see 3.2), which by definition locates these tasks squarely within Vygotskyan pedagogy.

Modern collaborative instruction, where pair or small team work is recommended, are intended to promote effective cooperation among the participants of the learning process (Finkbeiner, 2002; Kötter, 2002, 2003; Legutke & Thomas, 1991; Moreillon, 2007; Murawski, 2010; Rüschoff & Wolff, 1998; Ur, 2012). However, there are several criteria that need to be met in order for team cooperation to be successful. Firstly, all group members must assume responsibility for their own learning as well as the learning of other individuals. In this way, all members eagerly and fairly contribute to the team while working together to achieve a common goal. Secondly, productive cooperation requires interaction because learners are involved in problem-solving tasks and need to discuss and connect the material in use with prior knowledge, both procedural and declarative, and past experiences (see 3.1.1.1). Thirdly, cooperative learning necessitates the application of various social skills and competencies so as to ensure its effective operation. Among the valuable skills are: appropriate leadership, management, successful communication, trust, conflict resolution and responsible decision-making. The last factor to be taken into consideration is group reflection (see 2.3.2.2). This aspect entails an assessment of what has been learnt and a review of how the learning problem was approached or solved. Group reflection also allows for focusing on how a similar problem will be solved when a new opportunity arises.

The application of collaborative problem-solving activities in present day language classrooms is related to such constructivists as Dewey, Bruner and Vygotsky. For example, Dewey (1944) encourages teachers to stimulate learners' natural inclinations to explore and create, whereas Bruner (1986) considers the process of learning as a cultural interchange and sees collaboration as an occasion for culture members to negotiate meanings and share understanding. Problem-solving based instruction is also deeply rooted in Vygotsky's theory (1978), according to which language is a tool for communication and problem resolution. In pedagogical terms, problem-solving is appreciated since it encourages learners to think creatively and productively. Moreover, it empowers learners to assume responsibility for the future. Lastly, being engaging and challenging, problem-solving aids learners in the acquisition of leadership and team building skills (see 6.2).

The observations mentioned above have been confirmed by empirical studies of classroom collaboration and problem-solving. Some researchers have found that collaborative and problem-solving-driven learning contributes to the enhancement of interpersonal and problem-solving skills, increased motivation and enthusiasm, analytical thinking and decision-making, as well as the facilitation of inquiry-driven approaches to learning and cooperative interaction (Brooks & Swain, 2009; Kim & McDonough, 2008; Sert, 2005; Watanabe & Swain, 2007; Wigglesworth & Storch, 2009). The indications are therefore that collaboration and problem-solving should constitute an important part of a language course, and for this reason will be promoted in the complex tasks presented in Chapter Seven.

All things considered, it seems appropriate to perceive collaborative learning as part of personal growth. In addition to encouraging learners to personalise their learning experiences, collaborative learning provides a means for the learner to examine their own self-concept and its expression (see 6.1). Furthermore, collaborative learning boosts learners' self-esteem and enhances their confidence to use the target language in social interactions (see 2.2.1.2). Employing the previously discussed social constructivist assumptions, it must be clarified that "knowledge is grounded in language and arising from interchanges among the individual, the discourse community, and the material conditions of existence" (Nelson, 2008, p. 195).

2.2.2 EDUCATIONAL ROOTS OF LEARNER AUTONOMY

No discussion of the origins of the concept of learner autonomy would be complete without mentioning some evidence from various positions set forth by 20th century educational reformers. Accordingly, this part will deal with *Project Method*, *Transformative Learning* and *Deschooling*, all of which agitate for learner autonomy.

Kilpatrick (1925) contributed to the idea of learner autonomy through *Project Method*, often referred to as teaching thinking through problem-solving (see 2.2.1.4). To be more precise, children develop both intellectually and morally through solving problems in social settings. The four-step procedure for a classroom project guarantees meaningful and authentic learning experiences on condition that learners themselves are actively involved in establishing objectives, planning, executing and evaluating tasks (Kilpatrick, 1925). What is more, this method indicates that a classroom climate conducive to learning promotes personal interests (see 3.1.1.4), intrinsic motivation (see 3.2.1), collaboration (see 2.2.1.4) and real life experiences (see 3.2.1). It is clear therefore that Kilpatrick's view of education combines student-centredness, learner autonomy and personal growth. For a more recent discussion on project-based language education, see Beckett and Miller (2006).

A similar view was proposed by Freire (1970), who strongly considered education to be based on problem-solving, liberty and dialogue. The latter, as with Vygotsky and Feuerstein, was extremely important to Freire as it guarantees the communication needed for true education. His learner-centred and libertarian education was created to put an end to the common positivist view that education not only deprived learners of independence, but also stamped out their consciousness. Freire's (1970) *Transformative Learning* contributes to the theory of autonomy in that it highlights the issues of power and control in the classroom (see 2.3.2.1). This theory supports a climate of equality among learners. Students are able to become not only partners with their teachers and other class members, but also their personal autonomy (see 2.2.3) is fully appreciated in the process of knowledge creation.

The final position to be discussed here is *Deschooling*, presented by Illich in *Deschooling Society* in 1971. Illich's severe criticism of the idea of school indicated that school suppressed authentic learning since it was bound to a rigged curriculum, and hence did not guarantee radical social change. The proposed new model of education gathers learners of similar interests who acquire knowledge and various competences through, for instance, computer/Internet-based projects (Burbules, 2006), English corners (Gao, 2007, 2009) or literature clubs (Cirocki, 2012; Illich, 1971). Acknowledging that responsibility for learning lies only with learners and that real life tasks (3.2.1) provide the means for successful learning, the new model promotes the concept of learner autonomy, defining it first as learners' internal drive to make decisions about their learning (2.3.2.1) and second as learners' right to pursue what they are interested in rather than what somebody else finds worthwhile.

Having discussed the major influences from psychology and education, it is time to survey the roots of learner autonomy in political philosophy. The most relevant sources are the subject of the following subsection.

2.2.3 LEARNER AUTONOMY IN POLITICAL PHILOSOPHY

The construct of learner autonomy also derives from the political philosophy of the 20th century, in which liberal philosophers viewed people as autonomous agents. In their opinion, to be a person meant to utilise one's autonomy, defined as the human drive for individual choice, responsibility (van Lier, 2008) and agency (Lantolf, 2013; Lantolf & Pavlenko, 2001; Toohey & Norton, 2003). In this vein, autonomous beings approve of existing rules without any external interference or control and take possession of their resolutions, which remain under the influence of rational reflection (Lantolf, 2013; Little, 2008).

As can be seen, learner autonomy refers to the concept of *personal autonomy*, which goes back to Ancient Greece where people "were governed according to their own laws rather than those of a conquering power" (Benson, 2001, p. 43). Personal autonomy has been presented as a three-dimensional concept; the three coinciding facets are: *the intellectual, the moral* and *the emotional* (Crittenden, 1978). The first embraces the individual's beliefs about the surrounding world, the second subsumes the person's judgements and action, whereas the third is linked to the individual's control of their feelings and emotions.

As far as the liberal-humanist philosophy of personal autonomy is concerned, it shows that people attach value to independent choices they make on a day-to-day basis. People have the ability not only to act for a reason, but also to reflect on the reasons for their agency (Raz, 1986). Therefore, people treat personal autonomy as a prerequisite to politically unrestrained well-being. What is more, liberal-humanist philosophy emphasises that autonomous entities not only freely direct their lives (Young, 1986), but also have a plan or a strategy for existence (Waldron, 1993). This plan, in turn, is firstly based on democratic choices and decisions as well as knowledge of one's strengths and weaknesses (see 2.3.2) and secondly, dependent on human abilities, aptitudes and interests (see 3.1.1.4). Hence, individuals know best what is most or least important for them to construct their own world (Waldron, 1993).

The preceding discussion boils down to two conclusions. Firstly, the concept of personal autonomy lays strong foundations for human rights. Reference to political philosophy reveals that people have the right to freely put their own decisions and choices into practice to enjoy autonomous lives in which:

> *[they] chart [their] own course through life, fashioning [their] character by self-consciously choosing projects and assuming commitments from a wide range of eligible alternatives, and making something out of [their] life according to [their] own understanding of what is valuable and worth doing (Wall, 2003, pp. 307–308).*

Secondly, autonomy as a learning notion provides a basis for personal autonomy. Human beings must learn in order to be autonomous.

2.2.4 AUTONOMY AS A LANGUAGE LEARNING CONCEPT

Grounded in the psychological, educational and philosophical theories outlined above, the concept of learner autonomy was finally adopted in the EFL context. In Europe, it was Holec (France), Little (Ireland), Dam (Denmark), Dietrich and Wolff (Germany) as well as Droździał-Szelest and Michońska-Stadnik (Poland) who struggled initially for the establishment of learner autonomy in language pedagogy, and consequently for its great popularity in the language classroom.

However, it should be made clear from the very beginning that in the very early days, autonomy was erroneously associated with *individualisation*, yet, with time, clarification was provided. Despite the fact that both concepts have features in common, under no circumstances should they be equated or employed interchangeably. Individualised instruction or programmed learning, rooted in behaviourism (see 2.2), concentrates on the learner and adjusts the teaching-learning process to their needs, skills and motivations. Hence, instruction follows a structured and well-prepared programme that is designed in such a way that learners work on carefully chosen materials and tasks and proceed at their own pace, all under the guidance of teachers. This concise description reveals that individualised instruction deprives learners of the freedom of choice since the most important decisions belong to the teacher. Autonomy-orientated instruction, by contrast, leaves the vital decisions in learning to learners themselves (see 2.3.2.1), these decisions being made through negotiation (see 2.2.1.2) within cooperative learning groups (see 2.2.1.4) as well as "with respect to social and moral norms, traditions and expectations" (Kohonen, 1992, p. 19). This seems to imply that autonomy-focused instruction came into existence along with the present day *Communicative Approach* in language education. For a more detailed discussion of this approach, see Richards and Rodgers (2001).

Since communicative language teaching is an umbrella term for several interpretations of how the learning-teaching process can be realised in practice, it seems appropriate to differentiate at least between Howatt's (1984) *strong* and *weak* versions of the paradigm in question. According to the strong version of communicative language teaching, learners learn/

acquire the target language through communication, whilst the weak version of communicative language teaching asserts that learners learn/acquire a foreign language to express functions which satisfy their own communication needs, simultaneously developing both communicative and intercultural competences.

It is the weak version that has been in operation in recent decades, and is thus pivotal to the present volume. It promotes functional communication as well as such aspects as social interaction and meaning negotiation (see 2.2.1.2), mediation (see 2.2.1.3) and collaboration and problem-solving (see 2.2.1.4). All of these factors, as emphasised above, involve real communication through the integration of different language skills. The process of foreign language learning is thereby regarded as a creative construction (see 2.2) which learners are encouraged to monitor systematically and reflect upon individually or collaboratively (see 2.3.2.2). As a result, the weak version perceives the language classroom as a venue for democratic practices (see 2.3.2.1), simultaneously supporting learner-centred education, as well as paving the way for learner autonomy.

In summary, the concept of autonomy in the EFL classroom is not a new phenomenon. Despite the fact that it can trace its origins to a number of disciplines, it has lately been reborn and advocated by ELT experts. As mentioned before, mainstream foreign language pedagogy is a broad cluster of views, so it is time to analyse how current approaches to language instruction promote learner autonomy.

2.3 APPROACHES TO DEVELOPING LEARNER AUTONOMY

One of the intentions of the previous sections was to define learner autonomy from three different angles in order to show how versatile a construct it is and how it affects the profile of the autonomous learner (see 2.1), while at the same time disclosing how well-established it is and how it is conceived in the EFL context. Furthermore, the definitions presented above point to a significant conclusion that learner autonomy is perceived as both process and product, concurrently confirming the following observations: firstly, learner autonomy is a personal feature; secondly, learner autonomy relates to self-management, where students are both willing and able to perform the act of learning; thirdly, learner autonomy pertains to learner-control, that is, instruction organisation in formally established settings; and, finally, learner autonomy refers to intentional self-instruction which occurs beyond formal educational settings. For further explanations of these observations, see Candy (1991).

All these findings underscore the importance of learner autonomy in language education. The observation that it is impossible for autonomy to be taught or learnt since it is an ability which belongs to the learner is also confirmed (Sheerin, 1997). Accordingly, it is essential that teachers are aware that autonomous learning must be interpreted as an experience in which learners' capacity for autonomy is exploited and evidenced. This, on the other hand, indicates that autonomy can be developed. Hence, this section will focus on how teachers can cultivate autonomy by means of practices that enable learners to be actively involved in various styles of learning through which the capacity under study can easily evolve.

According to Brindley (1984, p. 15), "education should develop in individuals the capacity to control their own destiny". Therefore, any attempts made towards developing autonomy in the EFL context certainly fulfil part of the overall objective. The quotation is important for one more reason, namely, it cogently clarifies that learner autonomy is a dynamic process in which both learners and teachers have different roles to play (McGrath, 2013; Müller-Hartmann & Schocker-von-Ditfurth, 2011; Renandya, 2012; Willis & Willis, 2007). Despite the fact that autonomous learners are self-motivated meaning-makers and engaged agents in their own learning, teachers do not abandon their control over the process. On the contrary, it is the teachers who continually facilitate students' learning experiences, as well as encourage students' intrinsic motivation (see 3.2.1) and self-confidence, both of which condition autonomous learning. Also, it is the teachers who train students to become autonomous learners by selecting appropriate approaches in order to make their learning experiences rewarding and memorable.

A strong interest among researchers has contributed to the creation of numerous approaches to the development of learner autonomy (Benson, 2001, 2007, 2011; Benson & Cooker, 2013; Dickinson, 1987; Gardner & Miller, 1996; Holec, 1988; Nunan, 1997; Schwienhorst, 2008, 2011; Wilczyńska, 1999, 2002; Wolff, 2011). However, it is beyond the scope of this section to detail them all. Those that seem to be highly desirable in the mainstream EFL classroom, and thus the most relevant for the purposes of this book, can be arranged into four categories: *learner-related, classroom-related, resource-related* and *technology-related* approaches. All of them are discussed below.

2.3.1 THE LEARNER-RELATED APPROACH

The learner-related approach to developing autonomy seeks to empower learners to be self-reliant and more independent of their teachers, consequently putting them in charge of their learning by literally supplying them with all the required skills. The issue of advocating greater independence in language learners derives from thorough research into learner strategies (e.g. Chiu 2012; Cohen, 2011; Gu, 2008; Lan, 2008; Lee & Oxford, 2008; Nguyen & Gu, 2013; Oxford, 2011; Pawlak, 2011a; Wolff, 2003), defined as specific, higher or lower order, cognitive or social, conscious or unconscious procedures that learners employ not only to store, retrieve and appropriately use the information received, but also to respond to particular foreign language learning problems relevantly (Williams & Burden, 1997).

The preceding perspective of learning strategies can be enriched with the view that language learner strategies subsume both foreign language learning and foreign language use strategies. The latter refers to strategies as conscious steps which students resort to when they recognise new material, distinguish it from already acquired facts, categorise it for uncomplicated learning and commit unfamiliar information to memory, unless it is acquired naturally (Cohen, 1998).

Despite the fact that learning strategies appear under different names (e.g. *behaviours and actions* (Oxford, 1989, p. 235), *thoughts and behaviours* (O'Malley & Chamot, 1990, p. 1), *operations and steps* (O'Malley & Chamot, 1990, p. 99), *tools* (Scharle & Szabo, 2000, p. 8), *potentially conscious plan*

(Kost, 2008, p. 156), *problem-solving procedure* (Zhong, 2008, p. 53)) and the specialist literature offers their different typologies, the consensus model can be arranged around the following four categories: *cognitive*, *metacognitive*, *social* and *affective* strategies (Dörnyei, 2005, p. 169). Cognitive strategies involve interaction with the learning input (see 7.1.2.2); metacognitive strategies regulate the process of foreign language learning, for example, through planning, self-monitoring and assessing (see 2.3.2); social strategies entail interactions (see 2.2.1.2) and cooperation (see 2.2.1.4) with other people and, last but not least, affective strategies deal with emotional conditions and experiences in learning.

Complex as they may seem, the learning strategies have all been thoroughly researched. What is more, numerous studies on learning strategies have greatly informed research on the behaviours involved in autonomous language learning (e.g. Chiu 2012; Droździał-Szelest, 2008; Finkbeiner & Knierim, 2008; Michońska-Stadnik, 2008; Nguyen & Gu, 2013; Pawlak, 2011a). The findings of these studies make a generous contribution to the EFL context by emphasising that it is important for foreign language learners to be trained to become independent learners (see Task 4 and Task 5 in 7.3). This, in consequence, has led to the emergence of various approaches to classroom strategy training for autonomy.

For instance, one of the approaches lists three types of strategy training: *awareness training, one-time* and *long-term strategy training* (Oxford, 1990). The first of these aims is to make learners aware of language learning strategies and their role in assisting students to succeed in the language tasks they do. The second refers to both learning and practising strategies through active participation in language tasks. Due to this training, students know when and how to employ, as well as how to evaluate the success of a particular strategy or strategies. Finally, long-term strategy training, similarly to procedures in one-time strategy training, seeks to train students in a large number of strategies within a longer period of time, thus being more profitable and effective than the former one.

The next approach offers a three-objective training plan in which *learners' language culture, learners' learning culture* and *learners' methodologi-*

cal competence are developed (Holec, 1996). As a result, learners' language culture concentrates on those aspects of the target language which are indispensable for defining learning objectives, whereas learning culture focuses on language learning and acquisition aspects which are related to the determination of learning strategies. However, it is the training of learners' methodological competence that is of key importance to the development of learner autonomy. Thanks to this competence learners can take proper learning decisions (see 2.3.2.1). Therefore, the training is based on practising many categories of decisions (e.g. identifying learning objectives, selecting study resources and methods of evaluation), and includes two phases of decision-making, that is, "preparation and choice" (Holec, 1996, p. 97).

Another interesting position highlights the need to organise workshops for students where they can train themselves through reflection (see 2.3.2.2) and communication on their own learning experiences (Esch, 1997). The success of such an undertaking results from the fact that the participants are self-selected, relevant feedback is available during learning conversations and the participants themselves are in charge of selecting the syllabus.

An alternative perspective argues that strategy training is vital as it seeks to promote learner autonomy by enabling students to spontaneously choose their own strategies (Cohen, 1998). Therefore, teachers are advised to introduce strategy use by means of explicit instruction which would aim, among other things, at showing students how to identify both weak and strong points in their language education, encouraging them to employ successful strategies in new learning situations, monitoring their learning, assessing their performance in the target language and, last but not least, developing various problem-solving skills (Cohen, 1998).

The last approach suggests familiarising learners with a large variety of learning strategies through a three-stage process, namely, *raising awareness, changing attitudes* and *transferring roles* (Scharle & Szabo, 2000). The first stage focuses on the transfer of learners' intrinsic processes of constructing knowledge to "the conscious level of their thinking" (Scharle

& Szabo, 2000, p. 8), the second involves becoming aware of and exercising unknown roles in the learning process, and the last one is related to dealing with changes in classroom management. The end product of this gradual process is autonomous behaviour, which depends on the motivation (see 3.2.1) and responsible attitudes of the learners.

As can be seen, these approaches, despite having a common goal, are not the same, which necessitates the application of different materials and tasks (see 3.1.1.6). For instance, training in cognitive strategies requires tasks with note-taking, summarising and deductive reasoning, whereas training in metacognitive strategies calls for tasks that include designing schedules of work, creating language learning journals, self-reports, as well as different types of questionnaires (e.g. task or project self-evaluation questionnaires). Training in social strategies involves games, role-plays and simulations so that learners have a chance to cooperate with classmates (Chik, 2011; Legutke & Thomas, 1991; Siek-Piskozub, 1995; Thomson & Mabey, 2011). Finally, affective strategy training requires tasks which include stress questionnaires, or accomplishment and positive learning experience reports where students write brief comments about their work (Oxford, 1990).

Overall, it is suggested that teachers who want their learners to become autonomous engage them in strategy training, including the cognitive, metacognitive, social and affective strategies mentioned above. It is vital that strategy training be incorporated into normal classes (Cohen, 2011; Hedge, 2000; Johnson, 2013; Komorowska, 2002a; Legutke, Müller-Hartmann, Schocker-v. Ditfurth, 2009; Oxford, 2011; Ur, 2012). As will be seen soon, this idea will be promoted in this volume by encouraging teachers to design learner autonomy tasks (see 7.1). One of the aims of such tasks is to highlight different types of learning strategies (see Task 4 and Task 5 in 7.3). Only by including the tasks in the teaching-learning process can learners appreciate the relevance of the strategies for language learning tasks. What is more, such a pragmatic approach would be important for two reasons. Firstly, it would enable learners not only to experiment with various strategies and monitor or evaluate the strategies used, but also reflect on how different types of strategies affect their performance in the target language. Secondly, it would remain in agreement with research evidence which shows that connecting explicit strategy training with learner reflection is more effective in achieving both, rather than dealing with them separately.

2.3.2 THE CLASSROOM-RELATED APPROACH

Another approach to the development of learner autonomy that is expected to play a major role in language education is called the classroom-related approach. It refers to decision-making processes students make with regard to the supervision of their learning. As a result, two aspects will be discussed in this subsection. These aspects are: planning and assessing classroom learning.

2.3.2.1 PLANNING CLASSROOM LEARNING

In recent years, there has been an increasing amount of literature on possible reasons why teachers may wish to promote language learning autonomy. These studies discussed autonomy as an inherent part of educational practices (Boud, 1988), and also took into consideration various political implications (e.g. Benson, 1997; Crabbe, 1993; Pennycook, 1997; Widdowson, 1987). The latter conclude that autonomy is a privilege of those who exercise control (see 2.2.3); students, therefore, need to be given power and offered the chance to manage their own learning (Villa, Thousand, & Nevin, 2008). This finding is consistent with the *Democratic/Participatory Approach* to the teaching-learning process, Hofstede's (2001) *Model of Cultural Dimensions* and Nunan and Lamb's (1996) concept of *learner-centeredness*, all of which stress shared teacher-student power and put emphasis on the continuous and collaborative engagement of learners in all spheres of their democratic life in the classroom.

To be more exact, the democratic/participatory ideology is extremely important from the point of view of producing autonomous learners. Such an ideology successfully encourages learner empowerment and promotes learner participation in classroom decisions, for example, planning, implementing and evaluating language instruction (Oxford, 2001; Richards, 2001). Additionally, it encourages intrinsic motivation (see 3.2.1) and critical thinking, acknowledges individual differences in learning styles (see 3.1.1.4) as well as fosters learner self-esteem (see 6.1). Given this evidence, it can be seen that the approach in question, moving control from the educational organisation towards learners, establishes a learning community which is not only accelerated by its members' interests, knowledge and experiences (Lamb, 2013), but also demonstrates mutual respect and social commitment, all of which contribute to the formation of autonomous foreign language learner identity (Benson & Cooker, 2013; Block, 2007; Hawkins, 2005; Menezes, 2013; Morita, 2004; van Lier, 2004).

Similar ideas are voiced in Hofstede's (1980) cultural dimensions model, especially in the areas of *individualism-collectivism* and *power distance*. When transferred to the context of language education and learner autonomy development in particular, both dimensions take on pivotal importance. The former pertains to how people perceive themselves and their affiliations with others (Hofstede, 1980). Individualism, for example, regards education as preparing individuals for a society made up of other individuals, where the main goal of the learning process is to be cognisant of how to learn and how to deal with novel and unanticipated events. Therefore, it prioritises autonomy, individual attainment, the right to privacy and a personal choice. Collectivism, however, interprets education in terms of how to do things so as to enter into collective groups or society (Hofstede, 1980). As a result, this position highlights collective interests and the ideology of equality.

The power distance dimension is connected with the distribution of power between language teachers and learners. According to the constructivist philosophy of teaching discussed in the earlier part of this volume (see 2.2), power is expected to be equally shared in the classroom. It is essential that low-power-distance education be promoted. In this way, low-power-distance learners are produced. Such learners approve of information sharing, rich and diverse learning experiences, cognitive as well as social engagement in learning (see 3.2.1), full participation in classroom decision-making and course management and self-regulated language education.

To fully understand the notion of classroom decision-making, it must be linked to procedural negotiation (see 2.2.1.2). As disclosed earlier, this type of negotiation enables language instructors and students to reach agreement. In the classroom context, a number of curricular areas can be decided upon through negotiation. Some of these are: the content of the course (i.e. *What language aspects, topics, skills and strategies will be the focus of classroom work?*), teaching techniques (i.e. *What types of classroom work will be promoted?*), resources (i.e. *What type of texts and tasks will the work be based on?*) and the assessment procedure (i.e. *What type of assessment instruments will be employed in the teaching-learning process?*).

As can be seen, students can be involved in the decision-making process of various aspects of their language course. At the classroom level, however, students can be empowered and given opportunities to make decisions through *co-teaching*. Co-teaching regularly utilises students to offer help in an instructional capacity (Villa, Thousand, & Nevin, 2010). Both teachers and students share responsibility for teaching in the classroom. For example, it is recommended that students are systematically involved in: planning and teaching individual parts of a lesson, preparing and setting up tasks (see 7.2), monitoring and checking for class understanding, providing feedback on class work and setting classroom discipline procedures. All these activities are in agreement with Pearson and Gallagher (1983) and Guskey and Anderman (2008), who highlight the importance of gradually shifting responsibility for learning from the teachers to the classroom community members. Students evolve into competent individuals who can make sensible decisions, self-direct their learning and effectively communicate what they have learnt (see 2.1). This, in turn, reflects Popham's (2008, p. 81) position that reads as follows: "Student ownership of learning requires that students understand the evidence used to signify whether learning is taking place."

Syllabus negotiation is another interesting way through which learners can be involved in making decisions. It is a way through which learners can become more aware of the teaching-learning process. However, the process of negotiation is far from haggling; it is a joint scrutiny to which both teachers and learners bring different knowledge, skills and experience, and eventually reach consensus through constructive discussion (Nation & Macalister, 2010). It is advisable that such discussion be conducted in the target language. In this way, learners will have a chance to take part in meaningful interaction (see 2.2.1.2).

Attractive as syllabus negotiation may seem, several disadvantages can be listed. For instance, learners rarely possess a sound awareness of feasible tasks, materials and techniques; neither are they effective negotiators. What is more, foreign language learners do not show confidence in negotiations with teachers and are unwilling to take part in them, which is, more often than not, determined by their cultural background. On the other hand, negotiated syllabuses (also referred to as process syllabuses) are very likely to be successful because they come into existence in direct response to learners' wishes and motivations, and through their active engagement and commitment to the course. Also, syllabus negotiation pays attention to diverse needs and learning styles, at the same time contributing to an atmosphere of trust and respect between teachers and students. Finally, student participation in the process of syllabus negotiation has two other important benefits: learners become more cognisant of language education objectives and share ownership of the language course (Bloor & Bloor, 1988; Nation & Macalister, 2010; Richards, 2001).

The present discussion ends with a concise overview of several experimental programmes in which learners were involved in planning classroom learning. The studies detail considerable gains in terms of both autonomy and language learning. In most cases the researchers observed in their students: increased motivation (Stefanou, Perencevich, DiCintio, & Turner, 2004), learning (Harris & Noyau, 1990), strategy use (Carpenter, 1996), interaction between students (Carpenter, 1996), responsibility for learning (Littlejohn, 1982), as well as greater willingness to apply additional resources (Littlejohn, 1982). However, apart from all these successful outcomes, some problems have also been reported. For instance, Carpenter (1996), in her model of peer teaching, noted two difficulties, namely: the quality of classes delivered by students was unbalanced and some students did not participate in class activities.

2.3.2.2 ASSESSING CLASSROOM LEARNING

Self-assessment is another necessary part of both developing learner autonomy and the classroom-related approach. Self-assessment aims to involve learners in determining what constitutes good work. Learners can then evolve into true judges of their own output, as well as effective and reflective monitors of their own learning (Boud, 1995; Everhard & Murphy, 2015). There is a strong focus on self-assessment in learner autonomy tasks displayed in Chapter Seven (see Task 7 and Task 8 in 7.3). Self-assessment should be an integral part of classroom practice, for it not only encourages good learning, promotes learning strategies (see 2.3.1) and introduces an alternative form of assessment, but also allows learners to review their achievements and increase their self-knowledge and self-understanding (Boud, 1995; Everhard & Murphy, 2015; Komorowska, 2002a; Legutke, Müller-Hartmann, & Schocker-v. Ditfurth, 2009; Müller-Hartmann & Schocker-v. Ditfurth, 2011).

In order to be true judges of their own learning, it is recommended that learners partake in critical reflection which has much to offer as an internal dialogue that provides teachers or peers with various emic perspectives on language education and the learner's understanding of self as learner (see 6.1). It prompts learners to ask questions about their learning experiences and personal growth, as well as why and how they learn (Komorowska, 2002a). It reveals that learners think, how they think and how they feel about the foreign language teaching-learning process. Reflection also informs about the encountered learning difficulties, discovered solutions to problems and how these could be employed in future classroom experiences. Finally, it challenges traditional quantitative assessment types by finding solutions to problems that cannot be, or are hardly ever, settled through statistical measures. Examples of tasks related to self-assessment (see Task 7 and Task 8 in 7.3) and reflecting on learning (see Task 9 and Task 10 in 7.3) are presented in Chapter Seven.

As the preceding discussion indicates, reflective practice makes language learners more analytical, critical, observant and empowered. Since all these qualities contribute to the formation of an autonomous learner (see 2.1), there is a need for learners to be involved in reflection training. In its simplest design, it can take the form of the following five steps:
- tell your students what reflection is;
- tell your students how reflection operates;
- show your students how to perform reflection;

- assist your students in employing reflection to recent learning experiences; and
- enable your students to reflect in order to become effective assessors.

Language learners can self-assess their learning via different instruments, including: self-marked tests, progress cards, self-rating scales, diaries, can-do statements, criterion- and performance-based sheets and portfolios (see, for example, Harsch & Schröder, 2008; Komorowska, 2002b; Mews, Stute, & Uplawski, 2009). From the perspective of learner autonomy, they can all be incorporated into classroom procedures, yet teachers should bear in mind that self-assessment instruments ought to encourage both *planned formative assessment* (i.e. related to eliciting evidence of student thinking processes) and *interactive formative assessment* (i.e. reacting to student thinking in teacher-student interactions) and finally lead to reflection and re-evaluation of objectives. Put somewhat differently, learners need to be constantly provided with relevant information so that they can take control of both their learning process and progress (Benson, 2011; Komorowska, 2002a, 2002b; Müller-Hartmann & Schocker-v. Ditfurth, 2011).

Even though self-assessment can be conducted with different tools, the *European Language Portfolio* (ELP) merits special attention in the present analysis. It was proposed by the Council of Europe in order to fulfil two major aims: to foster learner autonomy and to promote plurilingualism. The latter is defined as the capacity to use a number of languages at varying degrees and for a wide range of purposes (Díez, Place, & Fernández, 2012). The ELP consists of three integral parts, that is, *a language passport*, *a language biography* and *a dossier*. The dossier allows learners to gather evidence of their foreign language learning and intercultural experiences (see Schärer, 2003), while the other two components promote learner autonomy, and thus are integral to the present discussion. For instance, the language passport enables learners to systematically assess foreign language proficiency, whereas the language biography involves learners in self-assessment with regard to learning objectives, styles and strategies, as well as schematic or narrative reflection (Claus, Grau, Legutke, & Rau,

2008; Kolb, 2007; Komorowska, 2002b; Legutke & Lortz, 2002; Lenz, 2003; Little, 2011; Pawlak, 2008).

The ELP appears to be an important tool as it links both *formative* and *summative* types of self-assessment (Müller-Hartmann & Schocker-v. Ditfurth, 2011). The former is related to learner weaknesses in language learning and aims to remedy those through constructive feedback (see 7.1.2.6). Formative self-assessment is found in the biography and dossier sections of the ELP. The latter, connected with the passport component of the ELP, seeks to summarise attainment at the end of a course book unit, a course or at a particular point in the learner's life. Both forms of assessment are of key significance since learners must be capable of assessing their strengths and weaknesses. The ongoing process of self-assessment is ensured by the ELP. Multiple sources of data (e.g. evidence of individual and group projects, tests or notes) encourage reflective awareness, which is a vital factor in developing learner autonomy.

Another aspect that speaks for the implementation of the ELP is the fact that it does assist learners to learn how to manage the complex process of foreign language learning. The ELP engages learners in such areas as goal-setting, decision-making, selecting and applying assessment criteria, monitoring and reflecting on learning. Growth can be documented, for example, in terms of skills, attitudes and performance. All these features contribute not only to intensified involvement in learning and assessment processes, but also to strengthening learners' feelings of ownership and responsibility for the portfolio.

Self-assessment is symbiotically connected with peer feedback, which tends to affect the former in a positive manner (Boud, 1995; Mann, 2006). For instance, through peer assessment sessions, learners develop both evaluative and critical thinking skills, and thus become more aware of their own task performance as well as learning in general (Mann, 2006; Rooke, 2015). A study by Gregory, Yeomans and Powell (2003) shows that peer feedback motivates learners to work more attentively, facilitates collaboration (see 2.2.1.4) and, ultimately, furthers learners' ownership of classroom assessment. The indications are therefore that peer assessment is a valuable complement to self-assessment, as it encourages learners to learn from their peers' successes and weaknesses, contributing positively to their own foreign language attainment.

To assist learners to successfully control their learning process and progress, it is advisable that teachers provide students with appropriate tasks (e.g. questionnaires on identifying learning styles, needs analysis tasks or appraisals of strengths and weaknesses). It is also important that training to facilitate the development of self-assessment is made available for the learners. The idea of student training is supported by Cram (1995), who points out that self-assessment practices advance with training and work best in a supportive ambience. Those who develop the ability to self-assess are both responsible for their actions and judgements and capable of individually monitoring their own foreign language performance (Boud, 1995; Everhard & Murphy, 2015; Komorowska, 2002a).

In conclusion, the classroom-related approach deals with *cognitive* (decisions about the learning process), *organisational* (decisions about classroom management) and *procedural* (decisions about learning materials) dimensions of autonomy, thanks to which learners assume control and make conscious choices about the planning and assessment of classroom learning. The degree of control, of course, depends on numerous factors (e.g. age, knowledge and experience), which strongly affect the ability to cope with learner autonomy. Therefore, if teachers want to efficiently facilitate the development of learner autonomy, it is vital that they first reasonably share power (see 2.3.2.1) with their students and, second, provide favourable conditions for autonomy development in their own classrooms. It is the classroom context that ensures productive collaboration with other learners and professional scaffolding (see 2.2.1.3) from teachers.

2.3.3 THE RESOURCE-RELATED APPROACH

The purpose of presenting the two preceding approaches was twofold: the learner-related approach concentrates on the production of behavioural and psychological changes, due to which learners are highly likely to gain fuller control over their learning experiences, whereas the classroom-related approach demonstrates how learners can be involved in the process of regulating their own learning. The resource-related approach, in contrast, focuses on providing learners with exact opportunities to direct their learning, yet it must be admitted that the feasibility and efficiency of the latter, to a large extent, rely on the former two.

Resource-related learning occurs in self-access centres which are mainly established for two reasons, namely, practical and ideological. The former is chiefly associated with individualisation of learning discussed earlier (see 2.2.4), whereas the latter focuses on fostering learner autonomy, and therefore becomes central to the following discussion. Hence, in this subsection, an attempt will be made to outline the place and role of self-access learning centres in the development of learner autonomy. The discussion will first focus on defining self-access learning centres and providing purposes for their establishment. A concise discussion of self-access learning materials and tasks will follow.

2.3.3.1 SELF-ACCESS LEARNING CENTRES

What then are *self-access learning centres* (SALCs)? SALCs, appearing under different names such as independent learning centres, self-directed learning centres and learning resource centres (White, 2003), can be defined as facilities with appropriate language learning materials students can choose and study from, as well as assess their foreign language performance themselves or with little assistance from their teachers (Geddes & Sturtridge, 1982). SALCs can also be defined as resource rooms which offer ample resources (e.g. printed, audio- and video-materials, computer software, games, posters and realia) and cater for learners who not only represent different learning styles (see 3.1.1.4) and levels of language proficiency, but also have different interests and needs (Cotterall & Reinders, 2001; Sturtridge, 1997).

The definitions presented above seem to indicate that learner autonomy and SALCs are closely related. The former allows learners to make choices and, consequently, assume responsibility for their learning, whereas the latter, offering learners diverse modes of learning, constitute a welcoming context in which autonomy can be developed (Ahmadi, 2012;

Chiu, 2012; Langner & Prokop, 2003; Littlewood, 1997; Sheerin, 1997; Sturtridge, 1997).

SALCs can take the form of completely independent educational units with their own staff (e.g. help desk, learning counsellors, librarians and technicians) and philosophy for engaging students (3.2.1), or semi-independent units (e.g. run by language teachers during office hours or before/after lessons) located next to, or even within a particular language classroom. Of course, not every institution can afford to possess an independent unit, but the most important thing is that the centres, be they independent or semi-independent, function properly and successfully serve their main purposes, that is, enabling learners to independently interact with various kinds of learning materials and tasks (Benson, 2001, 2011), allowing them to choose what, when and how they will study (Cooker, 2002), as well as assisting them to develop various skills in order to become more autonomous in their learning (Chiu, 2012; Gardner & Miller, 1999; Langner & Prokop, 2003; Law, 2011).

As far as the independent units are concerned, they can be categorised into different types, for example: *study centres, programmed learning centres, drop-in centres, controlled-access centres* and, finally, *open-access centres*. Despite the fact that these centres all strive to develop learner autonomy, there are certain differences. For instance, in study centres, learning materials are narrowly focused and seek to complement classroom instruction. Programmed learning centres, in contrast to study centres, do not supplement classroom instruction, but allow learners to enhance particular language skills, for example, reading skills. Drop-in centres, offering a large array of study materials, enable learners to choose as well as to pursue those aspects of the target language which are of personal interest. Controlled-access centres, compulsory for learners, are intended for homework-based activities. Open-access centres are designed for sophisticated language learners who are able not only to determine what they wish to engage in, but also successfully locate the materials and tasks they require.

No matter what type of SALC a school or university possesses, its effectiveness can be boosted by involving learners in their own development and how they function. This idea finds support in two studies, conducted in Italy (Aston, 1993) and Cambodia (Jones, 1995), in which learners were successfully involved in the management of SALCs. For instance, Aston's (1993, p. 226) research concludes that thanks to this experience the students involved take "greater control not only of their own learning, but also of the institution whose task it is to make such learning and control possible".

In light of the above, teachers should not hesitate to involve their students in the management of learning centres or class reading corners. In the case of the latter, teachers could appoint book monitors or classroom librarians to be in charge of loan cards, a reading record sheet or a wall record chart that would precisely track which students are reading which books, simultaneously giving details such as: titles and authors, borrow and return dates, genres, book levels and recommendation comments. All these extra items would be of great importance since they would provide learners with useful information about learning materials and help them to organise the entire system.

2.3.3.2 SELF-ACCESS MATERIALS

The discussion of developing autonomy through SALCs would not be complete without mentioning learning materials for self-study which stocked in different forms (e.g. print texts, audio/video tapes, CDs, ebooks, computer software, etc.) guarantee the success of SALCs. Unfortunately, SALCs generally focus on materials which frequently aim at supplementing classroom activities (e.g. extensive practice of problematic language items or specific skills) students can do in their own time and at their own pace. However, it should be noted that too many homogenous materials (grammar books, language skills books or pronunciation books) contribute to the fact that SALCs promote controlled practice only. In other words, SALCs reinforce explicit declarative knowledge, simultaneously defying the development of implicit procedural knowledge of the target language (Tomlinson, 2011a). This evidence seems to indicate that commercially produced materials are suitable only for studial learners, and does not appear to cater for experiential learners.

To cater to all the learning styles (see 3.1.1.4), SALCs should provide a large diet of authentic materials with complex tasks (see 3.2.2). The latter, when based on authentic texts, can increase students' learning potential by promoting intellectual, aesthetic and emotional engagement (see 3.2.1), at the same time stimulating both hemispheres of the brain (Rüschoff, 2010; Tomlinson, 2003a; Wolff, 1994). It is the autonomous learning context that appears to be the most appropriate in which to analyse authentic texts (see Mishan, 2005). For useful accounts of using literature in the language classroom, see Bredella and Delanoy (1996); Burwitz-Melzer (2000, 2007); Hallet and Nünning (2007); Legutke, Müller-Hartmann and Schocker-v. Ditfurth (2009) and Cirocki (2013a).

What then are authentic texts? Despite being extensively applied in ELT--orientated literature, the notion of *authenticity* is still in dispute, and therefore no general consensus exists among experts as to its meaning. However, I concur with Swaffar's (1985) and Widdowson's (1998) observations that pairing *authentic* with *written by and for native speakers* appears to be a serious misconception, since what gives texts written by and for native speakers their authenticity is that they are perfect examples of communication between writers and intended audiences. Thus, in the same manner, a similar conclusion can be drawn: when writers communicate with audiences of foreign language learners at specific levels of language proficiency, the resultant texts are absolutely authentic. It should also be added that authenticity deals more with relevant responses (Widdowson, 1978), and thus should be assessed in terms of the degree of learners' participation, highlighting that what counts is what learners *do* with texts rather than their occurring in real environments (van Lier, 1996).

Mishan's (2005) observation mentioned above firmly supports earlier research on the value of authentic texts in developing learner autonomy. For instance, tasks built around authentic texts enable foreign language learners to experience authentic decisions and truly existing issues. Such tasks also appear to be records "of any communicative act (...) performed in fulfilment of some personal or social function, and not in order to provide illustrative material for language learning" (Little, 1989, p. 4). In addition, frequent encounters with authentic texts make learners more confident about the target language, which is one of the prerequisites of autonomous language learning (Little, 1997). Also, exposure to tasks based on authentic materials guides learners towards authentic sources and more independent discovery and learning (Little, 1997). Research literature (e.g. Cirocki, 2013a; McGarry, 1995) on authentic texts in language education, in turn, lists the following important findings: authentic texts enhance positive attitudes to learning, promote the development of different skills and enable students to work independently of teachers. It is clear therefore that authentic-text-based tasks allow students to match foreign "language learning opportunities to the needs and interests of individual students" (McGarry, 1995, p. 3) and create "conditions under which students can most successfully exploit these opportunities" (McGarry, 1995, p. 3). Finally, in case studies on learner experiences in autonomy, Fernández-Toro and Jones (1996) observed that at higher levels of language proficiency, learners gain considerably from regular interactions with authentic texts in autonomous modes.

As I have explained elsewhere (see Cirocki, 2013a), I value literary texts, for they contribute substantial evidence to foreign language acquisition. They also provide the means for exploiting, as well as developing learners' knowledge and personal experiences. Genuine literature enables foreign or second language (L2) readers to interact with the target language, book characters and events. Literary texts link formal linguistic expression to wider sociocultural contexts.

Discussing the usefulness of literary texts in learner autonomy development, it should be noted that interactions between the texts and the readers are a game and there are four rules to be followed (Rabinowitz, 1987). *The rules of notice* refer to situations where readers pay attention to certain features of texts only. *The rules of signification* pertain to aspects in which readers assign meanings to aspects that attract their attention. Readers connect the latter with their experiences, simultaneously treating characters as ordinary people with specific psychological profiles. *The rules of configuration* allow readers to link different text fragments to one another, combining various textual patterns with their own expectations. Finally, *the rules of coherence* enable readers to transform texts into a coherent whole.

In a similar fashion, readers are in charge of the reading experience since it is only through their energies that the power of the texts can be freed (Rosenblatt, 1978). In order to illustrate the notion of transaction, Rosenblatt's (quoted in Weaver, 2002, p. 23) three key terms can be presented as follows:
- *the reader* – the person seeking to create meaning by transacting with any kind of text;
- *the text* – the collection of word symbols and patterns on the page, the physical object you hold in your hand as you read; and,
- *the poem* – the literary work created as the reader transacts with the text.

"Poem" refers metaphorically to any literary work. Meaning does not exist in the texts themselves but is rather constructed in the course of the transaction between readers and texts during the reading process.

It is also important to note that despite the various advantages authentic texts offer, they may turn out to be too difficult for learners at lower levels of language proficiency. In such a case, the choice appears to be confined to pedagogic or simplified readers (Day & Bamford, 1998). The latter, especially modern graded readers, are highly recommended for independent learning (e.g. Pulverness, 2007) because, in stark contrast to their outdated counterparts, they are published as comprehensive packages with a different focus, for example, on English-speaking cultures and their histories, dramatisation or literary expression. They serve many purposes, and therefore are gaining more and more popularity in language education. For instance, detailed examination of the place and role of graded readers in language education (e.g. Day & Bamford, 1998; Pulverness, 2007; Waring, 2009) showed that they enhance receptive skills, consolidate learning, strengthen comprehension and vocabulary, stimulate students' creativity, expose students to different historical and cultural perspectives, broaden students' horizons and generate interest in literature. In addition to this, most of these readers are accompanied with activity or project sections to help learners to analyse issues introduced in texts, audio CDs which provide fully dramatised recordings of stories, full-colour illustrations and full poster-size games, quizzes, biographies of authors and summaries of plot.

As can be seen, it is important that SALCs include different types of materials and tasks (see 3.1.1.6) so that users will find them attractive and effective. The same approach will be taken in the bank of learner autonomy tasks displayed in Chapter Seven (see 7.3). To successfully facilitate learner autonomy, it is essential that SALCs compete with good language teaching materials, offer a wide range of tasks and be distinguished by:

> *a clear statement of objectives, meaningful language input, exercise materials and activities, flexibility of materials, learning instructions, language learning advice, feedback and tests, advice about record keeping, reference materials, indexing, motivational factors, and advice about progression (Dickinson, 1987, p. 80).*

It is Tomlinson (2011a) who is the author of the most precise list of features of self-access materials (see Figure 1). Therefore, if schools, universities or teachers wish to manage a successful, vibrant and up-to-date SALC, they should treat this list as a signpost.

1.	The materials provide extensive exposure to authentic English through purposeful reading and/or listening activities.
2.	Whilst reading/listening activities are offered to facilitate interaction with the text(s).
3.	The post reading/listening activities first of all elicit global, holistic responses which involve interaction between the self and the text.
4.	The focus of the main responsive activities is on the development of such high level skills as imaging, inferencing, connecting, interpreting and evaluating.
5.	There are also activities which help the learners to fix selective attention in such a way that they can discover something new about specific features of the text, and thus become aware of any mismatch between their competence and the equivalent performance of target language users.
6.	Production activities involve the use of the target language in order to achieve situational purposes rather than just to practise specific linguistic features of the target language. These activities offer involvement in various types of personal expression (e.g. analytical, aesthetic, imaginative, argumentative, evaluative).

7.	The learners are given plenty of opportunities to make choices which suit their linguistic level, their preferred learning styles, their level of involvement in the text and the time they have available.
8.	Whereas self-access activities are typically private and individual, access-self activities include the possibility of like minded learners working together without reference to a teacher. That way the learners are able to choose between the tailor-made benefits of private work and the opportunity to pool resources and energy with fellow learners.
9.	Feedback is given through commentaries rather than answer keys. The commentaries give the learners opportunities to compare their responses to those of the material developers and of other learners. They can be consulted at the end of the activities to gain summative feedback or during activities in order to help learners to modify or develop their responses as they proceed through the unit.
10.	Learner training is encouraged through activities which involve the learners in thinking about the learning process and in experiencing a variety of different types of learning activities from which they can later make informed choices in determining their route through the access-self materials.
11.	Suggestions for individual follow-up activities are given at the end of each unit.

Figure 1. Features of access-self materials (adapted from Tomlinson, 2011a, pp. 417-418)

As can be seen, Tomlinson's access-self materials rest on a humanistic philosophy of language learning. This philosophy views language learners as whole persons who possess physical, emotional, social and cognitive features (Williams & Burden, 1997). What is more, the creativity of the learners is put to use generating views of the surrounding reality in unique ways. This very observation brings Tomlinson's list closer to constructivism. This philosophical framework stresses that human beings construct their own representations of the world (see 2.2). Accordingly, it is desirable that materials and tasks available in SALCs are designed in such a way that they enable learners to utilise their prior experience and allow for personal discoveries and development (Tomlinson, 1994, 2003b). To be effective, it is of key importance that such materials and tasks activate the entire brain so that both hemispheres are engaged in language learning and personal development. Additionally, such materials and tasks are expected to be based on a rich comprehensible input (Krashen, 1982) and offer a variety of open-ended questions (see 3.1.1.5). Opportunities for diverse responses will then be provided.

All in all, SALCs create favourable conditions for cultivating learner autonomy since they provide their users with countless opportunities to direct their own learning. However, teachers should note that SALCs successfully fulfil their role only when the following three requirements, namely, the bank of appropriate materials and tasks, the mutual involvement of teachers (or other staff) and learners in their effective operation and their close relationship with the curriculum, are fulfilled.

2.3.4 THE TECHNOLOGY-RELATED APPROACH

The discussion about crucial methods of developing learner autonomy in the EFL context closes with the technology-related approach. This approach has certain aspects in common (e.g. a wealth of learning materials and tasks) with the resource-related approach discussed above. The technology-related approach is distinguished from the resource-related approach in its examination of the technologies involved while accessing learning resources.

Learning technologies have always gone together with learner autonomy. For example, in the 1980s, communicative computer-assisted language learning (communicative CALL) promoted computers as tools to boost "the linguistic process in achieving non-linguistic goals" (Benson, 2001, p. 138). In the 1990s, communicative CALL took the form of integrative CALL, supporting the use of computer technology as a tool for meaningful interaction and collaborative project work (Cutrim Schmidt, 2008; Gruba, 2004; Kaupmann, 2012; Kötter, 2003; Krajka, 2007; Legutke, Müller-Hartmann, & Schocker-v. Ditfurth, 2009; Rüschoff, 2009). Today, there is a large variety of technologies available in language education. They range from tablets to mobile phones. As a result, the term CALL has become obsolete (Jarvis & Achilleos, 2013; Jarvis & Krashen, 2014) and has been replaced by such terms as *technology-assisted language learning* or *technology-enhanced language learning*.

Now that the terminology has been updated, it must be made clear from the very beginning that autonomy in a technology-mediated environment is not understood as individual work with computers or other technological devices. Rather, autonomy in a technology-mediated environment is associated with enhancing the learning capacity of those who are involved in foreign language education via computerised modes (Krajka, 2007). In other words, learners make use of the opportunities technology offers for developing not only autonomous behaviour, but also all the skills needed to incorporate technology in their experiential learning (see Task 1, Task 2 and Task 3 in 7.3). Thus, it can be inferred that in the context of technology in language education, learner autonomy can be defined as developing a capacity for involvement in and analytical reflection on the learning process (see 2.3.2.2). The definition of learner autonomy includes facilitating interdependence between learners and teachers, both of whom collectively assume charge and control of their classroom environment (see 2.3.2), as well as enjoying the outcomes of the decisions and choices they make (Blin, 1999; Schwienhorst, 2008, 2011; Shield & Weininger, 1999). The first three tasks displayed in the bank of learner autonomy tasks serve this very purpose (see 7.3).

By this token, learner autonomy can be developed in the technology-mediated setting through blended learning, which combines face-to-face teaching and learning situations with educational technology (e.g. CD-ROMs, the Internet, interactive whiteboards, email, HTML editors, Skype, tablets, laptops, mobile phones, digital voice recorders). In fact, in this type of instruction, different elements can be blended (e.g. in-class and on-line programmes or materials in different formats), yet the most important thing is that it improves instruction, taking the best from autonomy-orientated, teacher-led as well as in-classroom and out-of-classroom delivery (Driscoll & Carliner, 2005).

As can be seen, the technology-related approach, with its various tools, has a lot to offer to modern language education. For instance, interactive whiteboards, a strong catalyst in pushing language education away from the coursebook-based model (Cutrim Schmidt, 2008, 2009; Thomas & Cutrim Schmidt, 2010), enable learners to manipulate images (e.g. colour, size) and texts (colour, size, underlining, highlighting, shading, covering, etc.), create their own pictures and illustrations, save notes and store documents for later review, as well as promoting social interaction (see 2.2.1.2), active collaboration (see 2.2.1.4), decision-making (see 2.3.2.1) and creativity in classroom tasks. The evidence strongly suggests that interactive whiteboards are a useful tool for language classrooms with multiple learning styles and differing needs (see 3.1.1.4). They are not only ideal for visual learners, but can assist kinaesthetic learners in the classroom through activities involving touch and movement. Similarly, visually-impaired students can benefit from interactive whiteboards by manipulating objects or working with a large text option, for example.

Email and Skype, in turn, contribute to developing literacy in the classroom. They both allow learners to take part in social interaction and genuine communication (Gao, 2009; Krajka, 2007; Mullen, Appel, & Shanklin, 2009; Müller-Hartmann, 2000; Rösler, 2006). Learners construct texts and exchange information for a purpose with real-life partners (see 3.2.1). Furthermore, email and Skype change learners into critical thinkers. These forms of communication allow learners to assume the role of active creators of information and meaning (see 2.2). For instance, research conducted by Vilmi (1994) demonstrates that email-based and Skype-based instruction helps students to better understand speakers from different ethnic backgrounds. Students are encouraged to confidently participate in cross-cultural communication. Beauvois (1995, 1997) and Warschauer (1995) observed that foreign language learners who are shy and reserved in face to face classroom interactions participate more willingly in exchanges in the electronic context. Apart from major benefits in the target language literacy, email- and Skype-based tasks additionally promote cooperative team or pair work, independence from language teachers (or at least, reduced control on the part of the latter) and computer skills such as typing and hand-eye coordination.

On the other hand, researchers (e.g. Nagel, 1999; Robb, 1996; Vilmi, 1994) working within the area of educational technology present a number of difficulties that tasks related to foreign language keypal exchanges can create. Firstly, email exchanges are likely to produce a large amount of message output for both teachers and learners. Secondly, not responding promptly or not replying to emails at all may result in the decline of motivation on the part of the students. Hence, it is imperative that there be steady Internet access and a deep commitment on the part of all class members. Finally, non-response or inadequate communication may also stem from a disparity in the language level or learning purpose of the students involved.

Other tools that can be used to develop foreign language learning in technology-enhanced instruction are blogs or web logs. Blogs are online journals which can be easily established and run, as well as systematically updated with interesting thoughts or announcements. Web logs are gaining more and more popularity in the classroom these days because of their collaborative nature (see 2.2.1.4). For example, tasks that include web logging promote target language interaction, encourage literacy, facilitate learner autonomy and cultivate inquiry-based learning (Campbell, 2003; Godwin-Jones, 2003; Kaupmann, 2012; Krajka, 2007; Long, 2002; Raith, 2006, 2009; Schmitt-Egner, 2012; Trajtemberg & Yiakoumetti, 2011).

Likewise, classroom wikis are increasingly being used as versatile communication tools (Ebersbach, Glaser, Heigl, & Warta, 2008; Krajka, 2007). These wikis function as a group of web pages used for storing and modifying information. In contrast to blogs, wikis possess the unique feature of giving everyone the right to manipulate their content. Thus, anyone can add, revise or delete certain elements in a wiki. Permissions and passwords are not needed. In this vein, wikis are more democratic tools than blogs, which are controlled by the blog owner.

From the pedagogical point of view, tasks that involve designing wikis are effective in several dimensions. For example, they empower learners to create knowledge and facilitate creativity in the classroom by keeping students thinking, questioning and writing. Such tasks also enable language students to experience foreign language writing in a collaborative climate. The latter is extremely useful as it allows learners not only to learn from others, but also provides favourable conditions for building a class community. Finally, wiki-based tasks foster learners' critical thinking as well as investigative and negotiation skills.

Mobile phones have also been used in language education in different contexts. As research reports, mobile phones are particularly valued because of their ubiquity (Tindell & Bohlander, 2012). They are also held in high regard for engaging students in meaningful learning from literally anywhere. As research shows, mobile phones contribute to enhancing students' lexico-grammatical knowledge (Levy & Kennedy, 2005; Lu, 2008) as well as language skills (Smythe & Neufeld, 2010; Plester, Wood, & Joshi, 2009). Mobile phones also increase collaboration in the classroom and help to engage students in different types of interaction (Scornavacca, Huff & Marshall, 2009; Thomas & Orthober, 2011). Finally, mobile phones help students to manage their learning process by accessing, completing and submitting their school assignments (Purcell, Heaps, Buchanan, & Friedrich, 2013).

Another asset to blended learning is technology-based materials. These materials comply with the general principles for communicative materials design (Allwright, 1981; Breen & Waters, 1979). The materials have inherent features such as: interactivity, multidimensionality, large storage capacity, dynamics, as well as the unique ability to show and hide information at a given time (Levy, 1997, p. 110-111). This observation is also in agreement with the view (Ariew & Frommer's, 1987, p. 177-193; Doughty & Long, 2003, p. 52) that the attractiveness and effectiveness of technology-based materials rest on the fact that they:
- encourage learning by doing;
- provide rich visual and aural input;
- facilitate inductive learning;
- promote collaborative and interactive learning;
- engage students in authentic modes of target language use;
- supply various types of feedback (textual, kinaesthetic and aural); and
- stimulate independent action on the part of learners.

Additionally, both pedagogical and technical advantages of CALL or technology-based materials have been listed by Godwin-Jones (2005) and Zhao (2005), who emphasise that such materials enhance:
- digital literacy and communicative skills;
- authenticity via the Internet and video;

- analysis of learner conduct and errors; and
- empowerment due to the fact that learners have easy access to and substantial control over study materials.

The analysis of educational research indicates that technology-based materials and tasks exert a positive influence on learners. For instance, several studies report that technology-mediated instruction increases learners' motivation and self-esteem (Lynch, Fawcett, & Nicolson, 2000), boosts involvement and enthusiasm for learning (Nah, White, & Sussex, 2008; Solvie, 2004; Rooke, 2015; Wang, Shen, Novak, & Pan, 2009), promotes communication (Kötter, 2003; Schmitt-Egner, 2012), enhances confidence in managing their own learning (Li, 2000; Chen, Hsieh, & Kinshuk, 2008), develops learners' sense of responsibility (Kaupmann, 2012; Li, 2000) and facilitates collaborative work (Hsu & Ching, 2013; Kötter, 2003; Li, 2000; Rogers & Price, 2009; Rüschoff, 2009). All these findings are essential for learners in order to become autonomous. Also, according to Warschauer (2000) and Fang and Warschauer (2004), CALL provides ample opportunities for successful development of learner autonomy *per se*.

The general conclusion from this subsection is that the technology-related approach is vital in cultivating learner autonomy. Bearing in mind all the facts presented above, it is desirable that teachers make various attempts to promote blended learning in their own practice. This can be achieved by providing students with opportunities to collaborate in classroom projects (Cutrim Schmidt, 2008; Ebersbach, Glaser, Heigl, & Warta, 2008; Krajka, 2007; Wolff, 2002b). The projects could take the following two forms: *on-line research* where language learners conduct research on the Internet in order to explore matters of interest, or *on-line publication* where language learners work in small groups in order to produce and eventually publish web-based documentary reports from their countries.

2.4 CONCLUSION

Defining learner autonomy at the beginning of the discussion was not at all a simple task. The process of facilitating the construct in the EFL context at the end of the present chapter was not without difficulty.

Conclusion

The development of the capacity for independent language learning, as Chapter Two reveals, requires taking into account various psychological (e.g. characteristics of learners), sociocultural (e.g. social interactions with more knowledgeable others) and political (e.g. power structures) aspects. This complexity contributes to a very important conclusion, namely, intricate though learner autonomy may seem, it can be developed by means of precisely planned educational mediation. It is suggested that learner autonomy be incorporated into the classroom context, perhaps most effectively through a blend of approaches and tasks.

The literature review presented in this chapter discloses that there are numerous approaches to developing learner autonomy. Research outcomes convincingly demonstrate the effectiveness and pedagogical value of these approaches. What is more, the argument makes teachers aware that different approaches require different learner strategies, diverse types of work, specific instructional materials and well-designed tasks. Teachers are put in a difficult position because modern EFL course books do not contain a sufficient number of specific learner autonomy tasks. Teachers are required to either adapt existing materials or design their own tasks. Task design is complex and consists of several stages, as presented in Chapter Seven.

The next chapter will delve into and describe appropriate texts and complex tasks for developing learner autonomy.

CHAPTER THREE

MATERIALS AND PEDAGOGICAL TASKS FOR DEVELOPING LEARNER AUTONOMY

The theoretical considerations which concern learner autonomy discussed in Chapter Two led to the conclusion that a wide range of instructional materials and tasks is required to ensure successful learner independence. It is desirable that such materials combine print and digital sources as well as educational technology. As far as the tasks are concerned, it is vital that they promote, among other things, interaction, meaning negotiation, mediation, scaffolding, collaboration and problem-solving. Cogent though this observation may seem, it can turn out to be problematic. It is important not to forget that current course books are mainly produced with a large student population in mind. The books are made to fit as many teaching-learning contexts as possible (Hadley, 2014; McGrath, 2002; Müller-Hartmann & Schocker-von Ditfurth, 2011; Tomlinson, 2010). McGrath (2013, p. 9) shares the opinion described above and goes on to say that course books produced for the global market "derive from an anglocentric view of the world", and thus "have little relevance for the majority of learners studying English outside English-speaking countries". I could not agree more with this observation. I would also add that no matter how attractive modern course books appear, they contain a very limited number of learner autonomy tasks. This shortage of learner autonomy tasks in modern materials became the major incentive to create the collection included in Chapter Seven.

For example, in the Polish context, teachers have a range of course books to choose from. These course books are recommended by the Ministry of Education to ensure they meet general and specific criteria for evaluation, as suggested by Ur (1996) and Tomlinson (1999), respectively. The available course books are designed by leading publishers (e.g. Oxford University Press, Express Publishing) and aim at developing communicative competence. They are divided into a number of units, each of which mainly focuses on the systematic practice of both lexico-grammar and language skills. However, as this chapter will show, this is not sufficient for learner autonomy to be present in the classroom. It is recommended that teachers design their own tasks to supplement course books. This may be easier said than done as there are both advantages and drawbacks. For example, teacher involvement in task design means that local needs or conditions (e.g. time constraints or the classroom environment) must be taken into consideration. Such involvement is time-consuming and difficult, especially if teachers lack experience in creating tasks.

Another observation is that the concept of a traditional course book has recently changed in secondary schools in Poland. What once used to be considered supplementary materials are now treated as course books. For example, published collections of either past or exemplary Matura examination papers appear to be compulsory materials now. They seem to have replaced traditional EFL course books to a large degree. The new course books are normally used by Year 3 students. In some schools, Year 2 students are already familiar with these new versions of course books, too. The decision to use these materials in the final year, that is, Year 3, is to familiarise students with the Matura examination format and help them to be well prepared for the examination. Such a state of affairs is directly linked to the backwash effect (Farrell & Jacobs, 2010; McNamara, 1996). This means nothing less than teaching for the examination. This teaching practice appears to be a recent development in language education at the secondary level in Poland (Zawadowska-Kittel, 2013).

The main goal of this chapter is to provide teachers with useful information on instructional materials and pedagogical tasks to be used for the development of learner autonomy. As pointed out in Chapter Two, text-driven tasks play an important role in learner autonomy facilitation. Therefore, several important criteria for text selection will be examined. It is vital that English language teachers are aware of these criteria and utilise them while planning cognitively challenging tasks. Additionally, teachers are expected to be familiar with a number of crucial features of pedagogical tasks. Teachers will then be able to design their own tasks or adapt those of others. A detailed discussion of these features followed by a brief analysis of course books closes Chapter Three.

3.1 SELECTING TEXTS FOR FACILITATING LEARNER AUTONOMY

The discussion in Chapter Two stressed the importance of literature (e.g. short stories) in the successful development of learner autonomy. It is recommended that teachers bring authentic texts (see 2.3.3.2) into the classroom whenever possible because of the limitless benefits these texts offer. Attractive though text-based materials may seem, they must not be limited to literature and, unquestionably, should be perceived as more than language (Kress, 1999). Since texts appear to be a complex concept, what then is the definition of a *text*?

In order to answer this question, some would probably reach for Halliday and Hasan's (1976, p. 293) definition, which regards a text as:

> (...) a semantic unit. The unity that it has is a unity of meaning in context, a texture that expresses the fact that it relates as a whole to the environment in which it is placed. Being a semantic unit, a text is realised in the form of sentences, and this is how the relation of text to sentence can best be interpreted.

Others would refer to de Beaugrande and Dressler's (1981) perception of a text as a communicative occurrence described in terms of seven standards of textuality: cohesion, coherence, intentionality, acceptability, situationality, intertextuality and informativity. A closer look at the individual standards does show that de Beaugrande and Dressler's definition successfully combines syntactic, semantic and pragmatic aspects of text. It is, therefore, clear why both linguists insist texts be studied in their context of communicative use.

Bouissac (1976, p. 126), in contrast to Halliday and Hasan (1976) and de Beaugrande and Dressler (1981), appears even braver in formulating his concept of a text, and defines it as:

> (...) any permanent set of ordered elements (sentences, objects, or actions, or any combination of these) whose copresence (or collation) is considered by an encoder and/or a decoder as being related in some capacity to one another through the mediation of a logico-semantic system.

All three definitions of text are strongly related to language teaching, yet it is the third standpoint that is most relevant for the purposes of this chapter. Bouissac's perspective seems to resonate the social semiotic theory. This theory deals with social meanings and explores how human beings communicate via a variety of modes. These modes, also referred to as semiotic resources, include language and images. For example, Kress and van Leeuwen (1996, p. 44) elaborate that:

> What in language is realised by locative propositions is realised in pictures by the formal characteristics that create the contrast between foreground and background. This is not to say that all the relations that can be realised in language can also be realised in pictures, or vice versa, that all the relations that can be realised in pictures can also be realised in language. Rather, a given culture has a range of general, possible relations which is not tied to expression in any particular semiotic code, although some relations can only be realised in pictures and others only in words, or some more easily in pictures and others more easily in words.

In other words, social semiotics underscores that texts people construct (see 2.2), and then send to their interlocutors, particularly in social or cultural circumstances, promote multiple modes of representation, including print, visual images and design (Hassett & Curwood, 2009; Siegel, 2006; The New London Group, 2000) and in the case of multimedia sound and movement (Barthes, 1964; Bearne, 2009). A more detailed range of modalities has been presented by Cope and Kalantzis (2009, p. 178-179). Their list includes:

- *written language* (e.g. handwriting, the printed page, the screen);
- *oral language* (e.g. live speech, recorded speech);
- *visual representation* (e.g. still or moving image);
- *audio representation* (e.g. music, noises);
- *tactile representation* (e.g. touch, smell, taste);
- *gestural representation* (e.g. hand, arm or eye movement); and
- *spatial representation* (e.g. proximity, spacing, layout, landscape).

The transition from print-orientated to multimodal instruction is evidence of a big change in developing foreign language literacy. The way the socio-cultural reality requires that learners interact with texts and their various representational modes cannot be neglected (Siegel, 2006). Multimodal texts call for new ways of processing text-image relations since the printed word, more often than not, is no longer the primary carrier of meaning (Kress, 1999; Lanham, 2001; The New London Group, 2000). The focus needs to be shifted onto numerous textual components such as print, and graphics, plus the interactive conversations about the texts which occur in the social context of the classroom. The more modalities involved, the more complex the texts are, and consequently, the more challenging the tasks are for the reader to process. In other words, the various modalities incorporated into a text work together. Images or graphics become part of the discourse of text (Alsup, 2010). While reading multimodal texts, readers must not look at the language in isolation, because the written word interacts with the design elements used, simultaneously acquiring and giving new meanings (Cook, 1992).

It is notable that multimodal texts require a type of reading that radically differs from reading a traditional monomodal text. In traditional texts, also referred to as linear verbal texts, reading is an uninterrupted and progressive activity. By contrast, in multimodal texts, the different semiotic components integrated on one page cannot be processed in the same linear manner as mentioned above. Because of their inherent complexity, multimodal texts require the reader to be much more active. Such a reader must be capable of recognising interdependencies between the verbal and the non-verbal constituents. The reader must also be capable of constructing a fully integrated meaning out of them (Hallet, 2011).

The pedagogical implications of this new approach are immense, and therefore will be taken into account in the process of designing complex tasks in the later part of this volume (see 7.1.2). The purpose of this kind of instruction is to produce active meaning creators who are able to read multimodal texts, invariably relating to five dimensions of meaning (Cope & Kalantzis, 2009, p. 176). These dimensions are as follows:

1. *representational* (i.e. What do the meanings refer to?);
2. *social* (i.e. How do the meanings connect the persons they involve?);
3. *structural* (i.e. How are the meanings organized?);
4. *intertextual* (i.e. How do the meanings fit into the larger world of meaning?); and
5. *ideological* (i.e. Whose interests are the meanings skewed to serve?).

With the social semiotic approach to texts in mind, it must be clarified that all the pictures, posters, charts and graphs teachers present to students, with verbal support or without, are also instances of texts. These texts, sometimes referred to as visual communication, are meant to present messages graphically. When isolated from verbal elements, audio-visual materials may sometimes distract learners, eventually leading to conflicting messages. This stems from the fact that people utilise their background knowledge and cultural understandings to decode messages (Hallet, 2011; Ryan, Cooper, & Tauer, 2011). For this reason, no matter what texts are being used in a given situation, it is advisable that teachers invariably draw students' attention to the following communication components: the communicator, the receiver, the communication material and media used to convey messages (Ryan, Cooper, & Tauer, 2011).

As can be seen, texts can take different forms (e.g. written, drawn, painted). Regardless of their structure, they are created by diverse sign systems which convey messages. Individual signs are further governed by complex meaning-relations operating within texts, and thus contribute to the communication event (Crafton, Silvers, & Brennan, 2009). Another interesting observation is that the semiotic perspective of a text corresponds to the formerly discussed philosophy of social constructivism (see 2.2). Both positions emphasise that people, as social beings, are continuously involved in the creation and interpretation of meanings with other members of the surrounding world (Hill & Nichols, 2013).

It is the criteria for text selection that constitute the central theme of the following discussion. For this reason, it must be clarified that from this point on, the concept of text in this volume includes multimodal texts.

3.1.1 CRITERIA FOR TEXT SELECTION

Having clarified how the concept of text should be perceived in language pedagogy, the stage is set for text selection criteria. Such criteria have been specified in the literature on different occasions (Carter & Long, 1991; Dudley-Evans & St John, 1998; Wallace, 1992), but it is beyond the scope of this section to give an overview of them all. I will focus only on *connectivity, suitability of language, suitability of content, suitability for personalisation, exploitability* and *variety*. Although these criteria are not new in the field, there are several reasons why they need to be addressed now. Firstly, some of the criteria are not always successfully met in the modern course books or language courses taught in diverse teaching contexts (McGrath, 2013; Sepúlveda, 2009; Wong & Waring, 2010). Secondly, language instructors have a direct influence on these criteria. Teachers can improve materials by adapting them when a criterion is not given enough attention in ready-made sources (McGrath, 2013). Adapted materials (see 3.3.1) serve to provide high standards, and consequently guarantee better instruction and more interesting classes (Danielson, 2007). Thirdly, good quality provision and attractive materials affect student motivation (see 3.2.1), which conditions learning and performance outcomes (Ushioda, 2001). From a practitioner's point of view, the six indicators, to a large degree, decide which materials should be recommended and which should be discarded. It should also be remembered that properly selected texts provide a solid basis for designing high-quality tasks. The model for developing pedagogical tasks for learner autonomy is presented in Chapter Seven.

The six criteria carry important information for both teachers and materials writers. They both must know what aspects to take into account in the design process so that the final product is enjoyable for all. Teachers and materials writers are additionally expected to be aware of the essential know-how of selecting effective and challenging texts that could be used or modified to fit learner autonomy development. The key criteria are briefly discussed below.

3.1.1.1 CONNECTIVITY

With regard to the main tenets of social constructivism which have been thoroughly discussed in Chapter Two (see 2.2), learners are actively engaged in constructing worlds of texts. For example, both reading and listening comprehension are facilitated when schemata, defined as mental structures representing readers' knowledge (Alderson, 2000), are activated. This, in turn, means that foreign language readers/listeners draw on prior knowledge and experience to assist them in comprehending what they are reading/listening to. Consequently, that knowledge can be employed to make different types of connections.

Learners appear to be better comprehenders when they make at least three types of connections: *text-to-self*, *text-to-text* and *text-to-world* (Keene & Zimmerman, 1997; Moreillon, 2007). The first type focuses on the highly personal connections learners make between the texts they process and their own life experiences. The second occurs when learners connect to texts in relation to other texts they have already decoded. The third type, text-to-world connections, takes place when learners make connections between texts and ideas, issues or events that go far beyond their own personal experiences (Moreillon, 2007).

To cognitively interact with multimodal texts (see 3.1), it is important that students be provided with tasks that suit their schemata. For example, in a new learning situation, language data are processed in accordance with how the data correspond to the complex network of a learner's schemata (Piaget, 1952). If the new information matches the existent cognitive structures, it is approved and comprehended. If there is a divergence, the new information may be rejected or the learner makes an attempt to accommodate the new information by revising the existing framework of schemata (Piaget, 1952). As a result, using constructivist terminology, new schemata are created. The latter situation is the accommodation process (see 3.1.1.3). Intrinsic motivation (see 3.2.1) is triggered in the form of inquisitiveness to minimise the divergence between the new stimuli and the existing schemata (Gottfried, 2008). It can also be inferred that texts and tasks generating cognitive divergence provoke intrinsic motivation in the form of curiosity or willingness to explore.

The better the match between the new material and the learner's ZPD (see 2.2.1.1), the more connections are made. These connections are extremely important as they enable learners to synthesise and consolidate information and become actively engaged in learning the target language (Moreillon, 2007). High quality text-based tasks should generate different types of connections by encouraging learners to ask different types of questions (see 3.1.1.5). For example, text-to-self connections can be encouraged by asking the following questions: *Have you ever had a similar experience? Have you ever read/heard about this event before?* Text-to-text connections can be stimulated by questions such as: *Have you ever read a story in which similar events took place? Have you ever listened to a talk in which people behaved in a similar way?* Finally, learners' text-to-world connections can be boosted when the following questions are posed: *What do you think the author's purpose was in writing this text? In what way does the writer make references to current issues in the country?*

3.1.1.2 SUITABILITY OF LANGUAGE

Another criterion to be discussed is the *suitability of language*. The textual material language learners are exposed to should allow them to master their target language competence. The definition of *communicative competence* presented by Bachman (1990) states that language competence refers to knowledge of the language. More specifically, this definition consists of four sub-competences: *grammatical, textual, sociolinguistic* and *illocutionary*. Accordingly, grammatical competence in this model pertains to knowledge of vocabulary, morphology, syntax and phonology/graphology, whereas textual competence includes knowledge of the conventions to construct meaningful texts. These conventions include cohesion, rhetorical organisation and conversational routines. To be more precise, cohesion creates the readability of a text and affects the comprehensibility and clarity of the arguments. As a result, it is closely related to appropriate use of conjunctions, references and lexical relations in texts. Rhetorical organisation refers to such aspects as the composition of texts and text types (e.g. narrative or argumentative). Finally, conversational routines deal with phenomena such as topic-nomination, turn-taking and conversation maintenance.

The other two competences to be discussed are sociolinguistic and illocutionary. The former pertains to the sociocultural rules of language and discourse. It is clear therefore that sociolinguistic competence enables language users to perform illocutionary functions with regard to the context of specific language use. Hence, it requires both sensitivity to differences in variety or register and the capacity to interpret cultural references. Illocutionary competence, on the other hand, is associated with the knowledge of language functions described above and their appropriate use in communication. It is essential that language users be able not only to endow language with illocutionary force, but also to cogently interpret its illocutionary force.

Complex though the concept of language competence may seem, it is essential that all its components be systematically developed in the language classroom as part of the wider process of learning to communicate (Council of Europe, 2001). This means that it is the Communicative Approach (see 2.2.4) to teaching grammar, not the structural approach that should be employed in EFL courses today. The structural approach is inappropriate since it fails to address the communicative needs of learners. Discussing grammar structures in a discrete manner does not reflect SLA research of how language rules are normally developed (Ellis, Basturkmen, & Loewen, 2002).

The components of language competence require that grammar be perceived not at a sentence level but at a discourse level. In other words, language competence deals with how sentences are integrated into texts, including both written and spoken modes (Hedge, 2000; Widdowson, 1978). One of the main reasons why this position is advocated in modern language pedagogy is that the everyday linguistic behaviour of humans is not involved in constructing separate sentences; humans produce sentences to create discourse (Widdowson, 1978). In addition, when grammar is perceived as an element of discourse, the grammar structures are presented in context. Contextualisation is very important, especially when language learners focus on the pragmatic aspects such as implied meaning, politeness or formality (Cirocki, 2013b). Hence, a rich textual environment is keenly sought in the classroom.

As a result, it is recommended that class texts support a focus-on-form (FonF) approach to language instruction (Ellis, 2001). This approach promotes overtly directing the learners' attention to linguistic elements during communicative tasks as they randomly occur in classes where the focus is on communication (Long, 1991; Nassaji & Fotos, 2011). More specifically, the FonF approach primarily concerns message processing (i.e. form-function mapping) rather than formal aspects of the target language, namely its forms in the traditional sense. Texts which draw learners' attention to form while directing learners' primary focus to meaning are particularly helpful. It is also important that texts encourage learners to make the most of the target language they possess. Last but not least, texts distributed in the classroom are meant to inform learners about the target language system, assist learners in schematising their lexico-grammatical knowledge and develop awareness that the target language is grammatical but is not grammar in itself. Another point to keep in mind is that discourse is additionally made up of sounds/letters and words. As a result, it embraces lexical, semantic, phonological, orthographic and orthoepic competences. For more details, see Paltridge (2006).

The next category to concentrate on is vocabulary, which appears to play an even more important role than grammar. As Wilkins (1972, p. 111) observes:

> *Without grammar very little can be conveyed, without vocabulary nothing can be conveyed. If you spend most of your time studying grammar, your English will not improve much. You will see most improvement if you learn more words and expressions. You can say very little with grammar, but you can say almost anything with words.*

Good texts which students receive during their course of study will assist them in building a rich vocabulary. The texts are supposed to encourage students to learn new lexical items on a regular basis. First of all, it is essential that the vocabulary the texts contain is useful for learners' own needs (Ur, 2012). Usefulness of lexical items can be measured through *frequency*, that is, how often particular items occur in discourse. Classroom texts should use vocabulary from the available lists that are based on frequency. Some of the lists are: *Oxford 3000*, *English Profile* or *The Academic Word List*. Sometimes good dictionaries also indicate frequency levels, for example, *Cambridge Advanced Learner's Dictionary* or *The Longman Active Study Dictionary*. Further sources to be consulted in this respect are the *Collins Birmingham University International Language Database* (COBUILD) and the *Longman Lancaster Corpus* (LLC).

What should also be emphasised is the importance of multiword units. These units are expected to be regularly promoted in texts so that language learners recognise them as functioning strings of words rather than individual lexemes (Schmitt, 2000). These multiword units include: *idioms* (e.g. let the dust settle), *phrasal verbs* (e.g. put up with), *fixed expressions* (e.g. as a matter of fact), *compound words* (e.g. brainstorm) and *proverbs* (e.g. All that glitters is not gold.). According to psycholinguistic research (e.g. Schmitt, 2004), these units are stored in the long term-memory as individual wholes, often referred to as chunks. Since these multiword units act as individual units, they are easily retrievable. These chunks are stored as wholes and retrieving them imposes much less demand on cognitive capacity. Very little or no additional processing is required (Schmitt, 2000).

As with grammar, vocabulary must be contextualised. It is rich contexts that more often than not define words. Otherwise, lexical items are deprived of linguistic and psychological realities. Words must carry messages and emotions to engage learners (Schouten-van Parreren, 1989). The more engaging the texts, the better. Engaging texts allow language learners to convert their *passive vocabulary* (i.e. lexical items that are recognised, but not regularly used) into *active vocabulary* (i.e. lexical items frequently used in speech or writing). Learners can then perform better, for example, in productive post-reading communicative tasks (e.g. speaking or writing). The enhanced performance, though, is not only limited to this area.

The general conclusion of this section is that language education needs to provide learners with opportunities to use their lexico-grammatical knowledge in realistic situations (see 3.2.1). The more such opportunities in the classroom, the better. Lexis and grammar provide the basis for the successful development of the four language skills. It is important that textual input (see 7.1.2.2) supplied in the classroom also enables learners to progress in their language proficiency from one level to another. In Poland and in other countries of the European Union (EU), the *Common European Framework of Reference for Languages* provides the groundwork for learner performance, which differentiates three broad levels of language use (Council of Europe, 2001). The levels labelled *Basic User*, *Independent User* and *Proficient User* are detailed below (see Figure 2).

Proficient User	C2	Can understand with ease virtually everything heard or read. Can summarise information from different spoken and written sources, reconstructing arguments and accounts in a coherent presentation. Can express him/herself spontaneously, very fluently and precisely, differentiating finer shades of meaning even in more complex situation.
	C1	Can understand a wide range of demanding, longer text, and recognise implicit meaning. Can express him/herself fluently and spontaneously without much obvious searching for expressions. Can use language flexibly and effectively for social, academic and professional purposes. Can produce clear, well-structured, detailed text on complex subjects, showing controlled use of organisational patterns, connectors and cohesive devices.
Independent User	B2	Can understand the main ideas of complex text on both concrete and abstract topics, including technical discussions in his/her field of specialisation. Can interact with a degree of fluency and spontaneity that makes regular interaction with native speakers quite possible without strain for either party. Can produce clear, detailed text on a wide range of subjects and explain a viewpoint on a topical issue giving the advantages and disadvantages of different options.
	B1	Can understand the main points of clear standard input on familiar matters regularly encountered at work, school, leisure, etc. Can deal with most situations likely to arise whilst travelling in an area where the language is spoken. Can produce simple connected text on topics which are familiar or of personal interest. Can describe experiences and events, dreams, hopes and ambitions and briefly give reasons and explanations for opinions and plans.
Basic User	A2	Can understand sentences and frequently used expressions related to areas of most immediate relevance (e.g. very basic personal and family information, shopping, local geography, employment). Can communicate in simple and routine tasks requiring a simple and direct exchange of information on familiar and routine matters. Can describe in simple terms aspects of his/her background, immediate environment and matters in areas of immediate need.
	A1	Can understand and use familiar everyday expressions and very basic phrases aimed at the satisfaction of needs of a concrete type. Can introduce him/herself and others and can ask and answer questions about personal details such as where he/she lives, people he/she knows and things he/she has. Can interact in a simple way provided the other person talks slowly and clearly and is prepared to help.

Figure 2. Common reference levels: Global scale (Council of Europe, 2001, p. 24)

3.1.1.3 SUITABILITY OF CONTENT

There is another criterion that deserves discussion – *suitability of content*. One proposed framework for favourable outcomes for interest development consists of a lure and a ladder (Harris & Sipay, 1990). The lure is represented by gripping and fascinating materials which have been produced to enchant the learners. The ladder, however, ranges from simple to challenging texts. The students can then climb gradually as their language skills improve.

The attractiveness of texts is, to a large degree, determined by topicality, which is also referred to as up-to-dateness, originality and currency (Mishan, 2005). However, the analysis of course books shows (see 3.3) that they are all limited to neutral topics such as food, shopping, holidays and interests instead of promoting controversy (Tomlinson, Dat, Masuhara, & Rubdy, 2001). The excuse publishers often use is that course books are planned to have a repeat life of a number of years. Topics that may be very attractive, but are likely to expire soon, are avoided. Some topics, for example, racism, religion, gay marriage and abortion appear to be inappropriate for class discussions in some cultures. These topics are avoided in course books. Both teachers and materials writers should realise that by promoting this commonplace neutrality of topics, they do more harm than good. What should be emphasised is that provocative topics are essential to provide students with classroom situations which require active engagement and affective response (see 3.2.1). Controversial texts facilitate learning, whereas neutral texts do not (Tomlinson, 2013a). In addition, affective engagement guarantees deep or high-level processing, which deals with the intricate scrutiny of meaning and complex processes of elaboration, interpretation and integration of information (Craik & Lockhart, 1972). It is exactly the same kind of processing that is a requisite for effective and sustainable learning (Scott & Gough, 2003).

As can be seen, topicality is difficult to handle in modern course books for a number of reasons. This problem, however, can be easily resolved at the classroom level. For example, in the language classroom, topicality can be ensured by the use of educational technology and the Internet (McGrath, 2002; Motteram, 2011; Ur, 2012). Teachers can supplement course book texts with digital texts on current issues (see 3.3). Recordings of interesting and controversial talks or interviews can be made available to students in the e-learning space. Of course, students can be actively involved in improving the course content (see 2.3.2.1). The learning process will then be even more enjoyable, relevant, autonomous and effective.

Apart from topicality, a number of other aspects need to be taken into account. For instance, for EFL reading practice, young adult literature is recommended as suitable content (see 2.3.3.2). Fiction earmarked for teenagers is highly appropriate as the books possess uncomplicated plots and a small cast of characters, with a young adult as the central figure. The language of these books abounds with colloquialisms, which can be a drawback or a great bonus. Additionally, young adult literature dramatises life in unfamiliar environments as experienced by the characters. Language learners also become familiarised with other cultures through such literature (Cirocki 2009, 2012; Wu 2009).

In the case of listening skills, video-based listening activities are widely advocated (see Widodo & Cirocki, 2015). Interesting real-life social exchanges can be used to facilitate the successful development of sociopragmatic competence. While listening to real-life spoken discourse, students' attention can be drawn to such aspects as: politeness, directness or paralinguistic and prosodic aspects of communication. Visual support is also a powerful tool while teaching the skill of listening. As research literature reveals (e.g. Anderson & Lynch, 1988; Rost, 2013), listening is not only an aural activity. To be able to fully comprehend or rightly interpret a text, the exploration of various sources of information (including visual, audio, haptic) is required. Likewise, more efficient acquisition of new language items and better retention of the facts gathered are also boosted through audio-visually-supported texts (Sampath, Panneerselvam, & Santhanam, 2007). In other words, multimodal texts (see 3.1) not only engage students in active learning, but also offer them multi-sensory experiences in which both abstract and concrete concepts are presented in various forms.

For students to succeed in developing positive reading/listening habits in the target language and to become autonomous readers/listeners (see 2.1), teachers are encouraged to provide texts which are not only absorbing and motivating, but also relevant to the students' interests and age (Tomlinson, 2003a). It is the age of the learner that invariably requires extreme caution since intellectual processing as well as learning skills are age-specific. Learners acquire more elaborate information processing abilities with age. For example, Piaget (1978) believed that a child's cognitive development is a process of maturation where genetics and experience interact. The concept of the developing mind, on the other hand, is one that invariably pursues equilibration. The assumption is that individuals require a stable internal state in an extremely complex and constantly changing environment. Equilibration, as a balance between what is known and what is being experienced particularly relies upon two main processes: *assimilation* and *accommodation*. The first is the process in which interpretations of the external world are adjusted to fit individuals' existing cognitive organisation. The latter is the process by which individuals modify what they already know to include new pieces of information (Piaget, 1978). Working in conjunction, assimilation and accommodation contribute to what Piaget labelled the central process of cognitive adaptation, which is a vital aspect of learning. In this way, the process of learning appears to be a complex act of construction and reconstruction of knowledge where learners build knowledge through the developmental processes of adaptation, assimilation and accommodation (see 2.2).

A meticulous analysis of the cognitive development of children and adolescents led Piaget (1972) to distinguish four stages, qualitatively different from each other, namely: *sensorimotor* (birth - 2 years), *preoperational* (2 - 7 years), *concrete operational* (7 - 11 years) and *formal operational* (11 - 16 years). Piaget further claimed that all children pass through these stages in ascending order so as to successfully attain the next phase of cognitive development. The higher the level of cognitive development, the more advanced the intellectual abilities. At this high level, children are able to demonstrate a more increasingly complex understanding of the world. With this in mind, it is crucial that teachers provide students with content that is fine-tuned to their ZPDs (see 2.2.1.1). Ideally, content should be cognitively challenging, but not disheartening.

3.1.1.4 SUITABILITY FOR PERSONALISATION

Having just highlighted that it is desirable that the course content be fine-tuned to learners' ZPDs, it seems fitting to briefly introduce the concept of *personalisation* into language teaching. It goes without saying that classrooms are clusters of multiple intelligences, different learning experiences, mixed abilities and learning attitudes (Armstrong, 2009; Capel, Leask, & Turner, 2013; Hedge, 2000; Ur, 2012). Learners are individuals and must be taught accordingly. For this reason, appropriate texts and tasks are required. In language education, personalisation is defined as instruction that is adjusted to learners' abilities, individual ZPDs, needs, preferences, interests, cultural backgrounds and learning styles (Xiaoqiong, Guoqing, & Zeng, 2013).

For example, Willing (1988) identified four types of learning styles in the adult learner population he observed. *Concrete learners* prefer to use images, games and films while learning. *Analytical learners* enjoy studying grammatical aspects and learning through reading. *Communicative learners* are keen on learning through conversations. *Authority-orientated learners* prefer to be taught by teachers and to regularly use course books. This rather broad typology has been challenged by Tomlinson (2011b, p. 18), who distinguishes nine learning styles. He highlights that both in- and out-of-class texts and the accompanying tasks should take into account all of the learning styles. According to him, the nine styles are: *visual* (learners prefer to use images, maps and colours), *auditory* (learners learn through listening), *kinaesthetic/tactile* (learners learn through performing physical activities), *studial* (learners pay close attention to the linguistic features), *experiential* (learners learn from the experience of using the target language), *analytic/sequential* (learners take in information one piece at a time), *global* (learners respond to chunks of the target language at a time), *dependent* (learners learn from teachers or course books) and *independent/autonomous* (learners learn from their own experience and effectively use learning strategies).

Unlike a *one-size-fits-all* approach to schooling, personalised instruction embraces *individualisation, differentiation* and *inclusion*. More specifically, individualised instruction (see 2.2.4) is adjusted to the learning pace of the learner (Capel, Leask, & Turner, 2013; Thomas & Lowe, 2002). Sometimes the learning pace is slow and sometimes it is fast. It depends on how much time students require to go through a particular text. Some passages or grammatical structures used in texts need to be analysed a number of times to be comprehended or learnt, whereas others can be omitted as students already have sufficient knowledge in these respects.

Differentiation is related to learners' preferences with regard to the teaching-learning process (Tomlinson & Allan, 2000). As mentioned above, visual learners prefer to see the language in print. Kinaesthetic learners, also referred to as doers, prefer learning by doing things. Following game instructions is ideal for them. Dependent learners, in turn, learn from their teachers and course books, as opposed to autonomous learners who tend to rely on their own experiences and learning strategies (see 2.3.1).

There are a number of ways differentiation can be implemented in the classroom. Differentiation is linked with language education specifically based on or supported by tasks that will be discussed later on in this book. Differentiation may include adjustments to the content, pace or outcomes of tasks, roles within team work, type of scaffolding (see 2.2.1.3) tasks provide and access to resources. For more information on differentiation in the curriculum, see Capel, Leask and Turner (2013).

Inclusive language education, in turn, refers to the mixing of disabled and non-disabled students. In such teaching-learning environments, non-disabled students work together with, for example, dyslexic, ADHD, autistic, hyperlexic or physically-challenged classmates. The purpose of inclusion is to "enhance understanding and acceptance of diversity in the surrounding world" (Cirocki, 2013c, p. 232). In other words, inclusion rejects "social exclusion that is a consequence of attitudes and responses to diversity in race, social class, ethnicity, religion, gender and ability" (Ainscow, 2009, p. xi). For more information on inclusive pedagogy and inclusive curriculum issues, see Norwich (2013). A brief section on the use of a reading portfolio in inclusive language education can be found in Cirocki (2013c).

Since personalised language education has widely been promoted for the past few years (Huat & Kerry, 2008; Long, 2015), it must be ensured that it is appropriately embedded in text-driven tasks used in language courses. Students in a particular class represent different intelligences, abilities and learning styles. It is important that course books and pedagogical tasks (see 3.2) meet this challenge by using diverse texts (see 3.1.1.6). Texts at different levels of linguistic (see 3.1.1.2) and topical (see 3.1.1.3) complexity are suggested. For successful learning, it is essential that the ability levels of learners as well as the (meta)cognitive development of learners also be taken into account. The use of high quality tasks which support a variety of media (see 3.1), the use of different degrees of instructional support (see 2.2.1.3) and different types of interaction (see 2.2.1.2) are all recommended. The above will provide a conducive learning environment as well as successful development of the individual ZPDs in the classroom (see 2.2.1.1).

It is essential that all these aspects are addressed in language education on a regular basis. Teachers are also advised to have at their disposal a bank of texts and tasks that provide learning opportunities for diverse learners. Only then can teachers and students ensure that existing learning styles and ZPDs in a particular cohort of students are sufficiently satisfied. Such texts and tasks additionally enable teachers to decide on the programme of study that is most adequate in terms of learners' needs and abilities.

3.1.1.5 EXPLOITABILITY

This criterion is extremely important as exploiting texts means using them to develop successful and competent foreign language users. Spoken, written or graphically presented texts can be exploited in various ways. When carefully selected, they provide a good basis for developing creative, interactive and thought-provoking tasks for learners at different levels of language proficiency (see 7.1).

In order to allow for deep processing and learning, it is vital that texts provide the motivation for the use of authentic tasks (see 3.2.1). Such tasks include: researching aspects of texts to obtain insight into the stories read/listened to, writing letters to authors of the stories discussed in the

classroom, presentations of the problems shown in the selected texts and raising ideas for group discussions/debates. All these tasks are essential because they not only enable text exploration, but also help to:
- develop students' language skills;
- creatively stimulate language development;
- provoke engagement with different types of texts;
- encourage personal response to ideas and emotions communicated in texts;
- lead to the development of interpretive strategies which can be subsequently applied to other texts; and
- develop interactive language and critical thinking skills.

What should also be borne in mind is that for successful learning to take place, the tasks mentioned above cannot be too easy or too difficult. Following Vygotsky's concept of ZPD (see 2.2.1.1), it is important for students to be engaged in tasks that are slightly too difficult to be able to do them independently.

Additionally, while practising receptive skills, texts that allow for engaging students in pre-, while- and post-reading/listening tasks are required (Hedge, 2000; Ur, 2012). The three stages employed during intensive reading or listening practice are critical and have different roles to play. For example, the pre-reading/listening stage seeks to help students to generate ideas, set the context, activate current knowledge and predict the content. Some appropriate materials for this stage are: pictures, maps or slogans. The purpose of the while-reading/listening stage is to assist learners to comprehend the specific content, to analyse the structure of various genres and to actively interact with the texts provided (Hedge, 2000; Ur, 2012). For this stage, it seems apt to use tasks with skimming, scanning, listening for gist, reading/listening with visuals and making questions. The post-reading/listening stage seeks to enrich and heighten learner interests in a particular topic. In this stage, tasks are expected to include poster designs, illustration drawing, mini-projects, discussions and blogs.

High quality textual material activates learners' *thinking routines* (McLaughlin & Allen, 2009; Ritchhart, Palmer, Church, & Tishman, 2006).

These routines include synthesising and organising ideas. Some language educators would opt for the word *strategies* rather than *routines* in this particular context (see 2.3.1). The notion of thinking routines, though, is more complex than it seems. Their place and role in learner autonomy development must be perceived within the wider concept of "classroom routines as culture builders" (Ritchhart, Palmer, Church, & Tishman, 2006, p. 5). As mentioned previously, learning is an active and constructive process which occurs in the complex social context of a classroom (see 2.2). Routines are a permanent component of this context, and thus contribute to its enactment via the creation of socially shared behaviour (Leinhardt & Steele, 2005). In other words, through their continuous application, routines become a regular feature of classroom ambience. Strategies, unfortunately, do not qualify as they may be applied only once in a while (Ritchhart, Church, & Morrison, 2011).

Since there is a large number of thinking routines, it is advisable that teachers first select the ones they want to introduce to students. Then, teachers need to categorise and present thinking routines to students as a structure to follow. Taking text exploitation into account, thinking routines can be grouped as: *routines for introducing texts, routines for organising and exploring texts* and *routines for reflecting or elaborating on texts*.

Of course, developing thinking routines takes time, but the good thing is that when properly fostered, they will eventually become sound learning practices. Their usefulness will be of particular importance in problem-solving tasks (see 2.2.1.4), and highly valued in the social constructivist approach to teaching (see 2.2.1). At the beginning, however, the learning process demands effective scaffolding (see 2.2.1.3), defined as well-timed support (Wood, Bruner, & Ross, 1976). The latter, from the work of Vygotsky and later analysed by Applebee (1986), must satisfy a number of criteria. Firstly, students must have an opportunity to contribute to the learning event. Secondly, it is of key importance that the learning process builds upon the prior knowledge and skills of the learner. Thirdly, students must be part of a structured learning environment where a natural sequence of thought and language occurs. Fourthly, while learning, students and teachers solve problems together through interaction (see 2.2.1.2). Last but not least, classroom participants internalise new information and routines and become more independent in the learning process.

While exploiting texts in classroom tasks, autonomous learners are expected to independently utilise the right routines at the right reading/listening stage. For example, at the pre-reading/listening stage, autonomous learners need to employ such thinking routines as activating prior knowledge, making predictions and making connections to other texts (see 3.1.1.1). Some of the things independent learners do in the while-reading/listening stage are: organise information, make further connections, identify key concepts and analyse and summarise ideas. At the post-reading/listening stage, autonomous learners are expected to be involved in identifying perspectives around an issue, reflecting (see 2.3.2.2), questioning and discussing the content, plus going beyond the content.

The present discussion would not be complete without mentioning that one of the features of high-quality texts is that they provoke learners to ask different types of questions. For example, Maley (2003) studied the questions which are placed below texts in modern materials and concluded that they fall into three categories: *factual/referential, cause/effect* and *inference*. However, this number is not sufficient to fully exploit texts. Cognitively-challenging texts allow both teachers and students to ask seven types of questions. The additional four categories, as Maley (2003, p. 11) highlights, are: *opinion* (e.g. What do you think about their decision?), *interpretation* (e.g. What does the author mean by saying that ...?), *personalised* (e.g. What would you do if you were in her shoes?) and *speculative* (e.g. How do you think the problem will be solved at the end of the story?). In the case of multimodal texts (see 3.1), various tasks linking texts with audio-visual support are most desirable. Student attention must be drawn to the fact that both the language used and the provided images or sound are what organises texts as a whole (Cook, 1992).

Successful text exploitation is feasible when high quality multimodal texts and tasks built around them are used in the classroom. Such texts arouse learners' curiosity and provide for multi-sensorial experiences.

Of course, the conclusive selection of texts as well as classroom tasks and their sequencing is determined by the nature of the language course and individual preferences of both teachers and students. As far as assessing texts for exploitability is concerned, it is suggested that teachers select those which allow for "the integrated use of many skills together: the unitary skill of making sense of text" (Nuttall, 1996, p. 172).

3.1.1.6 VARIETY

The criterion of *variety* applies to an array of topics, text types and contexts which learners need to be regularly exposed to (Hedge, 2000; Ur, 2012). It is necessary for learners to work with different types of texts since textual features categorise texts, and thus pose different demands on the learners. For example, *narrative texts* (e.g. short stories) serve the purpose of entertainment and moral teaching, whereas *expository texts* (e.g. reports) convey factual information. Audio-visual materials, on the other hand, may successfully serve the purposes mentioned above, yet the demands posed will relate to different degrees of exploitation of a learner's senses, vision and hearing being the most common (Bastable, 2006).

It is essential that the criterion of variety is analysed in terms of individual units as well as across units in course books. Diverse and controversial topics (see 3.1.1.3) are vital for students to actively use and experiment with the target language. Popular themes allow students to reinforce new lexical and syntactical items as well as functional language in different contexts. Students exposed to fascinating subjects want to explore ideas and share feelings and opinions. Likewise, the implementation of different genres in the classroom is of great importance. The genre-based approach seeks to develop foreign language readers' awareness of rhetorical elements of texts and genre sensitivity (Hyland 2007; Johns, 2002). When provided with a large array of texts, students not only integrate language, content and context, but also realise that genres are context-bound (Hyland, 2003; Johns, 2002). Train timetables, airport departure/arrival boards, bus schedules and menus could be used for obtaining information, whereas short stories and plays could be used for pleasure reading. This interesting approach allows for an attractive combination of textuality, topicality and multimodality in the classroom (Hedge, 2000; Ur, 2012).

As for teaching listening, it seems sensible that students be provided with a variety of accents. It would be beneficial if the recorded or filmed material provided texts delivered by native speakers who represent different geographical regions (e.g. British English, American English, Australian English). It should also be pointed out that English is used as a lingua franca (Jenkins, 2007, 2012; Seidlhofer, 2011). This means it is no longer spoken by native speakers only. English is now used by non-native speakers all over the world, contributing to the emergence of new varieties such as Chinglish or Ponglish. This being so, it is of key importance that students be given plenty of exposure to different types of English accents, be they produced by native or non-native speakers. Students can then learn to easily understand different accents, and thus attain success in international communication (Kirkpatrick, 2007).

Admittedly, providing learners with a variety of texts during one lesson is a complex venture. The texts teachers offer to language learners must not be random or accidental under any circumstances. Texts must always be interrelated. *Intertextuality* corresponds to interdependence of texts (Barthes, 1977). A broader definition assumes that intertextuality is concerned with making links between present and past texts and interpreting one text through others (see 3.1.1.1). For this reason, it is imperative that teachers and materials writers take the concept of intertextuality into account whenever they develop complex tasks.

As discussed earlier, texts are meaningful entities that are shared with others through different modes in the act of communication. Intertextuality is nothing less than a process of constructing meaning. The philosophy of social constructivism (see 2.2) argues that intertextuality is essentially a metaphor for learning. Short (2004) has expressed a similar view. Rosen (1984), in turn, clarifies this observation by stating that learners' worldviews are made up of interrelated stories where any given story takes shape in relation to other stories. Because learners' stories are shaped by the socio-cultural context of which they are part, intertextuality is always socially created.

Another element that the variety criterion refers to is *different purposes*, which is tightly linked to the concept of genres discussed above. It is the structure of texts that requires people to read, listen and write for different purposes in specific contexts (Donovan & Smolkin, 2001). It has also been observed that people assume different processing goals to achieve their purposes when they read, listen and write (Hedge, 2000). For example, in the language classroom, students can read to search for information, for general comprehension or for quick understanding (Grabe, 2009). Listening can be practised for such purposes as obtaining specific information or appreciating pronunciation, rhythm and intonation (Hedge, 2000; Ur, 2012). In the EFL writing class, student attention can be drawn to aesthetic and imaginative points. Students can write to express feelings and emotions or develop a sense of audience and critical thinking (Fleming & Stevens, 2004). High quality tasks facilitate different types of writing, including descriptive, expository, narrative, persuasive, poetic, personal, social and institutional (Bearne, 2002; Hedge, 2000).

As the foregoing discussion reveals, language courses are more interesting and effective when they regularly promote a large range of texts with interesting topics and tasks. It is essential that the texts be presented according to their sequence of difficulty – advancing from easy to more difficult, but always remaining in a student's ZPD (see 2.2.1.1). It is also recommended that the variety of texts and topics be systematically practised over time to ensure progression in the acquisition of knowledge, skills and understandings of the target language and culture. To ensure steady progression in learning, teachers need to ask themselves the following questions:
- What do my students know and understand and what can they do at the beginning of the unit or module?
- What do I want my students to know, understand and be able to do at the end of the unit or module?
- What sequence of learning tasks may help my students to progress from their present state to my objectives?
- How do I know when my students have reached where I want them to go?
- Do my students recognise that they have made progress?

All these questions are extremely important. However, they need to be adjusted to individual teaching approaches that teachers adopt. For example, in the *unit* approach, the teaching-learning process is organised around stand-alone units (Aggarwal, 2009; Richards, 2001). These units are groups of lessons with well-structured teaching ideas (i.e. texts and tasks) that revolve around specific topics and lead towards appropriate learning outcomes. Each unit is linked to previous units which provide the basis for subsequent ones. Units tend to promote formative assessment where students receive feedback meant to help them to improve their performance (see 2.3.2.2).

The *modular* approach, on the other hand, consists of modules. Modules are defined as "independent learning sequences" (Richards, 2001, p. 165). These blocks, frequently thirty hours in a 120-hour course, have their own objectives, and therefore allow for a more flexible structure of a language course. This flexibility, however, may turn out to be destructive, and consequently, lead to unstructured courses (Richards, 2001). At the end of each module, there is an assessment section. The purpose of this section is to summatively measure language learners' achievement in the learning outcomes of a particular module.

The following section is a discussion of pedagogical tasks and their place and role in developing learner autonomy.

3.2 PEDAGOGICAL TASKS FOR DEVELOPING LEARNER AUTONOMY

Having presented various criteria for text selection, the discussion needs to become more specific and address the issue of learning tasks. It is through tasks that teachers "elicit language production, interaction, negotiation of meaning, processing of input and focus on form" (van den Branden, 2006, p. 1). It is also necessary that teachers be aware that pedagogical tasks cannot be discussed in isolation from texts. Texts become instructional materials only when teachers think of them in terms of classroom context and provide them with certain goals to be achieved in this context. More specifically, the moment teachers approach texts through the prism of student needs, cognitive development, language proficiency and interests, they transform texts into learning resources. It is no exaggeration to say that texts need tasks in order to become instructional materials in their own right.

On the other hand, tasks need texts so that the tasks can be brought to life in the classroom context. In other words, textual input constitutes a prerequisite for the successful completion of the tasks. Text discourses are represented by diverse topics and medial forms. Tasks connect text discourses with classroom discourses (see 3.2.2). What should be made clear is that texts do not contain meanings. Texts are meaning potentials that must be activated so that meaning can be constructed (Fenner, 2001). This activation is viable through complex tasks (see 3.2.2). Such tasks also support learners in uncovering hidden discourses in texts (i.e. sub-texts) which are then linked to the learner's world view (Müller-Hartmann & Schocker-v. Ditfurth, 2011). In social constructivist terms, a meaning-making activity is the reading of texts. Faced with linguistic or graphic textual input, readers create meaning (see 2.2.1.2). An interpretation or representation is produced as a completely new text whose comprehension is instrumental to successful task completion. Additionally, high-quality tasks enable learners to "move beyond the analysis of discourses and create something new in the process" (Müller-Hartmann, Schocker-v. Ditfurth, 2011, p. 184). The resulting change and coordination of perspectives contribute to a deeper understanding of texts.

What should also be pointed out is that it is wrong to classify texts as *good* or *bad*, especially when "bad" is synonymous with "old". I have seen teachers separate texts in this way. Value judgements of this kind are unfounded, because what counts is how texts are exploited in the classroom (see 3.1.1.5), not how old texts are. As a result, it is suggested that teachers do not discard old texts. These texts more often than not supply cognitively challenging and useful tasks. By the same token, it should be remembered that old course books are a treasure trove of multimodal texts (see 3.1). It is strongly suggested that they continue to be recycled. They contain a large number of images that can be used at regular intervals for different tasks.

This idea of exploiting old, also referred to as bad, course books in the classroom seems to derive support from Prodromou (2002, p. 27), who highlights that:

> It is the teacher, in collaboration with the class, who brings the material to life (...) a book that is considered mediocre for whatever reason can be transformed into motivating material by an enthusiastic and imaginative teacher but a boring book will remain boring if all the teacher does is plod through the material exactly as it is on the page.

There are a few reasons why the learning potential of tasks has become a central issue in language education. Firstly, language educators have become disappointed with explicit form-focused language teaching, which failed to promote language as a tool for communication (Kumaravadivelu, 2006). Secondly, the EU education policy, defining language as competence, stimulates language instruction that is not only action-driven, but also perceives language learners as rightful social agents who have tasks to perform (Council of Europe, 2001). What is more, these tasks must promote context-specific language needs (Council of Europe, 2001). For this reason, learning tasks are presented in the EU documents as progressing intercultural communicative competences that language learners are expected to master at particular educational levels. Finally, the role of tasks was strengthened in the language classroom when English developed as a lingua franca (see 3.1.1.6). This development holds that the goal of a learning task is to facilitate relevant and meaningful communication and to enable learners to mediate between diverse cultures through the medium of English (Kramsch, 1998).

A considerable amount of literature has been published on task-orientated language education (e.g. Breen, 1987; Bygate, Skehan, & Swain, 2001; Ellis, 2003; Hallet & Legutke, 2013; Long, 2015; Nunan, 2004; Samuda & Bygate, 2008; van der Branden, 2006; Willis & Willis, 2007). These sources have defined a *task* in a number of ways, thus making the concept somewhat elusive. For instance, tasks have been referred to as language learning goals (Bachman & Palmer, 1996; Long, 1985) and as educational activities (Breen, 1987; Bygate, Skehan, & Swain, 2001; Ellis, 2003; Skehan, 1998). For the purposes of this section, Nunan's (1989, p. 10) definition will be employed. It reads as follows:

> [A task] is a piece of classroom work which involves learners in comprehending, manipulating, producing or interacting in the target language while their attention is primarily focused on meaning rather than form.

In brief, task-orientated language education allows learners to attain specific goals while functionally employing language to do so. Nunan's definition appears to be specifically attractive for the present discussion since it complies with the tenets of social constructivism (see 2.2), around which this book is based. This definition promotes both active and interactive learning; it is through and around tasks that language learners engage in social interactions (see 2.2.1.2) and learn new information. It can be speculated that educational tasks assume the role of mediating tools (see 2.2.1.3), and consequently provide sound basis for the synergy between teaching and learning (Zaslavsky & Sullivan, 2011).

The discussion of learning tasks would not be complete without mentioning Nunan's *real-world* and *pedagogical* tasks. In real-world tasks (see 3.2.1), students are expected to experience, in the classroom, the sorts of behaviour required of them in the life beyond the school walls (Nunan, 1989). Pedagogical tasks, in turn, are those that are unlikely to be performed outside the classroom but can develop students' language proficiency (Nunan, 1989). The latter are extremely useful because they promote communication-orientated and problem-solving interaction in the classroom (Breen, 1987; Candlin, 1987). In other words, pedagogical tasks:

> require students to produce chunks of language as learners attempt to communicate by using the linguistic resources they currently possess in the target language. As participants talk, they modify their own and their interlocutors' speech. Learners thereby get and produce negotiated comprehensible input and output that are beyond their current level of communicative competence. This modified interaction sets up the necessary (…) preconditions for second language development to occur (Markee, 1997, p. 95).

In this sense, it must be acknowledged that both real-world and pedagogical tasks, though they seem dissimilar, actually appear to be on a continuum. Certain tasks may be more or less *real* to individual students. Hence, such an inauthentic task as writing a for-and-against essay may turn out to be authentic in certain circumstances.

It is notable that the intense interest in task-driven language education develops differently across teaching contexts (Samuda & Bygate, 2008; Müller-Hartmann & Schocker-von Ditfurth, 2011). Two central approaches can be identified. In *task-based language instruction (TBLI)*, tasks function as the foundation for the curriculum. In *task-supported language instruction (TSLI)*, tasks act as an additional component to a language syllabus that is traditionally based on topics, linguistic structures, texts and activities. What is interesting about these two approaches is that they both regard language as a vehicle to get things done. Teachers who work in task-supported language teaching contexts, for example in Poland, or in the European context in general, should be aware that globally produced course books are topic-based, not task-based (Müller-Hartmann & Schocker-von Ditfurth, 2011). They occasionally include tasks at varying degrees, though (see 3.3). As a result, teachers are greatly encouraged to design their own tasks (see 7.1) to provide learners with countless opportunities to engage in meaningful language use. It is the meaningful communication of meanings that distinguishes *tasks* from *exercises*, whose aim is practising discrete items (e.g. lexis or grammar) of the target language.

Teachers will obviously differ in their preferences for classroom tasks (Peterson, 2000). These preferences tend to be determined, among other things, by cultural influences, curriculum requirements, classroom limitations and learner types (see 3.1.1.4). Significant developments in TBLI and TSLI have also heightened the need for task classification. For example, Legutke and Thomas (1991) have suggested nine communicative learning tasks: *trust-building and relaxation; awareness and sensitivity training; information-sharing activities; thinking strategies and problem-solving; information-gap, fantasy and creative expression; role-playing and creative dramatics; interaction and interpersonality; values clarification and discussion* and *process evaluation*. Willis' (1996) typology of tasks consists of: *listing, ordering and sorting, comparing, problem solving, sharing personal experiences* and *creative tasks*. Richards (2001), in turn, lists: *jigsaw tasks, information-gap tasks, problem-solving tasks, decision-making tasks* and *opinion exchange tasks*.

It is worth emphasising that the classroom tasks listed above call for a new typology when approached from a SLA perspective. Findings from SLA research categorise pedagogical tasks into: *one-way* (Fujii & Mackey, 2009), *reciprocal* (Slimani-Rolls, 2005), *open* (Skehan, 1998), *closed* (Manheimer, 1993), *convergent* (Skehan & Foster, 2001), *divergent* (Skehan & Foster, 2001), *complex* (Gilabert, Baron, & Llanes, 2009), *planned* (Mochizuki & Ortega, 2008), *familiar* (Shintani, 2012) and *mixed-proficiency* (Kim & McDonough, 2008). For example, in one-way tasks, when students work in pairs, one of the students in each pair holds in front of them the information required to complete a task. One student may describe a photograph they have been given by the teacher, whereas the other student, listening to the description, is expected to draw a copy of this image. In reciprocal tasks, such as spotting differences, students exchange information by engaging in negotiation (see 2.2.1.2), which guarantees successful task completion. Open tasks, such as debates, allow for multiple answers. Extended turns (i.e. elaborative answers) and more complex language are thus promoted (Long, 2015). Closed tasks, on the other hand, are usually limited to one correct solution to a task problem. In convergent tasks, students need to reach an agreement to solve a problem posed by a task. In divergent tasks, students are involved in arguments or debates. Complex tasks are based on numerous reasoning demands, consist of a number of stages or contain unfamiliar content (3.2.2). Planned tasks allow students time to think about the tasks themselves. Students may also have time to think about the strategies (see 2.3.1) and language they will use to complete the tasks. Familiar tasks deal with familiar content or task structure, whereas mixed-proficiency tasks are earmarked for pairs with one student who is more proficient matched with one student who is less proficient.

Teacher preferences for classroom tasks can be additionally affected by the text types that language instructors have at their disposal. The selection criteria presented earlier (see 3.1.1) reveal that texts which teachers use in the classroom may, to a large degree, determine task features. Since the focus of the present volume is on fostering learner autonomy and developing pedagogical tasks for learner autonomy, the number of specifications that learner autonomy tasks are required to meet has to be narrowed down. Reference to the various theoretical aspects discussed in this volume discloses that tasks have the potential for fostering autonomous learning if they promote authenticity, are complex and foster purposeful learning. These specifications are briefly reviewed in the individual sections below. They are also taken into consideration in the process of designing complex tasks discussed in Chapter Seven.

3.2.1 TASK AUTHENTICITY

The issue of authenticity has already been addressed a number of times in this volume. The conclusion that can be drawn so far is that task authenticity rests on the learner's response to the input text (see 2.3.3.2). As Widdowson (1978) and van Lier (1996) emphasise, authenticity must be perceived in terms of what learners do with texts rather than in terms of the texts themselves. Yet the framework of task authenticity appears to be much more complex. What then makes a task authentic?

Task authenticity is a potential which enables language learners to experience what people may live through in real life situations (Nunan, 2004; Long, 2015). In other words, authentic tasks are based on learners' personal experiences. Such tasks bring relevant real-life problems into the classroom (see 2.2.1.4). Language learners are stimulated to be critical and creative in problem-solving (McGrath, 2002; Müller-Hartmann & Schocker-v. Ditfurth, 2011; Nunan, 2004). Authentic tasks give students the opportunity to experience deep conceptual learning, which is defined as an "intrinsically motivated process of personalised meaning construction" (Clare, 2007, p. 434). The gap is then filled between what language learners learn in the classroom culture and why this knowledge is vital to the social reality beyond school.

The criterion of task authenticity also indicates that good learning tasks stimulate social interaction (see 2.2.1.2), which is highly valued in Vygotskian psychology, discussed in Chapter Two (see 2.2). The process of genuine communication is not only limited to successful interaction between classroom participants. Genuine communication also refers to the relations between learners and texts in which tasks are immersed. In other words, authentic tasks create excellent opportunities for learners to engage in interpreting the communicative intentions of texts produced while performing tasks. The notion of communicative intention appeared together with the Communicative Approach (see 2.2.4) in the 1970s, whose main purpose was to develop communicative competence (see 3.1.1.2). Being inherent to speech acts, it is closely related to text functions (see 3.1.1.6). Because communicative intention may or may not be explicit, it must be properly inferred from the context of the text.

Task authenticity offers students a scope for being involved in a complex process of both meaningful and purposeful communication. In this process, information senders always have two types of intention at their disposal: *informative* and *communicative* (Littlejohn, 1992). Informative intention is employed to make receivers aware of something. Communicative intention, on the other hand, is utilised to get receivers to realise the informative intent. It follows that the process of communication consists in generating messages to communicate intentions (Sperber, 1994). It is vital that senders accurately communicate their intent so that receivers can easily discern them.

Unfortunately, the process of inferring communicative intentions sometimes fails and does not produce the intended effect (Niżegorodcew, 2007). In spoken discourse, the communicative intention can be checked by direct interrogation. In written discourse, the reader can utilise a number of graphic (e.g. the use of exclamation marks or punctuation), syntactic (e.g. cleft sentences) and linguistic devices such as carefully chosen verbs and adverbs to correctly interpret the writer's intended meaning. All these aspects are extremely important and should always be taken into consideration while designing learning tasks (see 7.1).

Apart from the classroom social interactions, authentic tasks ensure two other types of interactions: *learner-self* and *learner-tasks* (Hirumi, 2006). The first type of interactions comprises cognitive operations and metacognitive processes. These processes allow learners to be capable of monitoring and regulating their learning. The second type allows learners to receive information that is encoded in learning tasks. For instance, while reading/listening to foreign language texts, learners are involved in internal conversations with more knowledgeable others (Vygotsky, 1962). This kind of interaction, according to the philosophy of social constructivism, brings about changes in the learner's cognitive structures, and thus, in the learner's knowledge and skills. In particular, the changes in the cognitive structures reflect Piaget's (1952) processes of assimilation and accommodation (see 3.1.1.3). Due to these processes, the acquisition of knowledge occurs. In addition to the interactions with texts, students are also required to identify with their tasks. Students must feel that the messages the tasks convey are directed specifically at them. Engaging tasks activate the senses, prior experience and knowledge. Students are then able to make different types of connections with the surrounding reality (see 3.1.1.1).

The preceding discussion reveals that task authenticity requires a considerable degree of engagement on the part of the learner. Well-designed learning tasks are cognitively challenging and help learners to cross their respective ZPDs (see 2.2.1.1). Learners must be eager to devote mental energy to successfully perform tasks (Dörnyei, 2002; Ellis, 2003). At the same time, learners must be willing to make attempts to comprehend the target language input and generate comprehensible output linked to the tasks concerned. For this to happen, three stages of the motivational process must be considered: *pre-actional*, *actional* and *post-actional* (Dörnyei, 2002). In the first stage, motivation has to be provoked. After that, learners launch into action with clearly set goals. In the second stage, learners must succeed in maintaining the previously generated motivation and progress towards task completion. In the last stage, learners carry out evaluations of past experiences so that they can decide what future tasks they will be motivated to engage in.

Including a language learner's personal characteristics in the process of carrying out a learning task also deserves close attention (see 3.1.1.4). It is important that teachers be aware that the degree of task interactiveness is measured by estimating the extent to which tasks engage a learner's language ability, topical knowledge, affective schemata, communication strategies and personal characteristics to obtain their high performance (Bachman & Palmer, 1996; Purpura 2004). In the task-orientated framework, these individual components play different roles. For example, turning to the construct of language competence (see 3.1.1.2), language ability relates to organisational and pragmatic knowledge. Organisational knowledge enables language learners to produce and comprehend grammatically correct sentences. This knowledge also allows for organising sentences into coherent texts. Pragmatic knowledge, on the other hand, refers to the human ability to create and interpret discourse. Topical knowledge, often referred to as *know-what*, is nothing less than a complex network of the language learner's knowledge structures stored in the learner's long-term memory (Eom, 2006). Affective or emotional schemata are in charge of organising experience by integrating individual interactions of language learners with the surrounding world (Geva-Grofman, 2008). Communication strategies are the attempts by task participants to negotiate meanings in situations where required meaning structures fail to be involved (Gowans, 2012). Examples of personal characteristics include language learner age, gender, L1, personality and intelligence (see 3.1.1.4).

Consequently, tasks can evoke high or low degrees of engagement. Tasks with high degrees of engagement require active learner involvement in all areas of both language and personal knowledge while working on a task response. Tasks with low degrees of engagement require minimal involvement on the part of the learner. As a result, it is vital that teachers always aim for the first option. Also, bearing in mind the interrelatedness between texts and tasks (see 3.2), it is necessary that the concept of engagement be approached from two angles, especially when text-based tasks are involved. First, teachers need to decide whether efficient completion of particular tasks is determined by comprehension of the texts around which tasks are built. Second, the knowledge, skills and abilities required to both comprehend texts and complete tasks must represent the knowledge, skills and abilities available in the learner's ZPD (see 2.2.1.1).

Another thing to remember is that well-designed tasks involve learners in at least one out of five modes of engagement put forth by Wells (1990). Depending on the genre involved in a particular task, language learners may be engaged in the following modes: *performative* (i.e. decoding texts), *functional* (i.e. employing texts to get things done), *information* (i.e. using texts as a means of communication), *re-creational* (i.e. pleasurably utilising texts for creating and exploring a world with words) and *epistemic* (i.e. interrogating texts and offering alternative interpretations). This last mode appears extremely vital for language learners as it coerces them into thoroughly reviewing both their own and others' concepts and judgements. It can conceivably be hypothesised that the epistemic mode unlocks the potential of foreign language literacy, for it boosts the thinking of those who utilise it (Pappas & Barro Zecker, 2001).

Authentic tasks also move learners towards action and autonomy (Errey & Schollaert, 2003; Legutke & Thomas, 1991; Müller-Hartmann & Schocker-v. Ditfurth, 2011). Highly engaging collaborative tasks, for example, allow language learners to enter into meaningful discourse while negotiating a shared notion of end products. Cooperation (see 2.2.1.4), in turn, deals with organising the interaction using role appointment to distribute work that must be accomplished within a specific time frame. Fulfilling their roles, learners actively create and share knowledge (see 2.2). Learners also individually make decisions and take risks to achieve the intended outcomes (see 2.3.2). Briefly stated, action and learner autonomy are inherent elements of highly engaging tasks.

In summary, authentic tasks are advocated in the language classroom as they encourage learners to explore the world. This kind of scrutiny makes the learning experience intrinsically motivating. Intrinsic motivation is viewed as the human inclination towards both spontaneous exploration and mastery of novel skills or experiences (Dörnyei, 2001). This type of motivation is improved when learners are offered room for autonomy. This means that it is desirable that learning tasks engage learners in the learning process itself by encouraging them to: plan and monitor their learning (see 2.3.2.1), take risks, set goals and assess and reflect on their foreign language performance (see 2.3.2.2), individually or collaboratively and with computer technology (see 2.3.4) or without. Examples of such tasks are presented in Chapter 7 (see Task 1, Task 6, Task 7 and Task 10 in 7.3). Intrinsically motivated and autonomous learners demonstrate more interest, enthusiasm, confidence and self-determination about the tasks they are involved in (see 2.1). Also, such learners evidence increased performance, perseverance and creativity while learning (Dörnyei, 2001).

3.2.2 TASK COMPLEXITY

The second variable is *complexity*, whose importance is stressed by Hallet and Legutke (2013, p. 147) as follows: "tasks in the foreign language classroom must be structured in ways that develop the skills, knowledges and dispositions necessary for foreign language participation in lifeworld social and cultural discourses". This being so, language learners, whenever involved in pedagogical tasks (see 3.2), use and master "their cognitive, social-interactive and discursive capabilities" in the target language (Hallet & Legutke, 2013, p. 147). Thus, good tasks are always of a complex, challenging and experiential nature. Additionally, they allow for a combination of both classroom and real-world discourses.

Others (e.g. Nunan, 2004; Robinson, 2011) state that task complexity measures the manner in which a task is displayed. Designed content without too much technical vocabulary is preferable so that the learner is better able to understand the message. Thus, task design involves a semantic match between the tasks and the texts. It is desirable that tasks contain words from the same lexical field as the source texts; the better the lexical match, the easier the task. Likewise, small typeface or inaccurate visuals may prevent the target audience from understanding the task. As a result, it is important that teachers keep asking themselves the following questions: *Is the task cluttered with too much information? Is the uncluttered information logically ordered? Is the content adequate and realistic enough for the target group? Does the visual support correspond to the content of the proposed task and vice versa? Do the proposed images enhance or obscure the message? Will the target audience be able to respond to the task?*

The issue of complexity is also connected with task demands and task support (Cameron, 2001; Nunan, 2004; Duran & Ramaut, 2006; Müller-Hartmann & Schocker-v. Ditfurth, 2011; Skehan, 1998). While designing tasks for fostering learner autonomy, such issues as task simplicity or task difficulty must be taken into consideration. It is of key importance that teachers realise that learners invariably deal with *linguistic, cognitive* and *social* demands while accomplishing tasks. The linguistic demand is nothing less than the language, that is, grammatical complexity or vocabulary load required to complete a task (see 3.1.1.2). The cognitive demand is related to information processing, that is, understanding and working with the content. As far as the cognitive complexity of a task goes, there are two aspects of cognition (Skehan, 1998) that need to be analysed: the capability of the learner accessing familiar solutions to activity problems (also referred to as *cognitive familiarity*) and the need to find answers to uncommon situations (also known as *cognitive processing*). The social demand refers to social interactions (see 2.2.1.2) concerning the content. All these demands are dealt with in the learning process. However, it should be emphasised that the learner's processing system possesses a faculty to shift between the three dimensions mentioned above. Priority is given to the most pressing demands (Kumaravadivelu, 2006).

Task complexity is also described in terms of demands on learners (Cameron, 2001; van den Branden, 2006; Willis & Willis, 2007). For example, Cameron's (2001) typology of task demands includes the following: *cognitive, language, interactional, metalinguistic, involvement* and *physical* demands. Cognitive demands deal with conceptual information and the ways learners perceive the surrounding reality and people. Language demands involve the use of the target language, plus the use and the role of the native language in learning the former. Interactional demands are related to the social interaction that is required while completing tasks. Metalinguistic demands are related to understanding and using the target language to talk about the language and the learning process as such. Involvement demands refer to various levels of engagement that are crucial for successful task completion. Physical demands are related to the following types of motor skills: *gross motor skills* (i.e. running, jumping, etc.), *fine motor skills* (i.e. holding a pen, cutting with scissors, etc.), *sensorimotor skills* (i.e. kicking a ball or eye-hand coordination while writing, etc.) and *oral motor skills* (i.e. producing speech sounds).

Overall, well-designed complex tasks are both demanding and supportive, yet they need to be neither too challenging nor too supportive (Cameron, 2001). It is the difference between demands and support that provides room for growth and generates opportunities for deep learning (Cameron, 2001).

3.2.3 TASK PURPOSEFULNESS

Apart from tasks being complex, it is also important that they promote purposeful learning (Legutke & Thomas, 1991; McGrath, 2002; Nunan,

2004; Tomlinson, 2011b). Purposeful tasks are relevant and valuable tasks. The purposefulness of a task belongs to the individual who is fully engaged in performing the task and fully engaged in the task's context (see 3.2.1). The meaning of the task is unique to each learner since each task is affected by the learner's prior learning experiences, life baggage, age and cultural background (see 3.1.1.4). As can be seen, a purposeful task invariably requires active participation on the part of the learner. Attention must be given to the purpose and utility of the task being done. Learning combines the ability to carry out procedures and create meaning; ideas, language and skills related to the task also need to be developed. It is through purposeful learning that students become aware of why they learn. For example, particular skills and how to perform them successfully are learnt. It should be emphasised that in purposeful classrooms, the focus is not just on the learner's production of successful outcomes. What matters is that learners are actively involved in using the target language in ways that promote learning (Ellis, 2003). Purposeful tasks promote *intrinsic* (i.e. related to inherent satisfaction) rather than *extrinsic* (i.e. related to external rewards) *motivation*. Mastery-driven rather than performance-driven conditions for learning are thus created (Boekaerts, 2010). For this reason, purposeful tasks are relevant to the realities of students' lives (see 3.2.1). Learners are encouraged to set goals and strive to achieve their goals through meaningful interaction (see 2.2.1.2) and effective collaboration (see 2.2.1.4). These tasks are more often than not based on communicative purposes and enable students to assume the role of both senders and addressees of information (see 3.2.1). It is through purposeful tasks that learners learn how to initiate and partake in meaningful and real-life discourse and learn how to engage in high-quality learning (Bullen & Janes, 2007). For this reason, it is desirable that purposeful tasks become an integral part of language instruction. To make this happen, teachers must be trained in designing their own tasks and I will attempt to do this in Chapter Seven.

3.3 LEARNER AUTONOMY IN EFL COURSE BOOKS

Having already specified the key features of learner autonomy tasks, it is fitting to bring this chapter to a close with a short summary of an

EFL course book analysis. The summary is to verify the extent to which modern course books promote learner autonomy. As mentioned earlier, I have been involved in EFL/ESL instruction for a long time. I have used a large number of course books in my teaching practice. In general, they were very good at promoting vocabulary, grammar and skills practice. Unfortunately, very little attention was given to fostering learner autonomy.

The present analysis is based on six secondary school course books. Due to ethical and marketing issues, the titles will not be revealed, but all the course books have been published by well-known ELT publishers. For the purposes of this analysis, I looked at exactly the same course books as the teacher participants in the empirical part of the present project (see 4.5.2.2). The reason for this was threefold: (1) to compare my observations with those of the teacher participants, (2) to combine the observations gathered from a number of evaluators to produce a valid and objective analysis of the course books and (3) to support the present analysis with empirical evidence from EFL practitioners. Thus, to reiterate, the following analysis is a clear consensus reached on the basis of my observations and those of the teacher participants (see 4.5.1).

According to the analysis, the course books fell into two categories: standard EFL and examination preparation course books. As the analysis further disclosed, the course books were used at two different levels: Year 1 (four course books) and Year 3 (two course books). As the discussion at the beginning of Chapter Four will show (see 4.1), different approaches to teaching are adopted at these two levels. Hence, it seems appropriate to first describe the course books used in Year 1, and then those used in Year 3.

In Year 1, students use standard British EFL course books such as *New Headway* (Oxford University Press) or *Upstream* (Express Publishing). These course books provide systematic preparation for all the skills required for successful communication. In other words, the course books at this level seek to enhance learners' communicative competence (see 3.1.1.2). Some of the books promote topical syllabuses, whereas others promote structural syllabuses. The material is divided into units or modules (see 3.1.1.6). There are regular revision sections, after every three or four units or at the end of each module.

There is an even balance between the practice of receptive and productive skills in all the four course books. In receptive skills sections, the course books offer a broad range of texts, some of which include real life language (see 3.1.1.3), and engage students in pre-, while- and post-reading/listening activities (see 3.1.1.5). Activities focusing on the development of productive skills allow learners to practise a broad range of text types (e.g. discussions, conversations, letters, essays) and different registers. For example, two teacher participants made the following observations:

> *In my course book, there is a balance of skills practice. I really like that because my students systematically practice both receptive and productive skills. There are a lot of interesting activities students can do, for example, before, while and after reading or listening. I also enjoy the "Everyday English" sections. It is a pity that the course book does not include any controversial topics. If controversial topics were included, it would make the course book ideal for me.*

> *I like the multitude of activities related to practising all four language skills. The balance is almost perfect, and I like the combination of skills in various activities. The majority of the topics used in the course books are realistic and relevant. Not all of them are challenging and open to question, though.*

Syntax and lexis are important parts of the courses, too. Individual units introduce different structures and vocabulary and offer extensive and effective practice of the target lexico-grammar in workbooks. The grammar exercises help learners to see the link between forms and functions. The most popular exercises include: gap-fills, matching, multiple-choice, transformations, sentence-completion and cloze tests. For instance, one teacher participant commented on lexico-grammatical aspects in the following way:

> *This course book entirely satisfies my needs. Lexis, grammar and language skills get a lot of practice. I particularly value all the vocabulary and grammar sections in which students have an opportunity to practise the target language in many different ways.*

As far as developing learner autonomy is concerned, the course books do not fully succeed in this respect. This conclusion was drawn from my own as well as the teacher participants' analyses. The course books promote pair work and meaningful communication in sections devoted to speaking skills, yet there are very few well-designed tasks. In some units or modules, the course books offer explicit instruction of learning strategies (see 2.3.1), yet it is mainly limited to writing skills. For example, students are told how to write formal and informal letters and shown how the layout and language differs in both types of writing. Students are not always encouraged to use creativity and make decisions in L2 writing because the course book activities usually tell them exactly what information to include in individual paragraphs. Another observation is that process writing is not promoted in the selected course books. Learners are frequently asked to mimic model texts, examples of which are presented in individual units or modules. Likewise, the use of educational technology (see 2.3.4) is neglected in the course books concerned, as are collaborative projects (see 2.2.1.4) and meaningful learner autonomy tasks (see 3.2.1). Examples of desirable learner autonomy tasks include: self-assessment tasks (see Task 7 and Task 8 in 7.3), mini-project tasks with the use of educational technology (see Task 1 and Task 2 in 7.3), mini-project tasks integrating all language skills (see Task 3 in 7.3), tasks connected with reflecting on learning (see Task 9 and Task 10 in 7.3) and tasks based on learning strategy identification sheets (see Task 4 and Task 5 in 7.3). There are no activities that directly refer students to the Internet or any form of educational technology. Self-assessment (see 2.3.2.2) sections in which students could reflect on the learning process do not exist in the course books, either. There are revision sections after every few units, yet their purpose is slightly different. The revision sections are prepared in the form of a test and focus mainly on the lexico-grammatical aspects covered in particular units.

Materials used by Year 3 students, meanwhile, are completely different. Unlike Year 1 course books, the Year 3 course books offer authentic examination preparation only. These course books allow Year 3 students to familiarise themselves with the content and format of the Matura examination. Useful examination strategies are included for students to practise.

The two course books selected for instruction in Year 3 are earmarked for the extended level of the Matura examination and divided into thematic units (e.g. Home, School, Work), all of which match the list of themes suggested by the Central Examination Board. Each unit is a collection of typical examination questions (e.g. word building, transformations, true/false reading and listening comprehension, multiple-choice reading and listening comprehension, matching reading and listening comprehension, for-and-against essay, short story, review, article), plus exercises that are to help students to revise the required material for their final examination. All the units have more or less the same format and type of exercises; the classic sections in the units are: vocabulary, use of English, listening, reading, writing and speaking.

As the description above suggests, the Matura examination books resemble conventional supplementary materials. These examination books have gradually managed to replace standard EFL course books. The examination books consist of examples of examination papers and specially designed activities that train students in examination questions and strategies. The importance of the Matura examination in Poland and the importance of high marks in this examination have led to the negative backwash effect. As a result, various types of Matura preparation materials have been published to help students to practise for the examination. These materials have become the norm in the language classroom.

The quality of these books is good, and therefore they should not be discarded from language courses. Teachers should bear in mind, though, that the purpose for which these materials have been created is different, when compared to standard EFL course books. The Matura preparation books only aim to help language learners to revise the material for the final secondary school examination, plus practise a number of strategies to reach a high degree of automaticity in doing examination papers. Accordingly, these books should be used as an addition to a standard course book, not a replacement.

As far as developing learner autonomy goes, these books are only successful to a limited extent, as the current analysis showed. For example, two teacher participants made the following comments:

> Overall, it is a good course book, but I do not think it is successful in fostering learner autonomy, well perhaps to a limited extent.
>
> The course book generally meets my expectations. It does not fully promote learner autonomy, though.

The issue of the limited extent is mainly restricted to the promotion of pair work and meaningful communication in speaking activities. The analysis further reveals that Year 3 course books encourage learners to use different learning strategies in Matura examination questions. Another observation is that Year 3 course books share some of the weaknesses of Year 1 course books, particularly in terms of educational technology, process writing, self-assessment, collaborative projects and meaningful learner autonomy tasks. In general, the format and the purpose of Year 3 course books make them ideal for self-study. For this reason, these books should be treated as supplementary learning materials to be used in self-access centres (see 2.3.3.1) rather than as compulsory course books in the classroom.

Thus far, this section has shown the extent to which Year 1 and Year 3 course books assist in developing learner autonomy, despite the different purposes they have been designed for. The picture that emerges from the foregoing discussion is that activities included in Year 1 course books seem much easier to adapt (see 3.3.1) or modify to help to foster learner autonomy in the classroom than the activities in Year 3 course books. Whether teachers adapt or modify the existing materials to contribute to the fostering of learner autonomy or not depends on the teachers themselves. Their philosophy of teaching, their awareness of the importance of learner autonomy in language education and their creativity and resourcefulness are all contributing factors. It is hoped that the research project presented in the following chapters will shed more light on these issues.

In the next section, I will briefly demonstrate how teachers could change course book activities into complex tasks that promote learner autonomy. Chapter Seven, in turn, offers a detailed discussion on designing complex tasks for learner autonomy development.

3.3.1 TURNING COURSE BOOK ACTIVITIES INTO LEARNER AUTONOMY TASKS

Adapting course book activities is an indispensable process (Cirocki, 2011; Islam & Mares, 2003; Tomlinson & Masuhara, 2004; McGrath, 2013). It depends on a number of factors and objectives. The former may include classroom dynamics or syllabus constraints (Cunningsworth, 1995), whereas the latter can focus on personalisation (see 3.1.1.4) or modernisation of existing activities (McGrath, 2013). Considering the fact that modern ELT materials are globally produced and have an intended lifespan (Tomlinson, 2003b), teachers need to adapt them. Even if these materials are locally produced, adaptation still seems to be required. Materials need to be adjusted to either learner specific needs or individual teaching styles. Such observations have also been reported in various empirical investigations conducted in Japan, China and Greece (Dunford, 2004; Tsobanoglou, 2008; Yan, 2007). The focus of the discussion will now be narrowed down and will shift from ELT materials to activities included in commercial course books.

Figure 3 presents a typical course book activity in which upper-intermediate (CEFR B2) learners are asked to verbally respond to the following question:

> **Activity 1 What's Bothering You?**
> **Discuss.**
>
> *Do you have any moans and groans about anything that has happened recently in your country or in the world?*

Figure 3. What's bothering you?: An example of a course book activity

As can be seen, this activity allows students to practise speaking in the target language. It gives them an opportunity to make choices and discuss topical issues. However, the instruction is not very precise and does not tell the student whether they are expected to work on their own, in pairs or in groups. Additional information is needed to inform students whether this response is expected to be a brief 2-3-sentence utterance or a 15-minute presentation. The students need to know how to approach the activity and how much time they have to complete it.

The question that arises is: Is it possible for this activity to be improved and additionally promote learner autonomy? The answer is affirmative. In order for the process of adaptation to be successful, teachers are required to put the theory discussed so far into practice. The necessary theoretical aspects to be combined include the profile of the autonomous learner (see 2.1), the major tenets underpinning social constructivist pedagogy (see 2.2.1), the various approaches to fostering learner autonomy (see 2.3) and the characteristic features of pedagogical tasks (see 3.2).

How can the activity presented above be turned into a learner autonomy pedagogical task? The new task could be approached in terms of three constructs: authenticity (see 3.2.1), complexity (see 3.2.2) and purposefulness (see 3.2.3). Students could be asked to work in groups so that meaningful communication takes place. Group work also enables students to experience different types of classroom work. To make the choice of a topic easier for students, one area out of four possible options should be selected by the students themselves. The topics must be relevant to the age of the students, to their interests, language competence and intellectual maturity. Educational technology should also be integrated (e.g. computers, laptops, the Internet) into the teaching-learning process. Such integration would not only make the task more interesting and challenging, but also give students a chance to practise and demonstrate other skills or talents they have. Thus, each group would have a computer and Internet access while working on the task. In this particular form, the task would engage students in using the target language in ways that promote learning (Ellis, 2003). Students strive to achieve their goals through active participation and meaningful interaction (see 2.2.1.2). Also, the task would enable students to develop different types of skills, knowledge and dispositions required for successful target language use in social and cultural discourses in and outside the classroom (McKay, 2006; Hallet & Legutke, 2013). Finally, precise instruction would be provided and visual support would be added to make the task attractive. This is how the task would look (see Figure 4):

> **What's Bothering You?**
> *Do you have any moans and groans about anything that has happened recently in your country or in the world?*
>
> Work in groups of four and produce one of the following: an online blog, a dialogue, a poster or a diary entry. Decide who you would like to work with and form appropriate groups. As a team, choose one of these four areas to moan and groan about:
>
> 1. Music 2. Film 3. Education 4. Reality Shows
>
> Having decided on an area, divide the roles among your team members so that each person knows what to do and so that work is equally shared. Find useful information and images online to be combined with your opinions. You have 30 minutes to complete the task.
>
> When your final product is ready, make it available to other groups so that they can assess it. Assess the work of other groups in the next 15 minutes. Reflect on the assessed items and briefly present (2-3 minutes) your opinions to the class during the next lesson. Also, think how you could improve your work next time.

Figure 4. What's bothering you?: An example of a course book task

For more examples of pedagogical tasks and the discussion of the process of designing complex tasks, see Chapter Seven.

3.4 CONCLUSION

The preceding discussion discloses that learner autonomy tasks are not easy to design. They require that teachers take into consideration such aspects as language acquisition, language pedagogy and a current knowledge of how English is used. At the same time, teachers must be well aware of various criteria for text selection as well as specific features of pedagogical tasks. Insufficient knowledge of these may lead to the production of low-quality tasks, and thus jeopardise both effective learning and teaching.

The next three chapters take a look at how involved teachers are in developing learner autonomy and designing learner autonomy tasks in their teaching practice. It is also hoped that the discussion will reveal which materials or tasks teachers use or design to encourage autonomous behaviours in their students.

CHAPTER FOUR

LEARNER AUTONOMY IN THE POLISH EFL CONTEXT: A MIXED-METHODS STUDY

The previous chapters have had a theoretical focus. They have formed the background for the empirical part of the present book by explaining the topic of the research project, building a rationale for it, and locating the present study within the existing research on both learner autonomy and task design for learner autonomy development. More specifically, the purpose of this knowledge base was fourfold: (1) to define the concept of learner autonomy and autonomous learner, (2) to discuss constructivist roots for learner autonomy, (3) to explore various approaches to the development of learner autonomy and (4) to present several important criteria for text selection and a number of crucial features of pedagogical tasks that must be taken into account while designing cognitively challenging tasks.

The concept of learner autonomy is not new in language pedagogy. There is professional literature devoted to various learner autonomy projects which have been conducted in different parts of the world (e.g. Benson, 2007, 2011; O'Rourke & Carson, 2010; Pawlak, 2011b; Usuki, 2007). In the Polish context, however, this particular aspect of Applied Linguistics requires further research. Although conferences devoted to the theme of learner autonomy have been organised, there is a particular lack of research in the area of task development for learner autonomy. To fill this gap, a mixed-methods study was conducted among EFL comprehensive secondary school teachers and students. Both the quantitative and qualitative analyses of the gathered data as well as a detailed discussion of relevant research outcomes will be presented in the following chapters.

The current chapter begins with background information about the research project. A brief rationale for combining quantitative and qualitative methods in the present study is offered. Then, such issues as participants and time allocations, research tools and procedures, data analysis techniques, ethical issues and research limitations, are dealt with respectively. Additionally, a description of the pilot study precedes the presentation of the study proper.

4.1 BACKGROUND TO THE STUDY

Language education in Poland has undergone many changes in the past twenty years. The most significant transformation took place when Poland joined the EU in 2004. It was then that the education system faced a great challenge. The new system had to adhere to EU standards and regulations. It was also then that regular foreign language teacher and student exchange programmes were brought into existence. All these innovations contributed to a new perspective on language education and its social constructivist trends (see 2.2).

For instance, the new reform universally required that language competence be viewed as a broad notion which consisted not only of the grammar of the target language, but also its functions, discourse and sociolinguistic features, as well as strategic competence. As a result, the main objective of language learning and teaching was the use of the target language as the main medium of meaningful communication.

All secondary school students now study two foreign languages. The Matura examination can include tests of both languages. The examination consists of two parts: the written and the oral. The written part can be taken for the basic level or the extended level. These levels correspond to A2/B1 and B2/C1 levels according to the *Common European Framework of Reference for Languages* (CEFR). The oral examination lasts 15 minutes.

Examinees are asked to answer questions which relate to a particular topic, for example, to describe pictures, to discuss issues related to a picture and to produce an extended utterance based on two questions. This part of the Matura examination, not separated into the basic and extended levels, is based on both the general and specific requirements of the core curriculum. The written examination lasts 120 minutes when taken as a compulsory subject or 150 minutes when the foreign language to be tested is taken as an additional subject. Both examination papers include the following sections: listening comprehension, reading comprehension, writing and use of English.

The three-year foreign language courses at the secondary level are based on course books recommended by the Ministry of Education (see 3.3). The course content is presented in a syllabus "of a compound, eclectic nature [with] topics/ situations/ functions/ tasks" (Siek-Piskozub, 2004, p. 20). Classroom content and methodology, on the other hand, are designed to satisfy learner needs in real life situations (see 3.2.1). A proportional syllabus is frequently opted for as it includes a semantic-grammatical organisational base, a linguistic component grounded in language functions and topics parallel to learners' interests (Yalden, 1987). The proportional syllabus "specifie[s] the communicative functions [that learners] need [to] communicate effectively at a given level of competence" (Willis, 1990, p. 57). Individual functions and the exponents needed to express these functions are the underlying themes. An interesting observation, though, is that these courses change from typical EFL courses in Year One to examination-orientated language education in Year Three, as mentioned at the beginning of Chapter Three.

Recent discussions with my colleagues in Poland have revealed that foreign language teaching is now predominantly examination-orientated. Secondary school students are systematically trained in examination strategies to be able to answer examination questions with a large degree of automatic rote repetition. Such practices leave very little room for authentic learning, not to mention genuine communication in the target language and the successful development of learner autonomy. The teachers assign activities for students to accomplish in a set time period. Many of these activities are repeated again and again to ensure that students remember how and what to do or say in particular situations. With this in mind, it appears relatively difficult to describe the modern language classroom with the constructivist metaphors described in Chapter Seven (see 7.1.2.5). In a similar vein, the presented teaching-learning process does not seem to accurately reflect the philosophy of social constructivism discussed in Chapter Two (see 2.2). By implication, this means there is hardly any scope for fostering learner autonomy.

4.2 RESEARCH OBJECTIVES

To gain a deeper insight into the issues of developing learner autonomy as well as pedagogical tasks for learner autonomy in the Polish comprehensive secondary school EFL classroom, the study addressed eight research questions. These questions, provoked by the literature review in Chapter Two and Chapter Three, fall into two groups (see Table 1). Such a division seems justified because there were two groups of participants in the study. As a result, the project singled out *Inquiry 1*, which focused on teachers and *Inquiry 2*, which was related to students. The former was based on eight research questions, whereas the latter was based on three questions. The three questions from Inquiry 2 were also part of Inquiry 1. This enabled a comparative analysis of the data at a later stage.

Table 1. Research questions for Inquiry 1 and Inquiry 2

	INQUIRY 1		INQUIRY 2
1.	To what extent is the development of learner autonomy in the classroom important?	1.	To what extent is the development of learner autonomy in the classroom important?
2.	On average, what percentage of their classroom time do teachers devote to developing learner autonomy?		
3.	What methods, techniques and teaching resources do teachers employ to promote learner autonomy?		

INQUIRY 1		INQUIRY 2	
4.	What criteria do teachers use for selecting course books?		
5.	To what extent do current course books contribute to the successful development of learner autonomy?	2.	To what extent do current course books contribute to the successful development of learner autonomy?
6.	To what extent are teachers involved in task development for learner autonomy?		
7.	What types of tasks from modern course books do teachers look for to help students to become independent learners?		
8.	What possible problems impede the cultivation of learner autonomy?	3.	What possible problems impede the cultivation of learner autonomy?

As can be seen, the purpose of this study was to estimate whether learner autonomy is promoted in comprehensive secondary schools in Poland. If so, to what extent is learner autonomy promoted, by what means is it promoted and if there are obstacles, what are they? Also, the study sought to ascertain what types of tasks in-service EFL teachers look for to help students to become autonomous learners. The study was also designed to discover whether in-service EFL teachers develop such tasks themselves. As such, this project was to serve as a bridge between theoretical deliberations on the development of learner autonomy and its practical aspects at the classroom level. For this reason, the key features of social constructivism (see 2.2.1), learner autonomy development (see 2.3) and task-orientated instruction (see 3.2) were integrated into one framework. As evidenced in the first part of the book, the concept of learner autonomy is grounded in the philosophy of social constructivism and facilitated by complex learning tasks (see 3.2.2). It was hoped that critical reflection about English language teaching and a better understanding of various aspects of learner autonomy development would emerge, which, in turn, would inform decisions on what form the future of learner autonomy development should take.

4.3 WHY COMBINE QUANTITATIVE AND QUALITATIVE METHODS?

There are many approaches which deal with second language research. Nonetheless, as Grotjahn (1987) in his argument *On the Methodological Basis of Introspective Methods* observes, various parameters can be applied to distinguish research types. Such parameters include the type of data (quantitative or qualitative), the method of analysis (interpretative or statistical) and the manner of data collection (experimental or non-experimental). According to research literature (e.g. Benson, 2001, 2007, 2011; Usuki, 2007), some of these approaches have been employed in learner autonomy investigations. Furthermore, a combination of quantitative and qualitative methods has frequently been applied within individual studies. The latter relates to Denzin's (1978) concept of *triangulation*, which involves a blend of multiple research methods in dealing with one phenomenon.

The current study combined *quantitative* and *qualitative* methods in one framework. This was done so that various complex factors, such as teachers, students, materials, tasks and methods, that contribute to fostering learner autonomy could be adequately addressed. The problem in question could then be probed from different angles. The application of teacher and student questionnaires and teacher and student journals in both inquiries sought to generate a large body of data and provide a thorough and penetrating analysis of the concept under study.

The purpose of the quantitative part of the present research project was to gather numerical data through both teacher and student questionnaires (see Appendix A). The data were then analysed by means of statistical procedures (see 4.5.3). The purpose of this stage was to quantify the collected opinions about developing learner autonomy and task design for learner autonomy, and then generalise the findings from both the teacher and student populations. Various cause and effect relationships were sought. Hence, it can be inferred that the quantitative element of this project was influenced by the philosophy of positivism. This philosophy assumes that the world which exists around us is objective, and its objective exploration through the application of accurate instruments, is also possible (McNabb, 2010). As a result, the quantitative data analysis outcomes in Chapter Five will be presented in a numerical and objective manner.

The qualitative part, on the other hand, was based on teacher and student journals (see 4.5.2.2). Journals can be defined as individual reports of both learning or teaching occurrences recorded through systematic accounts (Bailey, 1990). In this study, the purpose of the journals was threefold. The journals were expected to:
1. supply personal accounts of language learning or teaching experiences in the Polish context;
2. keep records of details, feelings and various phenomena linked to learner autonomy development and task design for learner autonomy; and
3. reveal cyclical regularities and significant occurrences in language instruction, learner autonomy development and task design for learner autonomy in secondary schools.

The method used for analysing qualitative data was *thematic coding*. This method allowed for an investigation of the ways the language was used to communicate beliefs, attitudes and opinions about the development of learner autonomy and task design for learner autonomy (Jensen, 2002; Weathington, Cunningham, & Pittenger, 2010). What should be clarified here is that this investigation did not focus on the syntactic analysis of the research participants' language. Instead, the investigation dealt with the development of themes throughout the recorded texts, both in the questionnaires and journals, through critical reading of what was said and what was not said by the participants. The analysis of the gathered texts specifically focused on the reviewing of the textual material as well as comparing and contrasting various meaning elements in the participants' responses. The aim of this process was to observe how patterns emerged or recurred in the responses (Jensen, 2002; Weathington, Cunningham, & Pittenger, 2010).

Consequently, the conclusions in this part of the project were based on the participants' responses and observations. The observations were meaningful and culturally salient, as well as rich and explanatory in nature. It should also be remembered that qualitative research focuses on naturalistic and interpretive approaches (Denzin & Lincoln, 1994). The qualitative part was nothing less than an interactive process in which research participants, immersed in their natural setting, shared with me their numerous experiences. Such an approach is in line with Mackey and Gass's (2005) assertion that qualitative research is more often than not characterised by rich description, emic perspectives, few participants, and last but not least, ongoing and triangulated analysis of data.

The present project was deeply rooted in the constructivist framework adopted in this volume. As pointed out earlier, knowledge is socially construed (see 2.2.). In the current study, I made attempts to grasp the complex domain of experiences in which both teachers and students had been immersed in the Polish educational context. To find out what meanings both groups attributed to various teaching and learning activities and how these meanings affected behaviours in the groups concerned, I interacted with the individual participants through their texts in the questionnaires and journals. The process consisted of four stages: (1) preliminary consideration of the individual texts as a whole, (2) discerning connections and relationships among ideas within the texts, (3) relating personal knowledge to text ideas and (4) standing away from the texts to consider the objectivity of the texts (Campbell, Donahue, Reese, & Phillips, 1996). Having collected substantial data, diverse interpretations were made. The interactions were nothing less than a dynamic dialectal process whose main purpose was to obtain new perspectives on the concepts under study. The dialectal process was intricate. Often, the process required the comparison of contradictory ideas and a re-examination of previously adopted standpoints.

In summary, quantitative and qualitative methods are often seen as opposing poles (Hewson, 2007). In this project, both of them were used in a complementary way to investigate a complex phenomenon. By mixing both methods, the study in question linked two research models: the *analytical-nomological* and *exploratory-interpretative*. The former collects quantitative data through an experiment, and subjects the data to statistical analysis. The latter resorts to non-experimental methods, yielding qualitative data and their interpretative analysis. For a more detailed and comprehensive discussion of research methods in language pedagogy see Nunan (1992), Mackey and Gass (2005), Brown (2014) and Cirocki and Arceusz (2016).

In the next section, the pilot study that preceded the study proper will be presented.

4.4 PILOT STUDY

In general, a pilot study is closely related to the aim of the study proper of which it is part. It is meant to provide information about the feasibility of a research project as a whole. In other words, somewhat metaphorically, pilot studies are conducted to check whether or not "the beast will fly" (de Vos, 2002, p. 410) and to increase the likelihood of conducting the study proper "without tears" (Blaxter, Hughes, & Tight, 1996, p. 121).

The purpose of the present pilot study was threefold. Firstly, it sought to estimate the appropriateness of the quantitative method. Secondly, it aimed to assess the proposed data analysis techniques to uncover potential problems. Lastly, it was meant to give advance warning about feasible flaws in the design of the project as a whole, indicating which stages of the project could fail. Apart from these goals, two outcomes were expected of this pilot study. It was to provide evidence that the participants could understand all the questions in the questionnaires. The study was also meant to supply preliminary data about the issue under study. In addition, interesting observations recorded at this stage of the research project were intended to enrich the discussion of the findings in Chapter Six.

The pilot study was conducted at two comprehensive secondary schools in Gdańsk and Sopot (see Appendix B). The participants were twenty EFL learners and ten EFL teachers. These two schools were selected for the pilot study because my colleagues who worked at the schools expressed their willingness to help me with the pilot stage of the project. The participants were selected through a simple random sampling procedure in which each member of the population had an equal probability of being selected (Mackey & Gass, 2005). As a result, all the students in the second and the third grades were assigned a number. Then, a computer programme was used to select a sample from each group. The same procedure was applied to teacher participants. More specifically, there were ten respondents from the second grade and ten respondents from the third grade. Seven of the teachers had English MA degrees, the other three had English BA degrees (see Table 2).

Table 2. Pilot study data gathering

School	Date	Research Instrument	Subjects	Grade 2	Grade 3
Secondary School 1	September 2012	questionnaires	10 learners	5	5
Secondary School 2	September 2012	questionnaires	10 learners	5	5
				BA degree	MA degree
Secondary School 1	September 2012	questionnaires	4 teachers	1	3
Secondary School 2	September 2012	questionnaires	6 teachers	2	4

The pilot study was quite simple to administer. Only one research instrument – the questionnaire – was applied and it was only necessary to visit two schools. Firstly, I arranged a meeting with the group of twenty students in Gdańsk and Sopot. The meeting took place at their schools, in September 2012, and lasted twenty minutes. One teacher in each school introduced me as the researcher to the student participants. The teachers also helped me to hand out the copies of the questionnaire with the research consent forms (see Appendix A). The students were asked to reasonably answer all the questions. After the questionnaires had been collected, the data were analysed.

Secondly, on the same day, I provided the two teachers with an electronic copy of the questionnaire for teachers (see Appendix C) and asked them to email it to their school colleagues. The teachers were asked to spend about twenty minutes to complete their questionnaires and email them back to me on the same day. Then, the questionnaires were printed out and the collected data were read over and checked.

For the sake of clarity, it seems important to present a brief rationale and structure of the questionnaires used at the pilot stage. Questionnaires have a number of attractive features (Denscombe, 2007). They are easy to analyse when compared with other research techniques such as face-to-face interviews or telephone surveys. Many computer software packages are available for data entry and tabulation of almost all kinds of questionnaires. In addition to this, questionnaires are familiar to most people (Berdie, Anderson, & Niebuhr, 1986). Nearly everyone has had some experience completing questionnaires, so it was to be expected that this research tool would not make people feel apprehensive. The uniform question presentation of this technique reduces bias. Thus, the researcher's own opinions do not influence the respondents' answers.

It must be clarified that all the items in the questionnaires were developed based on the previously selected research questions. I generated, selected and edited these items myself. For example, the teacher questionnaire began with questions in English, pertaining to the importance and frequency of creating conducive conditions for fostering autonomous behaviour in the classroom (questions 1, 2 and 3). Then, the questionnaire addressed various methods, techniques and resources employed by language instructors to stimulate learner autonomy development (questions 4 and 5); selection criteria for course books and the extent to which course books promote learner autonomy (questions 6, 7, 8 and 9); desirable learner autonomy tasks to be included in course books (question 10); teacher engagement in task design (questions 11 and 12) and possible problems that are likely to impede the cultivation of learner autonomy (question 13).

The student questionnaire, on the other hand, was prepared in Polish. Similarly to the teacher questionnaire, it began with the question related to the importance of developing learner autonomy (question 1), and then asked the respondents about their satisfaction with the number of learner autonomy tasks offered in the classroom (question 2), their opinion about the extent to which their course books contribute to learner autonomy development (question 3), the frequency of using non-course-book-based tasks and the effectiveness of these tasks in learner autonomy development (questions 4 and 5) and possible problems that may prevent the fostering of learner autonomy in the classroom (question 6).

The resulting questionnaires consisted of thirteen questions for the teacher questionnaire and six questions for the student questionnaire. Since the student population consisted of second and third grade students, question three in the questionnaire differed in both groups. Second graders focused on their Year One course books, whereas third graders concentrated on their current, that is, Year Three course books.

The questions used in the teacher and student questionnaires were both open- and closed-ended, which means the respondents were to provide their own answers to the questions or choose from the existing answers. The open-ended questions were deliberately used as they allow respondents not only to supply detailed answers to presented questions, but also clarify their responses (Mackey & Gass, 2005). Another reason for using open-ended questions was that they offer respondents the possibility of giving unlimited answers, which provided additional information on their thinking processes, creativity and resourcefulness.

The use of the closed-ended questions, on the other hand, was to enable the respondents to answer all the questions easily and quickly. Closed-ended questions also ensure an easy comparison of answers from different respondents as well as uncomplicated codification and statistical analysis of the gathered data (Babbie, 2013).

Having prepared all the questions, the respondents' profile sections (i.e. questions about respondents' age, gender, etc.), plus the layout of the questionnaires were decided. All the pages were numbered and enough space was provided for the respondents' answers. Each questionnaire started with a research consent page.

The pilot study questionnaires provided interesting preliminary data. The analysis of the results indicated that the majority of the teachers (80%) and students (70%) considered the fostering of learner autonomy important. In practice, though, not much classroom time was devoted to developing learner autonomy. The majority of the teachers (80%) stated that they allocated not more than 20 percent of their classroom time to fostering learner autonomy. Those teachers who reported doing so said that they helped their students to become more independent learners mainly through homework tasks (90%) and learning strategy instruction (60%). The pilot study also revealed that course books were the most common sources used in learner autonomy development.

In the opinion of both teachers and students, course books helped learners to become more autonomous learners. This help, however, was somewhat limited. For example, the course books used by Year 1 and Year 3 students were believed to promote cooperative learning (see 2.2.1.4), learning strategy instruction (see 2.3.1) and critical thinking. Yet the same course books did not meet teacher and student expectations with regard to promoting self-assessment (see 2.3.2.2), learner autonomy tasks (see 7.3) and skills integration. Nor did they effectively promote the use of educational technology (see 2.3.4).

The pilot study showed that teachers (70%) did not regularly supplement course books. Similar observations were also made by students. As far as the design of learner autonomy tasks was concerned, almost all teachers stated that they were rarely involved in task design. Likewise, students agreed with the teachers that there were very few non-course-book-based activities in their classrooms.

Additionally, both teachers and students reported a number of possible problems that might prevent the development of learner autonomy. The most frequent response provided in both questionnaires was the lack of appropriate resources. On teacher questionnaires only, a common problem that was likely to impede the fostering of learner autonomy was the examination-orientatated curriculum.

Finally, the pilot study revealed three shortcomings. All the issues had to be addressed so as to increase the degree of success in the study proper (see 4.5). First of all, it was noted that the time provided for completing the questionnaire could have been a little longer. As a result, the participants were given twenty-five instead of twenty minutes to have enough time to fully answer all the questions. The second problem was related to the formulation of question 4 (*How do you go about fostering learner autonomy in your classroom?*) in the teacher questionnaire. As a consequence, the imprecise question was reworded to make it more specific. The final version of this question was as follows: *What methods and techniques do you employ to foster learner autonomy in your classroom?* The third problem pertained to the open-ended questions in the questionnaires. More specifically, the answers to these questions were either overly concise or completely neglected. Hence, in the study proper, before the distribution of the questionnaire took place, the respondents were encouraged to give their full attention to these questions. Likewise, the respondents were urged to provide additional information under "Other" items in some questions or whenever space for extra comments was provided. Next, the study proper was planned for the near future. The details of this study are described next.

4.5 LEARNER AUTONOMY IN THE SECONDARY SCHOOL EFL CLASSROOM: THE STUDY

The theoretical deliberations on learner autonomy development (see 2.3) and task design for learner autonomy (see 3.2) generated eight research questions and led to the design of the present study. The investigation was intended for teachers and students and, as mentioned earlier, led to the establishment of Inquiry 1 and Inquiry 2, respectively. This division was to ensure clarity and accuracy of the data analysis in the sections to come. A detailed description of the current research project will now be formed by a discussion of the following: participants and time allocations, research tools and procedures, data analysis, ethical issues and limitations of the research concerned, respectively.

4.5.1 PARTICIPANTS AND TIME ALLOCATION

The participants of Inquiry 1 were teachers of English who worked in comprehensive secondary schools. The schools were from the following four provinces of Poland: Zachodniopomorskie, Kujawsko-Pomorskie, Warmińsko-Mazurskie and Mazowieckie. All the teachers were invited to take part in this study during ELT conferences and workshops. One session at each conference or workshop was related to task-supported language teaching.

The teacher population (see Figure 5) consisted of 104 (87%) females and 16 (13%) males. There were 32 (27%) BA, 84 (70%) MA and 4 (3%) PhD degree holders. Fifty percent of the teacher population was over 33.9 years old. In addition to this, 76 percent of the teachers were employed full-time, whereas 24 percent were part-time teaching staff (18 percent with more than 50% of full-time hours and 6 percent with less than 50% of full time hours). The statistics showed that 74 percent of the respondents had been teaching English for five or more years.

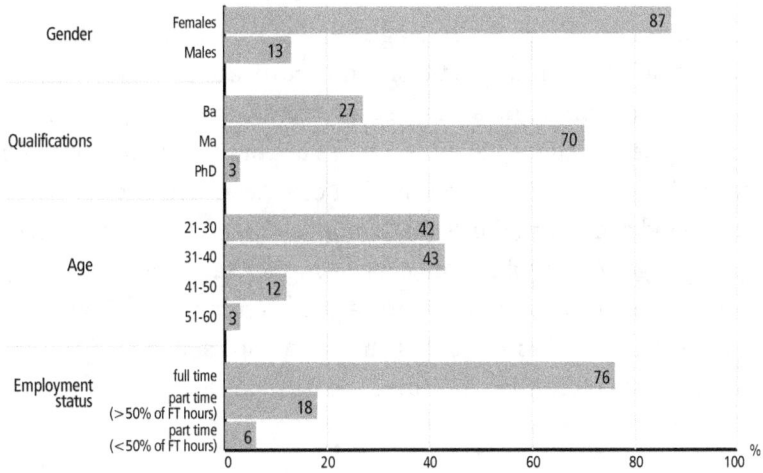

Figure 5. The teacher population: Age, gender, qualifications and employment status

Inquiry 2 was addressed to students. All the students were taught by the teachers introduced above. Three teachers from each province volunteered to involve ten students in the learner autonomy research. Hence, the student population (see Figure 6) in this study consisted of 120 participants: 66 (55%) female and 54 (45%) male. All of them were voluntary participants from the second grade (60 participants) and the third grade (60 participants) of twelve different schools. Eighty five (71%) participants were planning to take the extended Matura examination in English. Thirty five (29%) participants were planning to take the basic English level examination.

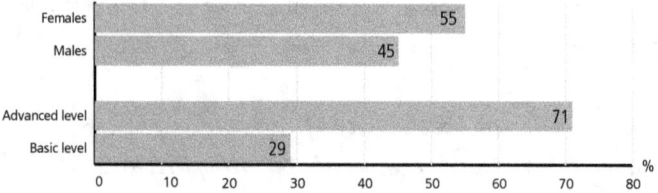

Figure 6. The student population: Gender and Matura examination preferences

As the respondent's profile section in the student questionnaire disclosed, the students had a motivated outlook towards learning English. A lot of them had private English language tutoring or were taking Cambridge examination courses (i.e. FCE or CAE) in local language schools.

Recent discussions with my colleagues have revealed that the students are aware that in Poland, apart from communication, there are political, economic, educational and social reasons for learning English. Since Poland joined the EU, there have been more opportunities for employment in international companies and foreign countries. All such possibilities require a good command (i.e. level C1 or level C2 according to CEFR) of the target language. These jobs often carry a higher salary and better opportunities for promotion. For students, a good command of English means easier access to better universities and to various scholarships. In short, a good command of English may directly determine a person's social status and power.

4.5.2 RESEARCH TOOLS AND PROCEDURES

The study sought to provide answers to the research questions from the perspective of the teacher (see 5.1) as well as the student (see 5.2). The questionnaires along with the teacher and student journals were the instruments used. More details about the application of both types of tools are briefly presented below.

4.5.2.1 THE QUESTIONNAIRES

The questionnaires used in the pilot study did not signal major problems. After the pilot stage (see 4.4), one question in the teacher questionnaire required a slight amendment. Having rephrased the question, both the teacher and student questionnaires were then employed in the study proper. More specifically, the questionnaires were distributed in two different settings. Inquiry 1 was intended for teachers and its quantitative part took place at the end of ELT conferences or workshops. I informed all the teachers that my research focused on the development of learner autonomy. I then selected the participants through convenience sampling. In other words, I involved teachers that were readily available and willing to participate in the study. Next, the participants were provided with the questionnaires and research consent forms. They were asked to complete the forms on the spot and return them to me in twenty-five minutes.

Inquiry 2 was intended for students. It took place in the natural classroom setting of regularly scheduled classes. The student participants were from twelve different secondary schools, which meant much more time and organisation were needed to collect all the data. As agreed during the ELT conferences and workshops, I posted the Polish language version of the research consent forms and questionnaires to the representative teachers. These teachers had agreed to distribute the material among the study participants on my behalf.

The participants for Inquiry 2 were selected through convenience sampling, as in Inquiry 1 above. Having selected the required number of participants in their schools, the teachers invited them to a 60-minute group meeting. The meeting was conducted in Polish. During this meeting, the participants were informed about the focus of the research and its procedure. The teachers used a brief and general discussion to check whether the participants were familiar with the notion of learner autonomy. The questions used in this discussion were: *What does learner autonomy mean to you? Are you an autonomous learner?* and *Does our school provide opportunities to develop your autonomy?* Some time was also devoted to the concept of a task. The teachers explained to the participants the difference between typical course book activities and tasks. The students were then involved in an activity in which they had to identify tasks. Subsequently, the consent forms and questionnaires were collected from the research participants and sent to my address. The questionnaires were analysed. The answers to the open-ended questions were translated into English and used to support the quantitative data.

Following up on the pilot study, before completing the questionnaires, the participants in both inquiries had been greatly encouraged to give true answers and to avoid wild guessing so that all the data would be as reliable as possible. The open-ended questions and the importance of giving detailed answers to contribute to the success of the entire study were pointed out to the respondents. The participants were informed that the questionnaire data would be pooled and included in an academic publication.

4.5.2.2 THE JOURNALS

The second type of instrument employed in this study was teacher and student journals (see 4.3). Teacher and student journals were deliberately chosen for the current project because of the distinct advantages they offer. Journals not only provide a thorough history of the entire research project, but also encourage participants to reflect on the various practices that were put to use (Mackey & Gass, 2005; Cirocki & Arceusz, 2016). The writings are naturally introspective, and thus reflect learner and teacher perspectives on the instructional factors that affect language learning and teaching. Lastly, journals are inexpensive research tools. They are convenient for research participants because of their portability. In this way, the employed teacher and student journals allowed the participants in this study to record personal feelings, reflections and thoughts about the issue under study.

Twelve teachers kept journals for two months. The participants were selected through convenience sampling (see 4.5.2.1). In their journals, written in English, the teachers were asked to reflect on learner autonomy, list the teaching materials they used to develop learner autonomy in their teaching practice and store properly referenced learner autonomy tasks they either had borrowed from non-course-book-based sources, had adapted or had designed for their students. The participants individually decided about the layout of their journals. The participants were also informed that the journals must be carefully kept as they would undergo external analysis and the data would be part of an academic text. The participants were to make comments every time teaching materials or tasks helped them to develop learner autonomy in the classroom. Finally, the participants were requested to evaluate one modern EFL course book in terms of how well it promoted learner autonomy (see 3.3). The participants were supposed to decide on the form of the evaluation, but a list with prompt questions had also been provided (see Appendix D). The participants were also encouraged to suggest how the course book of their choice could be improved to successfully develop learner autonomy. After two months, the research participants posted their journals to my address. Then, I confirmed that I had received the material and thanked the participants for their cooperation and contribution to my future publication.

Journals were also kept by learners for two months. After they had completed the questionnaires, but before they started writing their journals, twenty four participants had attended a workshop on learner autonomy. As with the teacher participants, the workshop attendees were selected through convenience sampling and represented twelve schools. The selection process had been organised by their teachers. This workshop was an introductory part to Inquiry 2. I designed and ran this workshop in a comprehensive secondary school in Gdańsk. It was the same school that had taken part in the pilot study (see 4.4).

The workshop focused on both the theory and practice of developing learner autonomy in a task-based learning environment. The three major sections of this workshop focused on defining learner autonomy, describing autonomous learners and analysing materials and tasks promoting learner autonomy. The closing section focused on the importance of introspective tools in classroom research. It was in this section that the participants were familiarised with the concept of a journal. The whole event was conducted in a student-friendly manner and involved a lot of interaction and collaboration.

The first aim of this workshop was to help the participants to better understand the concept in question. The second aim was to provide them with all the necessary information for appropriately writing a journal. It was up to the participants, though, to individually decide on the layout of their journals. These journals, written in Polish, were used for reports on tasks which helped the participants to become more independent learners. Additionally, the participants were asked to include comments about situations in which autonomy could have been developed in the classroom by modifying activities, but was not. Similar situations had been simulated during the introductory workshop. The participants were also encouraged to include copies of learner autonomy tasks used in the classroom. Every time the participants included a task in their journals, they had to ask their teachers about the source. This procedure enabled me to group the tasks into those taken from other sources and those designed by the teachers themselves. After two months, the research participants were requested to put the journals in sealed envelopes and hand them to their teachers. Those teachers posted them to my address. Subsequently, I thanked all the participants and their teachers for their cooperation. I also reminded them that the journal data would be analysed and included in an academic text.

I also kept a journal in which I recorded interesting observations that I had encountered at different stages of the project. In addition, my journal contained detailed information about the course books used by the participants and the potential of the course books for developing learner autonomy. I compared some of my findings with the observations recorded in the teachers' journals. The results were briefly presented in Chapter Three (see 3.3). My entries were also intended to enrich the discussion of the research results in Chapter Six.

4.5.3 DATA ANALYSIS

All the data, collected by means of elicitation and introspective methods, underwent both quantitative and qualitative analyses. The process consisted of four phases which are presented below:

PHASE 1	All the data were classified by date.
PHASE 2	All the data were read through a number of times to specify themes defined by the research questions. Relationships among the themes and the research questions were established.
PHASE 3	All the non-numerical data, that is, journal entries, were cut out of the journals, linked to the appropriate research questions and analysed. However, all the numerical data were placed in contingency tables (Microsoft Office Excel 2007) to arrange them into a manageable base of information, eventually providing proper frequencies.
PHASE 4	The statistical analysis was conducted with PQStat software which allows for a simple and accurate data analysis in both large and small samples. The questionnaire outcomes were presented in frequency tables, multiple response tables and on graphs. Before all the data were presented on charts, arithmetic rounding had been employed. Accordingly, the five digits 5, 6, 7, 8 and 9 were rounded up, as opposed to the four digits 1, 2, 3 and 4 which were rounded down. The present analysis was based on two statistical instruments: the z-test testing for the significance of a difference between two proportions and Fisher's exact test. The first test allowed for the comparison of the frequency of multiple responses. This statistical test analyses the differences between two groups by examining the proportion of items in each group that are in a particular category. Put simply, in this type of analysis, two different proportions are compared to determine whether the difference between them is significant or not. In the present analysis, the significance level was chosen to be 5% ($p<0.05$), whereas $p<0.01$ was considered highly significant. Fisher's exact test, in turn, was used to compare frequencies in questions where respondents could choose only one option. This test, also known as a statistical significance test, was used to determine non-random associations between two categorical variables that result from classifying objects in two different ways. Fisher's exact test was preferred in this study because the sample was rather small and the collected data were very unequally distributed.

The described approach to data analysis made it possible to become familiar with the entire body of obtained details. The information could be sorted into manageable patterns and structures based on the research questions.

It should also be stressed that all the data were gathered and analysed in two languages: English and Polish. The teacher participants used English. The student participants provided responses/comments in Polish, yet from time to time English was used. As requested by the teachers in the study, all the entries presented in Chapter Three and in Chapter Five were edited to provide a uniform style, clarity of ideas and accurate language. Likewise, all of the students' responses/comments were translated into English.

4.5.4 ETHICAL CONSIDERATIONS

The design of the mixed-methods study presented above demonstrates that ethical conduct was maintained at all stages of the research. Firstly, all the participants were clearly informed about what to anticipate in the course of the research. Secondly, according to the *Ethical Guidelines for Educational Research* (BERA, 2011), signed consent forms were collected from both research populations before the teachers and students became part of the study. Thirdly, the questionnaires and the journals were anonymised to make sure individuals could not be identified. Additionally, the school authorities requested that a special clause be included in the consent form stating that the research data would not under any circumstances be accessible to third parties. It was also emphasised that all the completed research tools were the sole property of the researcher and the research participants. Finally, both research findings and conclusions were precisely communicated to the participants.

4.5.5 LIMITATIONS OF THE STUDY

Before presenting and discussing the findings of the present study, there are a number of limitations that must be taken into consideration. For example, in this study, the concept of developing learner autonomy was limited to a small number of comprehensive secondary schools. A much clearer picture of the studied phenomenon as well as more empirical generalisations would have been attained had more schools been invited to take part in the project. Also, the investigation of the issue of developing learner autonomy and task design for learner autonomy would have been more thorough if interviews and lesson observations had been incorporated into the study. For instance, interviews permit unanticipated themes to emerge, which may reveal interviewees' attitudes and behaviours towards studied phenomena (Mackey & Gass, 2005). Observations, in turn, allow the researcher to get an emic perspective on the construct under study, and thus find detailed information on what people do in a particular situation, how and why (Mackey & Gass, 2005).

4.6 CONCLUSION

This chapter is devoted to routine practices in classroom-based research. The discussion promotes a mixed-methods approach. Such an approach appears to be one of the underlying principles for progress in the ongoing investigation of not only how foreign languages are learnt or acquired, but also how they may be best taught.

It is now time to turn to the analysis of the outcomes of the study. The quantitative and qualitative results are presented in Chapter Five.

CHAPTER FIVE

PRESENTATION OF THE RESEARCH DATA

The research outcomes displayed in this chapter were derived from the analysis of all the data relevant to the research questions gathered throughout the entire period of the study. For the sake of clarity, the presentation will be divided into two parts. As pointed out in Chapter Four, there were two groups of participants. *Inquiry 1* was focused on the Polish secondary school EFL teachers. It will be dealt with first. The data analysis of *Inquiry 2* was related to the Polish secondary school EFL students, and will be presented next. In both parts, the statistical analysis of data will be supported by qualitative data collected through questionnaires as well as teacher and student journals. Qualitative data seek to provide information about the beliefs, feelings, motivations and observations that underlie participant behaviours and actions. Additionally, on a number of occasions, some of the data collected in the course of the study will be compared with the observations recorded in my journal.

5.1 LEARNER AUTONOMY IN THE EFL CLASSROOM: INQUIRY 1

In Inquiry 1, both quantitative and qualitative data collection instruments were used. The results of this part of the research project are presented in four subsections related to participant: (1) opinions on the importance of developing learner autonomy, (2) ways to go about developing learner autonomy in the teaching practice, (3) engagement in using diverse materials and designing their own tasks and (4) observations about possible problems that may hinder the development of learner autonomy in the Polish context. The four issues are detailed below.

5.1.1 IMPORTANCE OF DEVELOPING LEARNER AUTONOMY

According to the teacher questionnaire, the majority of respondents believed that developing learner autonomy in the EFL classroom is important. The respondents' opinions were as follows: very important (13%), important (81%) and neither important nor unimportant (6%). The results are presented in Table 3 and Figure 7 below.

Table 3. The importance of developing learner autonomy

	Is developing learner autonomy in the EFL classroom important?	No of responses	[%]
a)	Very unimportant	0	0
b)	Unimportant	0	0
c)	Neither important nor unimportant	7	6
d)	Important	97	81
e)	Very important	16	13

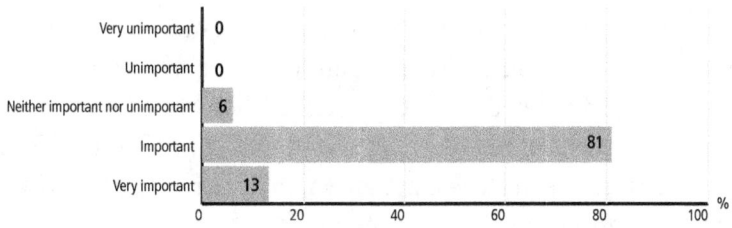

Figure 7. The importance of developing learner autonomy

A number of the participants also provided thought-provoking written comments on the importance of developing learner autonomy. Some of the opinions included in both questionnaires and journals were as follows:

> *Developing learner autonomy is extremely important. We need to prepare our students for their future lives. They will need to be able to act as independent citizens.*
>
> *Learner autonomy is very important, especially when we think about our students in terms of employability. The more independent they*

are, the more attractive they will be to employers. Thus, if we do not help them, who will?

Learner autonomy is essential. Students need to be provided with many opportunities of practising independence in the classroom. They need to be able to direct their own learning when they leave school. If they are not offered appropriate training or given enough practice, their lives outside of school will be very difficult.

It is very important to develop learner autonomy in the classroom because it encourages students to activate academic, intellectual and (inter)personal skills. Students must understand that they themselves must take ownership of their learning. Otherwise, they will never be successful learners.

Students must be aware that assuming responsibility for learning is a complex process. It is related to identifying learning goals and outcomes, offering self- and peer assessment as well as organising the entire process of learning. Therefore, it is important.

It is clear that the respondents are aware of the importance of developing learner autonomy in the language classroom. However, when asked about fostering learner autonomy in their own teaching practice, the respondents' answers were more varied. For instance, 51 percent of the respondents stated that they devoted no more than 20 percent of their classroom time to encouraging autonomous behaviour in their students. Forty percent of the teacher population reported that they allocated between 21 and 40 percent of their time in the classroom to promoting learner autonomy. Five percent stated that they spent between 41 and 60 percent of their classroom time on fostering learner autonomy, whereas 2 percent admitted to devoting between 61 and 80 percent of their time for the same purpose. Only 2 percent of the teachers stated that they allocated from 81 to 100 percent of their time to learner autonomy cultivation. The results are presented in Table 4 and Figure 8 below.

Table 4. The frequency of fostering learner autonomy

	What percentage of your classroom time do you devote to fostering learner autonomy?	No of responses	[%]
a)	0-20%	62	51
b)	21-40%	48	40
c)	41-60%	6	5
d)	61-80%	2	2
e)	81-100%	2	2

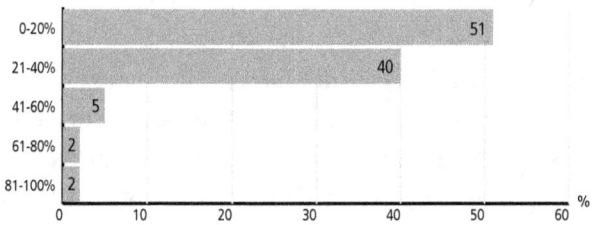

Figure 8. The frequency of fostering learner autonomy

The next question on the questionnaire referred to the amount of classroom time the respondents thought should be involved in developing learner autonomy. Thirty-six respondents (30%) showed their full approval for this idea by saying that they would be happy to allocate from 80 to 100 percent of their classroom time to fostering learner autonomy. The same number of respondents revealed that they would like to devote between 61 and 80 percent of their classroom time to integrating learner autonomy into the teaching-learning process. Forty-eight respondents (40%) were interested in employing the same procedure by allocating it from 41 to 60 percent of their classroom time. None of the respondents opted for the first two intervals, that is, 0-20% and 21-40%. The results are presented in Table 5 and Figure 9 below.

Table 5. Readiness of teachers to develop learner autonomy in their teaching practice

	What percentage of your classroom time would you like to devote to developing learner autonomy?	No of responses	[%]
a)	0-20%	0	0
b)	21-40%	0	0
c)	41-60%	48	40
d)	61-80%	36	30
e)	81-100%	36	30

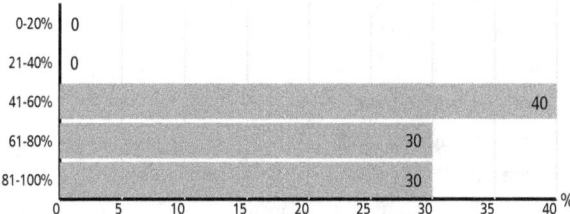

Figure 9. Readiness of teachers to develop learner autonomy in their teaching practice

5.1.2 UNDERTAKING LEARNER AUTONOMY DEVELOPMENT

This section centres on the issue of undertaking learner autonomy development by secondary school teachers. The respondents were asked about what methods and techniques they employ to foster learner autonomy in their teaching practice. It turned out that the teacher population – all 120 respondents – promote learner autonomy through pair/group work and homework assignments. A large percentage of the respondents also foster learner autonomy via dialogues, role-plays and simulations (93%) and by offering learning strategy instruction (81%). Thirty-seven (31%) respondents reported encouraging learner autonomy through presentations. Twenty-three (19%) respondents use project work, whereas 18 (15%) respondents foster technology-assisted teaching/learning. A very small part of the population promotes learner autonomy via self-access centres (3%); extensive reading (2%); learner portfolios, journals, self-reports and diaries (2%); self-assessment sessions (2%); syllabus and course content negotiation (2%) and drama, skits and plays (2%). The respondents do not seem to use extensive listening, reflecting on learning sessions nor literature and discussion clubs in learner autonomy development. None of these options were selected. The results are presented in Table 6 and Figure 10 below.

Table 6. The methods and techniques teachers employ to foster learner autonomy

	What methods and techniques do you employ to foster learner autonomy in your classroom?	No of responses	[%]
a)	Pair work/group work	120	100
b)	Extensive reading	2	2
c)	Extensive listening	0	0
d)	Project work	23	19
e)	Learner portfolios/learner journals/learner self-reports/learner diaries	2	2
f)	Self-assessment sessions	2	2
g)	Learning strategy instruction	97	81
h)	Reflecting on learning sessions	0	0
i)	Self-access centre	3	3
j)	Syllabus and course content negotiation	2	2
k)	Technology-assisted teaching/learning	18	15

What methods and techniques do you employ to foster learner autonomy in your classroom?	No of responses	[%]
l) Dialogues/role-plays/simulations	111	93
m) Drama/skits/plays	2	2
n) Literature club/discussion club	0	0
o) Presentations (e.g. PowerPoint, Prezi, poster, etc.)	37	31
p) Homework tasks	120	100
q) Other	0	0

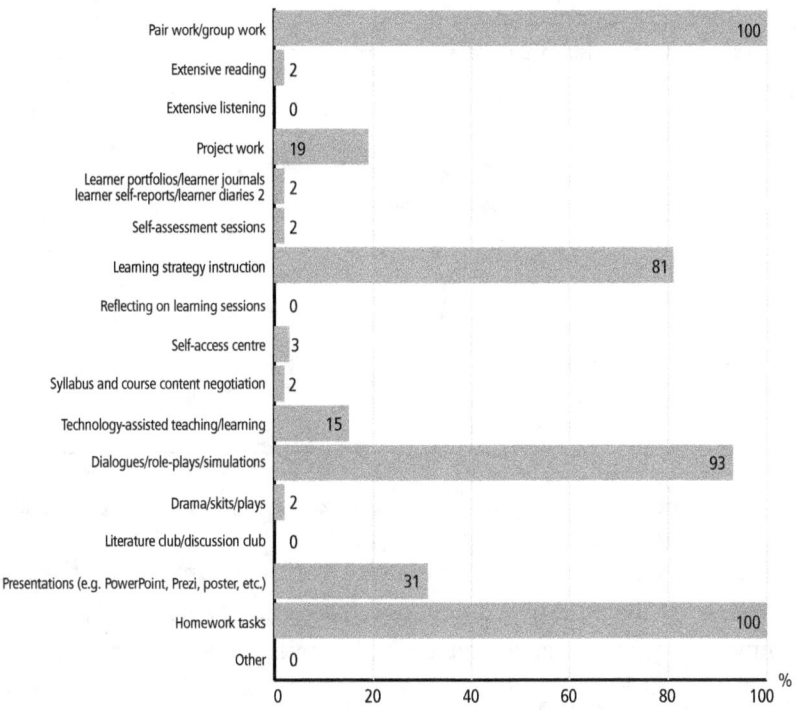

Figure 10. The methods and techniques teachers employ to foster learner autonomy

Next, the respondents disclosed what kind of teaching resources they utilise to foster learner autonomy in their classrooms. For instance, the entire population makes use of course books. Less popular teaching resources were listed in the following order: resource packs (26%), real-life texts (19%), technology-assisted language learning resources (15%) and graded readers (4%). Audio books and self-assessment questionnaires/sheets were not selected by the respondents at all. All the outcomes are presented in Table 7 and Figure 11 below.

Table 7. The teaching resources EFL instructors use to foster learner autonomy

	What kind of teaching resources do you use to foster learner autonomy?	No of responses	[%]
a)	Course books	120	100
b)	Resource packs	31	26
c)	Graded readers	5	4
d)	Audio books	0	0
e)	Real-life texts (prose, poems, newspaper articles, recorded interviews, etc.)	23	19
f)	Self-assessment questionnaires/sheets	0	0
g)	Technology-assisted language learning resources	18	15
h)	Other	0	0

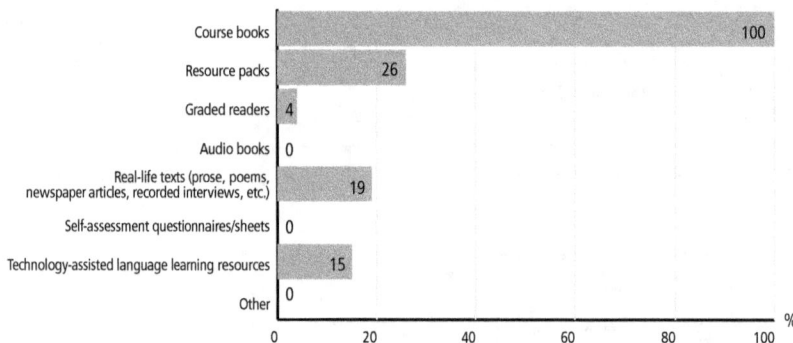

Figure 11. The teaching resources EFL instructors use to foster learner autonomy

A number of the participants made interesting comments on the teaching resources they use or would like to use while developing learner autonomy. The questionnaire and journal entries were as follows:

> I often use Internet-based materials. To prepare them requires a lot of time. I print these materials or record interviews so that I can use them in my classroom. The equipment I have at my disposal is not very high-tech. I cannot use computer rooms as they are not for language teachers. The most interesting thing is that my students enjoy these materials. They appear to be a nice addition to course books. They develop student critical thinking and promote collaborative learning.

> I read English newspapers on a regular basis. Whenever I find something interesting and suitable for my students I always copy it. This can be an article, a nice headline or an image. Then, I use it in a creative way. I try to use these materials in different ways so that I do not repeat a course book style. They often help me to develop autonomous behaviours in my students.

I use activities from resource packs that I received from my regional Oxford University Press ELT consultant. These activities are extremely useful and can be used in so many ways. They do help to promote learner autonomy. You sometimes have to adapt them to a large degree, though.

I would be happy to use other resources such as graded readers, but my school does not provide such resources. We do not have a library with English books. I myself cannot afford to buy enough copies for my students.

Graded readers sound like an interesting idea, but I cannot afford them. My school does not have a library with English books.

In order to use computer/Internet-assisted language learning resources, I would need a computer room. There are three computer rooms in my school, but they are not for language teachers. They are occupied by Computer Technology teachers all the time.

The previous question revealed that course books, despite their various weaknesses (see 3.3), are the most common resources employed to promote learner autonomy. This response was easy to predict, though. To get more detailed information, the next two questions aimed to find out what criteria the respondents use to choose course books for Year 1 and Year 3 instruction. These questions were to determine whether the notion of learner autonomy was considered as a course book selection criterion by teachers, and if so, to what extent. As the acquired data showed, the criteria for selecting the Year One course book were as follows: suitable language and content (98%), well-prepared teacher's book and test book (95%), reasonable price (90%), a balance of all four skills (66%), clearly presented grammar (61%), attractive activities and tasks (59%) and Matura examination practice (18%). As this question showed, the respondents do not take learner autonomy into consideration while selecting the Year One course book. The results are presented in Table 8 and Figure 12 below.

Table 8. The criteria teachers use to choose the Year One course book

What criteria do you use to choose the Year One course book?	No of responses	[%]
a) Reasonable price	108	90
b) Well-prepared teacher's book and test book	114	95
c) Suitable language and content	117	98
d) Clearly presented grammar	73	61

What criteria do you use to choose the Year One course book?	No of responses	[%]
e) A balance of all four skills	79	66
f) Learner autonomy	0	0
g) Attractive activities and tasks (games, songs, quizzes, real-life texts, etc.)	71	59
h) Matura examination practice	22	18
i) Other	0	0

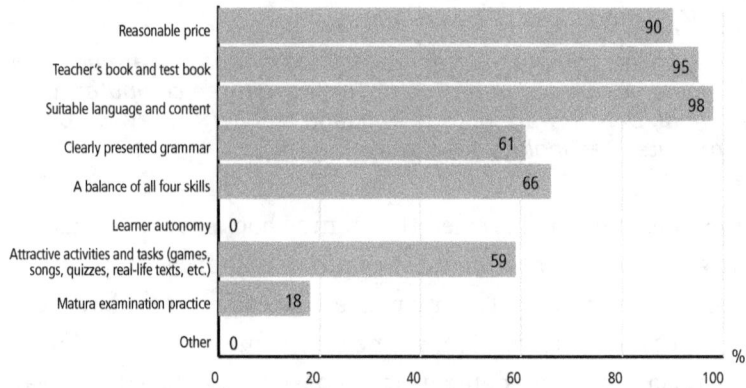

Figure 12. The criteria teachers use to choose the Year One course book

Other interesting observations on the criteria the respondents use to select the Year One course book were gathered from teacher questionnaires. These were:

> The most important criterion, obviously, is the price. My students come from different backgrounds. I know that for quite a few of these families, it is difficult to make ends meet.

> Apart from the price, I must have a teacher's book, preferably with ready-made tests. A teacher's book makes a teacher's life so much easier. It gives you hints about interesting ways of teaching and testing student progress. The tests are particularly useful. All you need to do is make the required number of copies. Marking these tests is not a big problem either because all the answers are provided.

> For my first year students, I usually select course books with well-presented grammar. Many of my students find grammar difficult. The main problem is that middle schools do not prepare students well for their further study. Of course, the balance of the four skills is also important, but modern course books handle this problem successfully.

> I always look for materials that familiarise my students with the Matura examination. The more activities that reflect the examination, the

better the course book is, in my opinion. I think students should be provided with all the examination techniques soon after they have started secondary schools, ideally in Year One. Otherwise, they may be somewhat surprised during the examination.

Having identified a number of criteria for selecting the Year One course book, the subsequent question addressed the same issue with regard to Year Three course books. Following the gathered data, the criteria were as follows: well-prepared teacher's book and test book (100%), Matura examination practice (100%), reasonable price (93%), suitable language and content (84%) and a balance of all four skills (78%). As with the previous question, learner autonomy was not a criterion for course book selection. All the outcomes are presented in Table 9 and Figure 13 below.

Table 9. The criteria teachers use to choose the Year Three course book

What criteria do you use to choose the Year Three course book?	No of responses	[%]
a) Reasonable price	111	93
b) Well-prepared teacher's book and test book	120	100
c) Suitable language and content	101	84
d) Clearly presented grammar	0	0
e) A balance of all four skills	93	78
f) Learner autonomy	0	0
g) Attractive activities and tasks (games, songs, quizzes, real-life texts, etc.)	0	0
h) Matura examination practice	120	100
i) Other	0	0

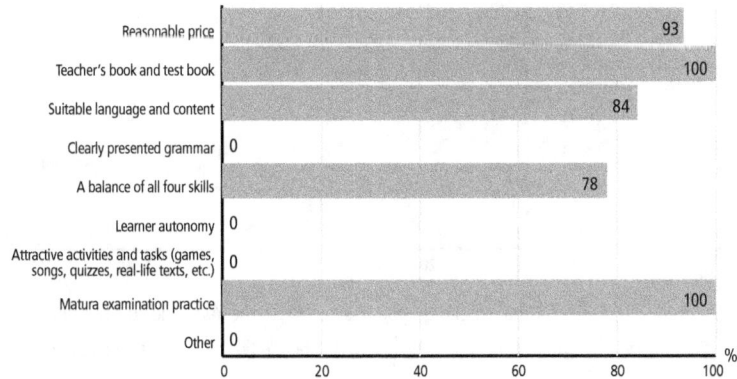

Figure 13. The criteria teachers use to choose the Year Three course book

Next, the statistical analysis will be supported by textual data delivered by the respondents who teach the final year students. For instance, two respondents stated that:

> There are quite a few examination preparation books on the market, so choosing one of them should not be a big issue. Of course, I always try to choose the most attractive one in terms of content, yet I also think about the price. The budget of many of my students is rather tight. They attend various extra-curricular courses outside school as they want to be admitted by their ideal universities.

> I use one of the most popular Matura examination preparation books. My students like it, but sometimes they complain about the repetitive pattern of the examination papers that we follow every week. The book contains suitable language and content because it has been designed with Matura examinees in mind. Another advantage is the answers section, which is extremely useful when students feel like working independently.

In order to determine the preferred criteria for course book selection in Year One and Year Three, the provided responses were compared (see Figure 14).

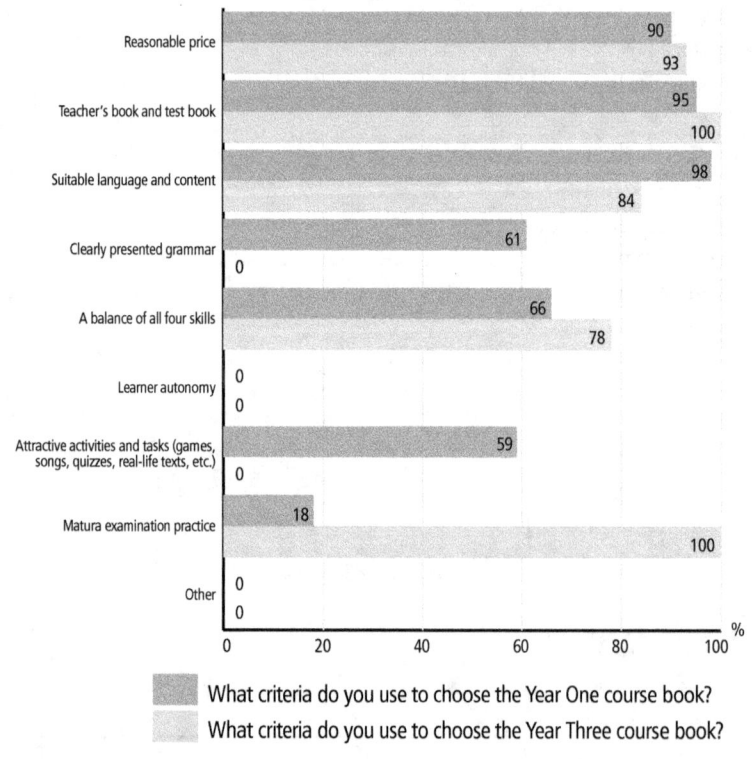

Figure 14. The criteria teachers use to choose Year One and Year Three course books

According to the gathered data, the respondents chose five common criteria for both levels. In no particular order, these were: reasonable price, well-prepared teacher's book and test book, suitable language and content, a balance of all four skills and Matura examination practice. There were two distinct criteria for the Year One course book: clearly presented grammar (61%) and attractive activities and tasks (59%). These two criteria were not taken into consideration while selecting Year Three course books. The learner autonomy criterion was not taken into account by the respondents at all.

Additionally, the course book selection criteria were compared to ascertain to what extent they differed in Year One and Year Three and whether or not this difference was statistically significant. The analysis revealed that no significant difference was observed for the "reasonable price" criterion. In the "well-prepared teacher's book and test book" criterion, a significant difference ($p=0.0387$) was reported towards Year Three course books. In other words, this criterion was used to determine Year Three course book selection. The next criterion, "suitable language and content", indicated a highly significant difference ($p=0.0008$) with a higher result for Year One course books. Likewise, the "clearly presented grammar" criterion marked a highly significant difference ($p<0.0001$) in favour of Year One course books. "A balance of all four skills" criterion showed a statistically insignificant difference. The observed proportion for "learner autonomy" criterion did not record any difference as this response was not selected by the respondents. As for the "attractive activities and tasks", a highly significant difference was noted ($p<0.0001$), with a higher result for Year One course books. In the last criterion, "Matura examination practice", a highly significant difference was observed ($p<0.0001$) in favour of Year Three course books.

The previous questions revealed that EFL course books constitute an essential part of the teaching-learning process. As a result, the next question focused on secondary school Year One course books. In particular, this question explored the respondents' thoughts about the extent to which these course books contribute to successful learner autonomy development. As a result, the respondents were asked about the following seven aspects (see Figure 15): cooperative learning (A), learning strategies

(B), critical thinking (C), self-assessment (D), educational technology (E), integrated-skills projects (F) and learner autonomy tasks (G).

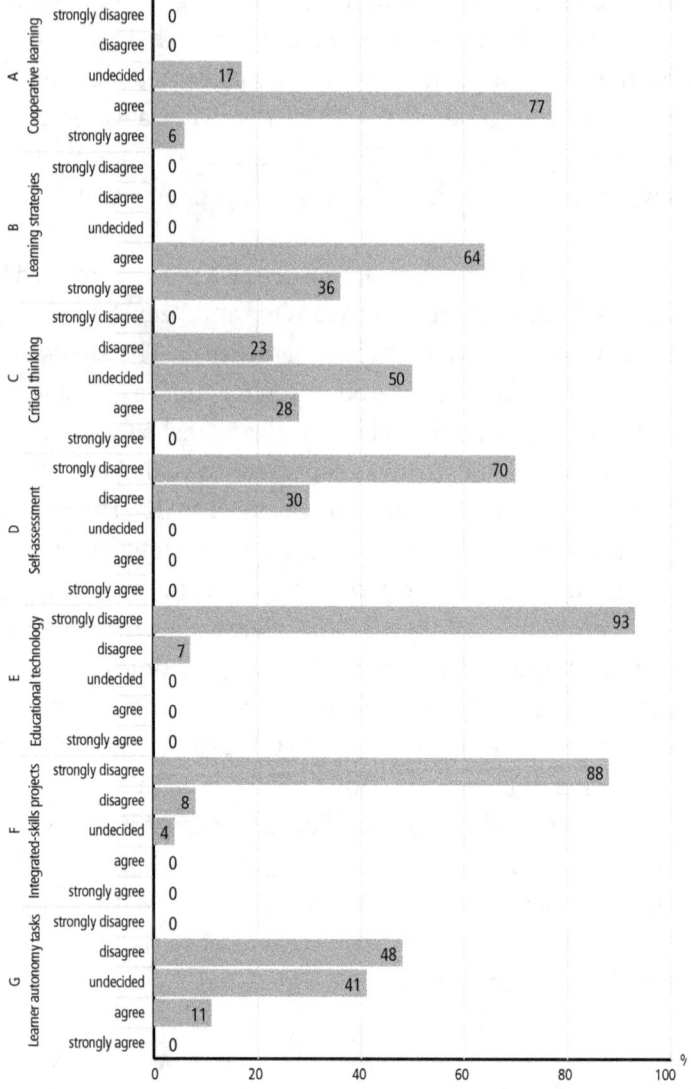

Figure 15. The effectiveness of Year One course books in promoting learner autonomy

Firstly, the respondents were asked to estimate whether or not the course books encourage their students to work cooperatively. As the data revealed, 100 (83%) respondents agreed and 20 (17%) respondents were undecided about whether course books encourage their students to work cooperatively. In the former group, 8 respondents expressed strong agreement. Secondly, the respondents were to decide whether or not the course books they use help their students to choose a variety of learning strategies. As the data showed, the entire population stated that the course books meet their students' expectations in this respect. More precisely, 64 percent of the respondents chose the answer "agree" and 36 percent preferred the answer "strongly agree". The next aspect was related to whether or not the course books at issue prompted students to develop critical thinking through problem-solving tasks. According to the collected data, the respondents' answers were as follows: agree (28%), undecided (50%) and disagree (23%). None of the respondents opted for the extreme answers, that is, "strongly agree" and "strongly disagree". Additionally, the respondents were asked whether or not the course books encourage students to assess themselves. All the respondents gave negative answers: 36 (30%) disagreed and 84 (70%) strongly disagreed. The next aspect was related to finding out whether or not the course books promote technology-assisted learning. All the provided answers were negative; 7 percent of the respondents disagreed and 93 percent strongly disagreed with this statement. The integration of language skills for in- and out-of-class projects was another issue linked to Year One course books. The majority of the respondents provided negative answers again: 10 (8%) disagreed and 105 (88%) strongly disagreed. Five (4%) respondents remained undecided about this issue. The last aspect analysed in this question was the extent to which the course books assist students to perform relevant and meaningful learner autonomy tasks. As the gathered data showed, only 13 (11%) respondents expressed a positive opinion. The other two groups were made up of 49 (41%) respondents who remained undecided and 58 (48%) respondents who disagreed with the statement that modern course books engage students in relevant and meaningful learner autonomy tasks.

Before moving to the analysis of Year Three course books, it must be pointed out that in general, the respondents' observations were in agreement with my journal entries (see 4.5.2.2). The respondents and I agreed that modern course books succeed in encouraging cooperative learning (e.g. pair and group work). We also agreed that course books do not offer self-assessment sections or collaborative projects using educational technology. There were two discrepancies in the collected data. I wished to see more explicit learning strategy instruction related to all language skills, not just limited to writing skills. The respondents, however, unanimously stated that modern course books met their expectations in this respect. By way of explanation, modern course books seem to provide a lot of guidance and support on how to succeed in EFL writing. They include various sections on writing letters, essays, CVs or covering letters. Also, there are parts on paragraphing, linking words and phrases or essay structure. However, what is missing is the explicit promotion of strategies aimed at helping students to succeed in speaking, reading and listening.

Another inconsistency observed in modern course books was related to the promotion of meaningful learner autonomy tasks. As my journal revealed, "learner autonomy tasks are neglected in modern course books". In contrast, 11 percent of the research population were content with the tasks their course books offered. The major problem is that modern course books do not successfully promote learner autonomy tasks. A similar observation was recorded in the teachers' journals (see 3.3). More interestingly, a number of course books have the potential to encourage learner autonomy. Many of the activities available in these course books could be adapted (see 3.3.1) to incorporate the requirements of complex tasks (see 3.2.2). The adaptation process, however, lies within a teacher's competence and is not always perceived as a prime concern.

Next, Year Three course books were analysed (see Figure 16). As with the previous question, the respondents were questioned about the same seven aspects: cooperative learning (A), learning strategies (B), critical thinking (C), self-assessment (D), educational technology (E), integrated-skills projects (F) and learner autonomy tasks (G).

Firstly, the respondents were to state whether or not Year Three course books encourage students to learn cooperatively. According to the tabulated data, 81 (68%) respondents were positive about this statement. However, there was a group of respondents that was not so optimistic. More explicitly, 21 (18%) respondents were undecided and 18 (15%) respondents thought that Year Three course books do not promote collaborative learning. Not a single respondent opted for "strongly agree" and "strongly disagree" answers. Secondly, the respondents had to decide whether or not the course books they use assist students to choose a variety of learning strategies. As the collected data showed, the respondents either agreed (30%) or strongly agreed (70%) with the statement in question. The next issue was related to developing critical thinking through problem-solving tasks. As the respondents noted, Year Three course books do not succeed in this respect. The selected answers were: undecided (17%), disagree (44%) and strongly disagree (39%). Also, the respondents were questioned about the degree to which the course books enable students to assess themselves. As with the previous issue, the respondents answered negatively. To be more precise, the respondents only expressed disagreement (16%) and strong disagreement (84%). In the next section, the entire population strongly disagreed with the statement that the course books encourage students to relate to educational technology. The integration of language skills for in- and out-of-class projects was non-existent in course books. In the entire research population, not a single respondent produced a positive answer. The last aspect that needs to be statistically presented is the promotion of relevant and meaningful learner autonomy tasks in the course books. As the respondents observed, Year Three course books do not involve students in such tasks. There was not a single respondent in the entire population who stated otherwise. Seven respondents (6%) expressed disagreement and 113 (94%) respondents expressed strong disagreement in this case.

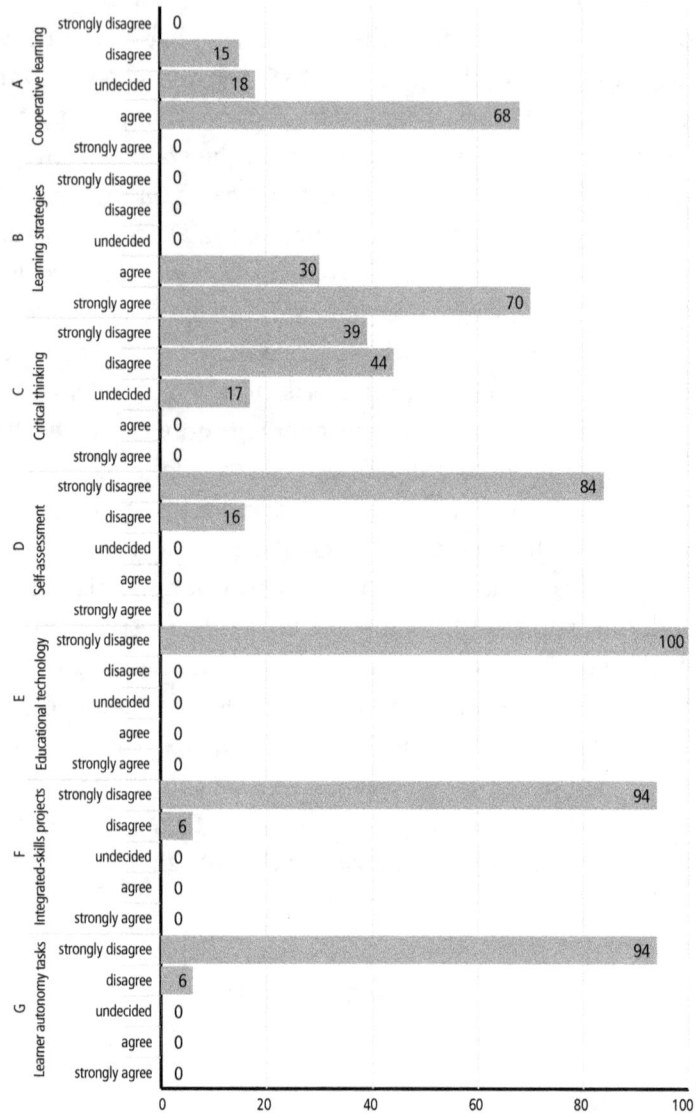

Figure 16. The effectiveness of Year Three course books in promoting learner autonomy

The collected responses from the respondents about Year Three course books will now be compared to my observations to show similarities and differences. This time, the analysis showed that the respondents and I agreed on six issues. We agreed that Year Three course books successfully promote learning strategies. It must be clarified, though, that I emphasised in my journal that learning strategy instruction was limited to only Matura examination exercises. The respondents agreed with me that the course books did not promote self-assessment, integrated skills projects and meaningful learner autonomy tasks. Likewise, we all agreed that the course books did not encourage students to relate to educational technology. The only inaccuracy was related to the issue of cooperative learning. While I was content with this aspect, 18 percent of the respondents were undecided and 15 percent thought that Year Three course books do not popularise collaborative learning.

5.1.3 TEACHER INVOLVEMENT IN TASK DEVELOPMENT

This section deals with teacher involvement in developing pedagogical tasks. When asked about the frequency of designing their own tasks, the respondents offered the following answers: usually (7%), from time to time (29%), rarely (55%) and never (9%). The results are presented in Table 10 and Figure 17 below

Table 10. The frequency of designing pedagogical tasks by teachers

	How often do you design tasks for your students?	No of responses	[%]
a)	Never	11	9
b)	Rarely	66	55
c)	From time to time	35	29
d)	Usually	8	7
e)	Always	0	0

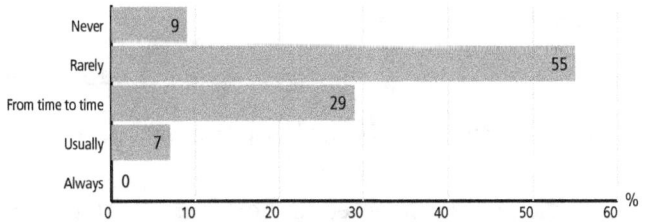

Figure 17. The frequency of designing pedagogical tasks by teachers

Some textual data related to teacher involvement in developing pedagogical tasks were also recorded. For instance, some of the questionnaire and journal entries showed that:

I only design tasks for my students from time to time. The reason for this is that I use very good course books which meet my students' needs. My students seem to enjoy learning from these materials.

I usually prepare tasks for students as EFL course books are not ideal. There are a lot of interesting activities in them, though. I like to have something extra for my students – something that is produced specially for them.

The next question was slightly more specific and referred to designing tasks aimed at fostering secondary school students' autonomy. The majority (75%) of the respondents stated that they never develop learner autonomy tasks. Sixteen respondents (13%) said that they rarely design learner autonomy tasks. The answers "from time to time" and "usually" were selected by 8 (7%) and 6 (5%) respondents, respectively. The outcomes are presented in Table 11 and Figure 18 below.

Table 11. The frequency of designing learner autonomy tasks by teachers

	How often do you design tasks aimed at fostering your students' autonomy?	No of responses	[%]
a)	Never	90	75
b)	Rarely	16	13
c)	From time to time	8	7
d)	Usually	6	5
e)	Always	0	0

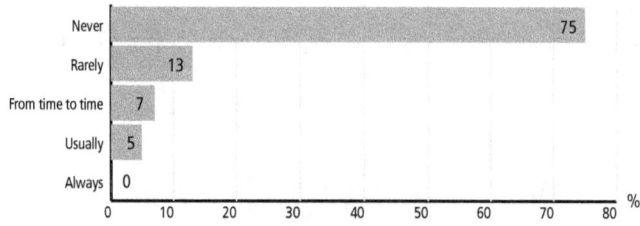

Figure 18. The frequency of designing learner autonomy tasks by teachers

Two teacher participants also noted in their journals that:

I design my own tasks only from time to time. This process always takes me a lot of time. Today's learner autonomy task took me ages to prepare, but it was worth it. The students liked the class very much. They had a chance to meaningfully communicate in English. Also, they had a chance to integrate different skills. They behaved differently

> than while doing course books activities. I think today's project was successful because the story appealed to everyone.
>
> In general, I have noticed that teachers do not design their own tasks. They entirely rely on recommended course books which consist of both student books and workbooks. The available variety of ready-made activities makes many teachers believe that is all they need for their students to succeed.

As far as student journals (see 4.5.2.2) were concerned, they also provided interesting findings on teacher involvement in learner autonomy task development. Out of a total of twenty-four student journals, only three contained learner autonomy tasks developed by teachers. On closer inspection, this means that altogether four learner autonomy tasks were designed in the period of two months. This situation appears to be a clear reflection of the quantitative data presented above.

Despite the fact that the respondents are not systematically involved in designing learner autonomy tasks, the next question revealed that the respondents would expect to see certain learner autonomy tasks in EFL course books. What is more, the respondents' opinions correlated with the comments recorded in my journal (see 4.5.2.2). The respondents' list of learner autonomy tasks included: self-assessment tasks based on questionnaires (91%), mini-project tasks with the use of educational technology (73%), projects integrating all language skills (59%), real-life texts with tasks which aim to develop all language skills (57%), tasks based on learning strategy identification sheets (48%), video/film-based tasks (14%) and tasks connected with reflecting on the learning sheets (6%). The outcomes are presented in Table 12 and Figure 19 below.

Table 12. Learner autonomy tasks that should be included in course books

	What type of tasks do you think should be included in EFL course books to help students to become independent learners?	No of responses	[%]
a)	Self-assessment tasks based on questionnaires	109	91
b)	Mini-project tasks with the use of educational technology	87	73
c)	Mini-project tasks integrating all language skills	71	59
d)	Real-life texts with tasks which aim to develop all language skills	68	57

What type of tasks do you think should be included in EFL course books to help students to become independent learners?	No of responses	[%]
e) Tasks connected with reflecting on learning sheets	7	6
f) Tasks based on learning strategy identification sheets	57	48
g) Video/film-based tasks	17	14
h) Other	0	0

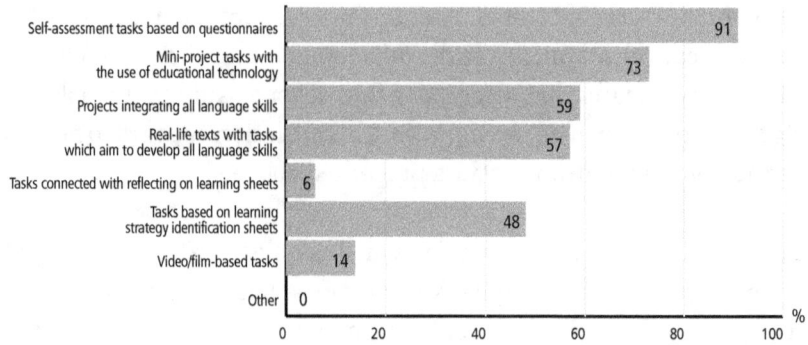

Figure 19. Learner autonomy tasks that should be included in course books

Also, a number of the journal entries focused on weaknesses of modern course books with regard to developing learner autonomy (see 3.3). According to these entries, modern course books could be improved by including certain types of tasks in them. More precisely, the participants stated that:

> There are a lot of interesting activities in the course book, but I would like to see more complex problem-solving activities. Small projects would be ideal. Of course, some of these activities can be adapted to become small projects, but I think ready-made tasks should be an important part of course books. Students should be encouraged to work in groups, make decisions, negotiate various positions, practise critical thinking and reflect on their actions.

> In my opinion, the main problem is self-assessment. Students have no chance to assess themselves. There are revision sections in test format every four units, which is fine. What needs to be added, however, is a section, for example, with 'can do' statements. Another option is a table with grades from 1 to 6 where students tick the right boxes. Such a section should also draw students' attention to various aspects of metacognition (e.g. planning and evaluation).

> It is a pity that modern course books do not promote activities with educational technology. Students are keen on Internet-assisted learning, so why not suggest activities that will encourage students to surf the Net? Such activities would be much more motivating and, if properly designed, could considerably boost autonomy.

5.1.4 OBSTACLES TO THE SUCCESSFUL DEVELOPMENT OF LEARNER AUTONOMY

The last section of data analysis in Inquiry 1 focuses on possible problems that may impede the fostering of learner autonomy. The respondents identified a number of dilemmas. As the collected data revealed, the main reason why the development of learner autonomy is neglected is lack of time on the part of teachers. This observation was made by 111 respondents (93%). Another obstacle to the successful development of learner autonomy is the examination-orientated curriculum (85%). According to 101 (84%) respondents, a lack of sufficient ready-made resources to develop learner autonomy poses a serious problem. A large group (64%) of the respondents additionally stated that the current state of affairs is the consequence of insufficient teacher training in the area of learner autonomy. Some respondents (38%) also listed the restricted number of classes as an impediment to the effective development of learner autonomy. Finally, a number of respondents pointed out that teachers prefer not to implement learner autonomy in their teaching because learner autonomy development methods cause disorder and contribute to a lack of discipline in the classroom. The last observation was made by 31 (26%) respondents. The outcomes are presented in Table 13 and Figure 20 below.

Table 13. Possible problems that prevent teachers from fostering learner autonomy

	Can you think of any problems that prevent you from fostering learner autonomy in your classroom?	No of responses	[%]
a)	Lack of time	111	93
b)	Examination-orientated curriculum	102	85
c)	Lack of sufficient ready-made resources to develop learner autonomy	101	84
d)	Lack of appropriate training in this area	77	64
e)	Restricted number of classes	46	38
f)	Learner autonomy development methods often contribute to lack of discipline and chaos in the classroom	31	26

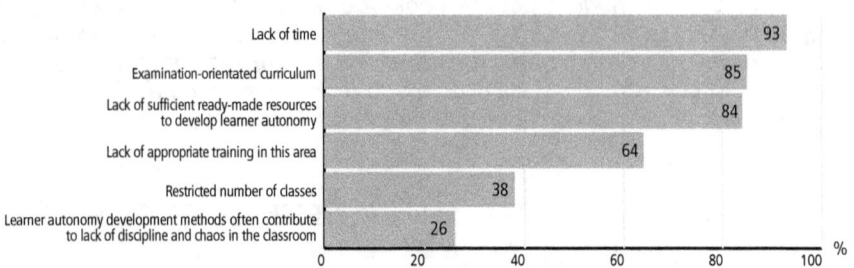

Figure 20. Possible problems that prevent teachers from fostering learner autonomy

The following seven remarks on the possible problems of developing learner autonomy in the Polish EFL classroom were additionally recorded in teacher questionnaires and journals:

> Developing learner autonomy is a rather difficult task. I really have no time to look for appropriate activities. My course book is not really successful in promoting learner autonomy. My priority is the Matura examination. I want my students to be well-prepared, so we regularly pore over examination papers. This is what my students need most now.

> Developing learner autonomy requires special skills, so workshops for teachers would be a good thing. I doubt teachers have time to design their own activities. We are all so busy: teaching, marking, holding teacher-parent conferences and, of course, writing EU projects. No time for learner autonomy for the time being.

> I believe it would be good to regularly develop learner autonomy in the first two years as the last one focuses on the Matura examination. My course book does not promote learner autonomy well. Are special resource packs available for developing learner autonomy? I think such materials would make teachers' lives much easier. Teachers are too busy to design their own tasks. Many teachers do not have any experience in developing their own tasks. Normally, we use ready-made tasks or adapt available materials.

> In order to prepare students well for the final examination I need to be very cautious with time management. Developing learner autonomy requires time and specially designed tasks. The number of hours I now have with my classes is hardly sufficient, so developing learner autonomy is out of the question. If I had two extra hours a week, I could think about it.

> The number of hours my classes have per week for practising English is not enough to prepare them very well for the Matura examination. Many of my students really struggle with this language. I cannot imagine doing extra things, for instance, developing learner autonomy. we can only afford time for examination practice.

> *Learner autonomy sounds great in theory. When you think about learner autonomy in terms of classroom management, it is not that exciting. I avoid group and project work, both of which promote learner autonomy as often as I can because they always cause a lot of commotion and mess in the classroom. It is difficult to control the class and students are often busy doing other things, for example, texting friends.*
>
> *Developing learner autonomy is certainly important, but, in practice, it leads to various problems. One of them is a lack of discipline. Group work that is conducive to fostering learner autonomy often creates disorder in the classroom, which I cannot tolerate.*

5.2 LEARNER AUTONOMY IN THE EFL CLASSROOM: INQUIRY 2

As with Inquiry 1, this part of the research project employed quantitative and qualitative data collection tools. The qualitative part was preceded by a learner autonomy workshop (see 4.5.2.2). This workshop was organised for those participants who had agreed to write journals on the fostering of learner autonomy in their classrooms. The results of Inquiry 2 are presented in three subsections related to participant: (1) beliefs about the importance of developing learner autonomy, (2) views on how the available learning resources help them to become autonomous learners and (3) thoughts about possible reasons for obstructing the development of learner autonomy. The three sections are presented below.

5.2.1 IMPORTANCE OF DEVELOPING LEARNER AUTONOMY

The first question in the student questionnaire was related to the importance of developing learner autonomy at the secondary level. As the collected data revealed, the students, as well as their teachers (see 5.1.1) responded positively to the first question. Forty-seven (39%) respondents agreed with the above statement, whereas 70 (58%) respondents expressed strong agreement. Only 3 (3%) respondents were indecisive. None of the respondents disagreed with this idea. The results are presented in Table 14 and Figure 21 below.

Table 14. The importance of developing learner autonomy

Do you agree that developing learner autonomy is important?	No of responses	[%]
a) Strongly disagree	0	0
b) Disagree	0	0
c) Undecided	3	3
d) Agree	47	39
e) Strongly agree	70	58

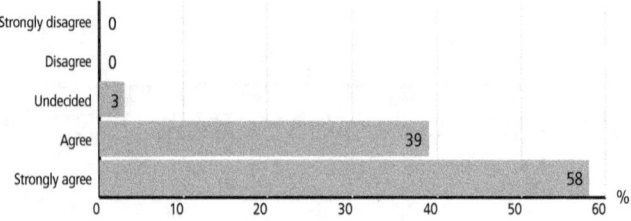

Figure 21. The importance of developing learner autonomy

Additionally, three respondents commented on this issue in the following way:

> To develop learner autonomy in the classroom is very important. It encourages negotiation and decision-making. Students have a say in the classroom and to some extent influence classroom life. It is good to be allowed to decide about course materials or types of work. The classes are more interesting and students are more motivated.

> I think developing learner autonomy is important as it prepares me for future challenges. In my opinion, if my teacher shows me how to become an autonomous learner, I will use it outside school, and even later, when I am at university. The more I know about learner autonomy, the easier it will be for me to manage my learning.

> Developing learner autonomy is essential. I wish my teacher was like the native speaker teachers who teach me every summer in the UK. The courses over there are based on projects, games and real life activities. I learn so much there; learning is very spontaneous and natural. In Poland, we only do course book activities, and students become bored very quickly.

5.2.2 LEARNING RESOURCES AND LEARNER AUTONOMY DEVELOPMENT

The issue of the importance of developing learner autonomy has been analysed. This section will focus on available learning resources and how these resources, in the opinion of the respondents, assist them in becoming autonomous learners. For instance, in the second question, the respondents were asked about their satisfaction with the number of learner autonomy tasks that they receive from their teachers. According to the tabulated data, the level of satisfaction was rather low. Eighty-five (71%) respondents disagreed with the statement that they are given enough tasks that aim to promote their independent learning. In this group, 29 (24%) respondents expressed strong disagreement, 28 (23%) respondents remained undecided about this issue and only 7 (6%) respondents gave a positive response to this question. None of them showed strong agreement, though. The results are presented in Table 15 and Figure 22 below.

Table 15. Student satisfaction with the number of learner autonomy tasks received in the classroom

To what extent do you agree that your teacher gives you enough tasks to develop your autonomy?	No of responses	[%]
a) Strongly disagree	29	24
b) Disagree	56	47
c) Undecided	28	23
d) Agree	7	6
e) Strongly agree	0	0

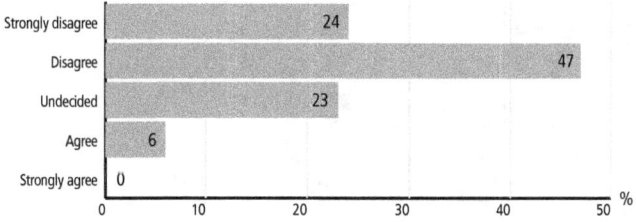

Figure 22. Student satisfaction with the number of learner autonomy tasks received in the classroom

Question 3 consisted of seven sections and referred to Year One and Year Three course books. More specifically, the respondents who were Year Two students were asked to express their opinions on the extent to which their Year One course books had encouraged them to become autonomous learners (see Figure 23). Respondents who were Year Three students were asked the same question about the course books they were currently using. The seven sections the respondents took into consideration in this question were as follows: cooperative learning (A), learning strategies (B), critical thinking (C), self-assessment (D), educational technology (E), integrated-skills projects (F) and learner autonomy tasks (G).

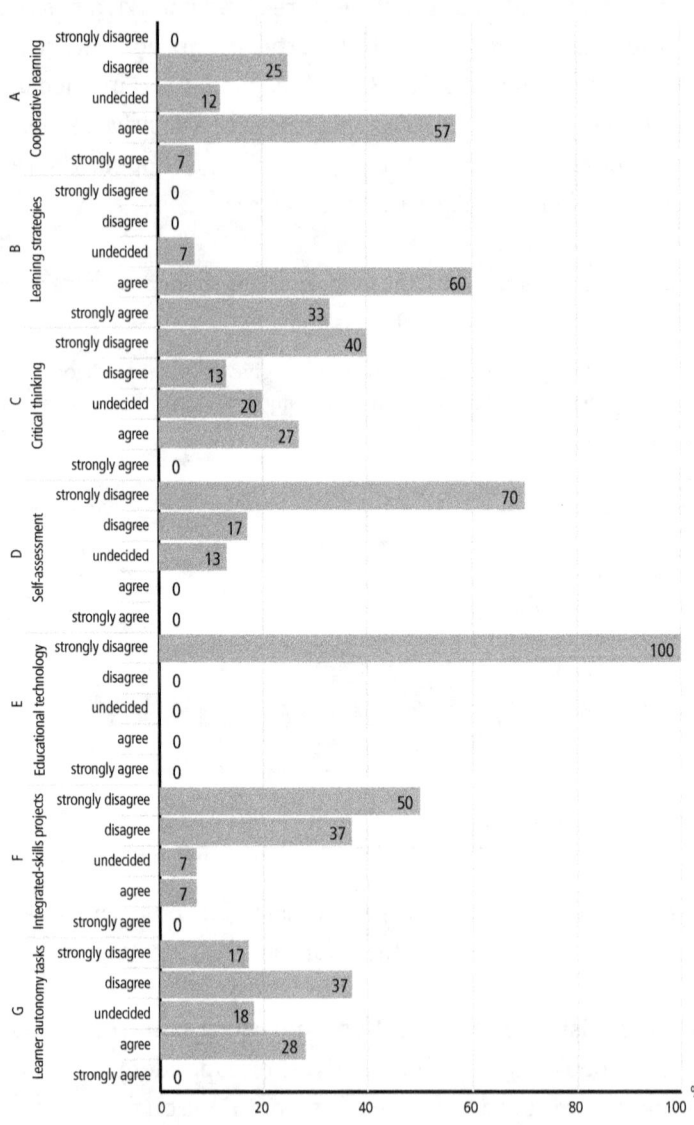

Figure 23. The promotion of learner autonomy by Year One course books: A student perspective

As far as Year One course books are concerned, Year Two respondents were firstly asked whether they agreed that their course books encouraged them to work cooperatively. As the analysis revealed, 63 percent of the respondents agreed with this statement. More explicitly, 7 percent expressed strong agreement, 12 percent of the respondents were undecided and 25 percent disagreed that their course books encouraged them to work cooperatively. Secondly, the respondents were asked to estimate whether or not their course books helped them to choose a variety of learning strategies. The three responses provided were: undecided (7%), agree (60%) and strongly agree (33%). Thirdly, the respondents were questioned about the extent to which Year One course books helped them to develop critical thinking through problem-solving tasks. The responses to this question varied, ranging from "agree" to "strongly disagree". More precisely, 27 percent of the respondents agreed, 20 percent remained undecided, 13 percent of the respondents disagreed with the statement in question, whereas 40 percent expressed strong disagreement. None of the respondents chose the last response, that is, "strongly agree". Fourthly, the respondents were asked to what extent their course books offered self-assessment. According to the gathered data, 13 percent of the respondents were undecided about this statement. The majority of the population strongly disagreed with it. None of the respondents agreed that their course books provided good opportunities for them to self-assess their development and progress. The next issue in this question was the integration of educational technology into the learning process. All the respondents were unanimous and strongly emphasised that technology-based tasks were not found in their course books at all. The last two sections were related to skills integration for in- and out-of-class projects and the promotion of relevant and meaningful learner autonomy tasks. In the former, the four supplied responses were: agree (7%), undecided (7%), disagree (37%) and strongly disagree (50%). In the latter, 28 percent of the respondents were positive about the statement in question and expressed agreement, 18 percent of the respondents were undecided and 54 percent of the respondents expressed disagreement. In sections F and G, none of the respondents selected the last option, that is, "strongly agree".

In order to check the differences between student and teacher responses regarding the promotion of learner autonomy by the Year One course book, all the data in question 3 in the student questionnaire and question 9 in the teacher questionnaire were compared. Section A, which was related to cooperative learning, indicated a highly significant difference ($p<0.0001$) in the provided responses, with a larger number of negative responses in the student questionnaire. Likewise, section B, focused on learning strategies, and showed a significant difference ($p=0.0262$) in response distribution, with a higher level of disagreement in the student questionnaire. Section C, in turn, was related to the development of critical thinking. Section C showed a highly significant difference in response distribution, with a higher level of disagreement in the student questionnaire. A highly significant difference ($p<0.0001$) in response distribution was observed in section D (dealing with self-assessment) and section F (pertaining to integrated-skills projects). The analysis indicated a higher level of disagreement in the teacher questionnaire. Section E showed a statistically significant difference ($p=0.0303$), with a large number of negative responses in the student questionnaire. The last section, focusing on relevant learner autonomy tasks, indicated a highly significant difference ($p<0.0001$) in response distribution, with a larger number of negative responses in the student questionnaire.

Similarly to Inquiry 1, the correspondence between the responses gathered from Inquiry 2 respondents and my observations based on the course book analysis was established. The respondents and I fully agreed in one aspect only; the observation was that Year 1 course books do not encourage students to integrate educational technology into their learning. In all the other cases (i.e. variables A, B, C, D, F and G), the gathered opinions tended to agree, yet the frequencies of the collected responses in Inquiry 2 varied more than in Inquiry 1.

Having examined the responses received from Year Two respondents, it was necessary to analyse how Year Three respondents perceived their current course books with regard to learner autonomy development (see Figure 24).

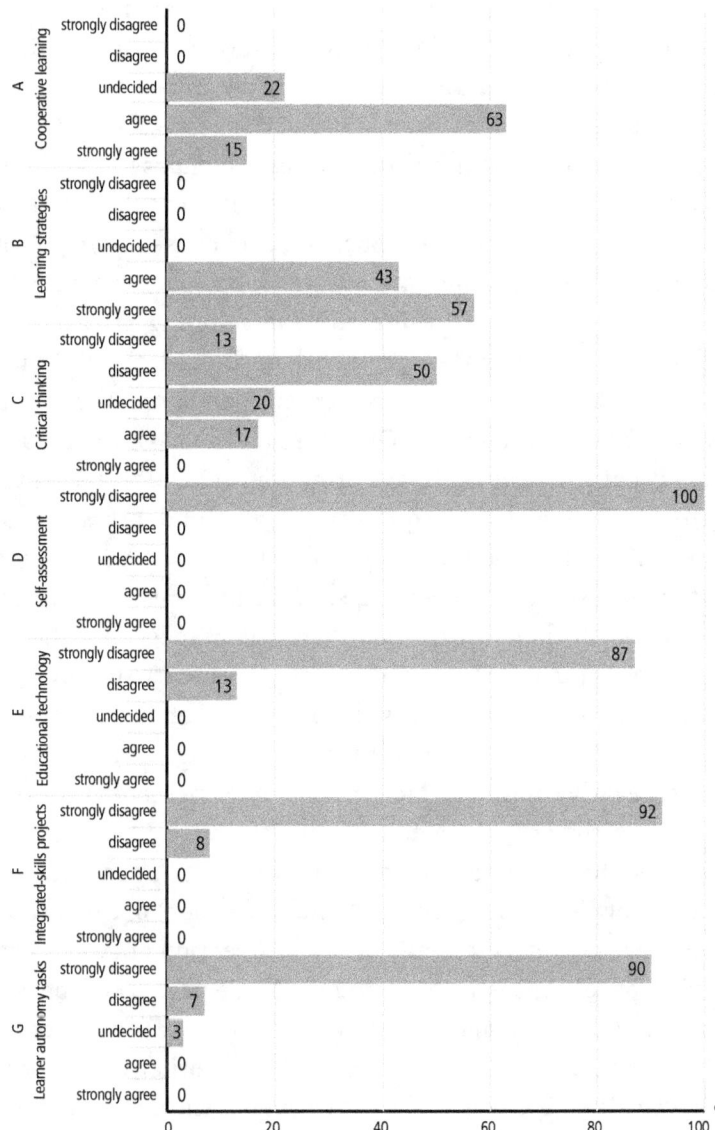

Figure 24. The promotion of learner autonomy by Year Three course books: A student perspective

In section A, the respondents were asked to state whether their Year Three course books were promoting cooperative learning in their classroom. According to the collected data, 78 percent of the respondents thought their course books met their expectations in this respect.

Strong agreement with the given statement was expressed by 15 percent of the respondents, while 22 percent were undecided. None of the respondents expressed disagreement. The second section was related to learning strategies. More specifically, the respondents were asked whether their course books allowed them to choose a wide range of strategies in the learning process. As the gathered data revealed, all the respondents' opinions were positive, and consequently expressed agreement only. The respondents' opinions, however, were much more varied in section C, which referred to developing critical thinking through problem-solving tasks. As the data showed, the majority (63%) of the respondents expressed disagreement and 20 percent of the respondents remained undecided. Only a small group (17%) of respondents confirmed that their course books promoted critical thinking through problem-solving tasks. Subsequently, the respondents were asked to decide whether their course books enabled them to assess themselves. As the analysis showed, the entire student population expressed dissatisfaction with their course books in this respect. In other words, all the respondents expressed strong disagreement. Moreover, the respondents stated that their course books did not encourage them to integrate educational technology into their learning. All the respondents expressed negative opinions. More precisely, 87 percent of the respondents showed strong disagreement. As with section E, the respondents did not agree that their course books were promoting integrated skills projects. According to the tabulated data, 92 percent of the respondents expressed strong disagreement. In the last section of question 3, only three types of responses were provided. Three percent of the respondents could not decide whether or not their course books were offering them relevant learner autonomy tasks. All the other respondents had no difficulty making a decision. As the analysis showed, 7 percent of the respondents expressed disagreement. The expressed disagreement was strong for 90 percent of the respondents.

Subsequently, all the data in question 4 on the student questionnaire and question 10 on the teacher questionnaire were compared. This procedure was used to check whether the student and teacher responses regarding the Year Three course book statistically differed, and if so, to what extent. As the analysis disclosed, three observations were made. Firstly, the distribution of responses in both student and teacher questionnaires indicated a highly significant difference (p<0.0001) in sections A (related to cooperative learning), C (focusing on the development of critical thinking) and E (pertaining to the promotion of computer technology). The analysis further showed that teachers tend to express more disagreement in these three sections than students. Sections B (related to learning strategies), F (pertaining to integrated-skills projects) and G (focusing on relevant learner autonomy tasks) showed there was no statistically significant difference in the response distribution in both questionnaires. Section D, in turn, indicated a highly significant difference (p=0.0004) in response distribution. In this particular case, there were more negative answers concerning the possibility of self-assessment in Year Three course books than were observed in the student questionnaire.

Additionally, the respondents' observations about Year 3 course books were compared with the comments recorded in my journal (see 4.5.2.2). Unlike in the Year One course book analysis, there was full agreement about four variables. The respondents and I agreed that Year 3 course books contribute to the promotion of learning strategies (limited to the Matura examination in my opinion). Year 3 course books also do not meet our expectations with regard to promoting self-assessment, educational technology and integrated skills projects. As far as cooperative learning and meaningful learner autonomy tasks are concerned, the data received indicated a tendency for agreement, yet there was no absolute compatibility in figures.

The next two questions in the student questionnaire focused on the extent to which their teachers were independent of course books. More specifically, in the fourth question, the respondents were to estimate how often their teachers provided them with tasks taken from sources other than their course books. According to the gathered data, the responses ranged from "never" to "usually". The exact distribution of responses was as follows: never (9%), rarely (63%), from time to time (23%) and usually (5%). None of the respondents opted for "always". The outcomes are presented in Table 16 and Figure 25 below.

Table 16. The frequency of receiving non-course-book-based tasks

	How often does your teacher provide you with non-course-book-based tasks?	No of responses	[%]
a)	Never	11	9
b)	Rarely	76	63
c)	From time to time	27	23
d)	Usually	6	5
e)	Always	0	0

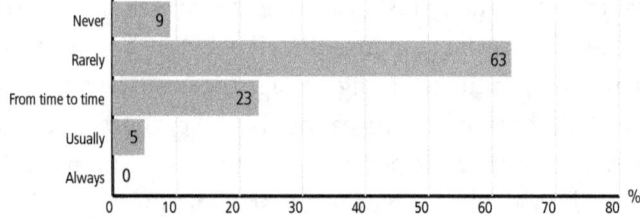

Figure 25. The frequency of receiving non-course-book-based tasks

The subsequent question was a little more specific. The respondents were to state whether or not the non-course-book-based tasks helped them to become independent learners. The statistical analysis showed that 90 (75%) respondents indicated that the tasks in question did not assist them in developing their autonomy. Nine (7%) respondents found it difficult to say whether these tasks helped or did not help them to become more independent in their learning. Twenty one (18%) respondents, in turn, considered the non-course-book-based tasks to be helpful in fostering their autonomy. The outcomes are presented in Table 17 and Figure 26 below.

Table 17. The contribution of non-course-book-based tasks to learner autonomy

	To what extent do you agree that the non-course-book-based tasks help you to become an independent learner?	No of responses	[%]
a)	Strongly disagree	76	63
b)	Disagree	14	12
c)	Undecided	9	7
d)	Agree	21	18
e)	Strongly agree	0	0

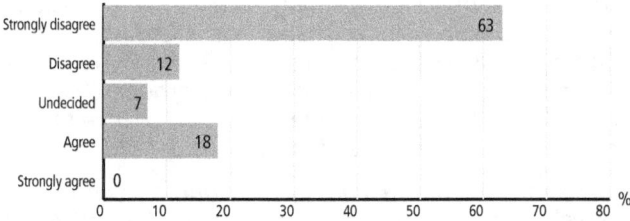

Figure 26. The contribution of non-course-book-based tasks to learner autonomy

An interesting point is that the last two questions confirm some of the observations made in Inquiry 1 (see 5.1.2). For example, course books appear to be a commonly used resource in the classroom. Another observation is that teachers do not seem to supplement course books, despite the various weaknesses of the books (see 3.3). However, when teachers do use non-course-book-based tasks in the classroom, students generally feel that the tasks do not help them to become more autonomous learners. The same findings have been found in the pilot study and student journals. For example, three entries from the student journals reveal the following:

> *Our teacher uses the course book tirelessly. However, once or twice a semester there is a surprise, and we do something different. Today, the teacher brought a general knowledge quiz for us to do. The activity was designed by the teacher himself. The lesson was a lot of fun as we were all bored with the books. The quiz was an interesting activity, based on recent events. Quite a few questions were about the UK. The only disappointment was the way the quiz was carried out. The teacher gave us 15 minutes to individually think about the questions. Then, he read the questions one by one and the students who knew the answers raised their hands and shared the information with the class. On reflection, my teacher in the language school would have done the activity in a completely different way. There would have been a lot of group work, positive competition, team spirit building and collaborative contribution.*

> *My teacher rarely designs tasks or brings activities from other sources. Yesterday, we watched an interview with Rod Stewart. We liked it, because it was different from our regular classes. Some students thought, though, that the teacher could have chosen a group or a singer more suitable for the teenage audience. Having watched the interview, we were asked to individually choose one of our favourite groups/singers and prepare a list of questions we would like to ask them if we had an*

opportunity to interview them. Then, a few students read their questions out loud and sometimes had to explain why they would like to ask these particular questions. In retrospect, it would have been better if only we had been allowed to role-play this activity. For example, students could have worked in pairs or in small groups. They could have assumed new identities. It is a shame we had no chance to be in charge of this activity. The lesson would have been a lot of fun!

In the past two weeks, our teacher gave us only two non-course-book-based activities. Neither of them was a task. We had no chance to converse in English. Both activities focused on reading comprehension. The teacher found interesting texts on the Internet, and then added a couple of questions below each. We were supposed to read the texts and answer the questions. The content of the activities was very interesting and controversial, so it was a shame we did not explore the texts further. It would be good to see my classmates' comments in a blog.

These three accounts, additionally, correlate with another observation in Inquiry 1, which stated that classroom time allocated to learner autonomy development is very limited.

5.2.3 OBSTACLES TO THE SUCCESSFUL DEVELOPMENT OF LEARNER AUTONOMY

The last question in the student questionnaire sought to identify possible problems that may impede learner autonomy development. The respondents selected the following responses: examination-orientated curriculum (94%), lack of sufficient ready-made resources to develop learner autonomy (78%), lack of appropriate training in this area (74%), lack of experience in designing tasks for learner autonomy (51%) and lack of teachers involving students in making decisions in the classroom (41%). The results are presented in Table 18 and Figure 27 below.

Table 18. Issues that may prevent the fostering of learner autonomy

	Can you think of any problems that prevent the fostering of learner autonomy in your classroom?	No of responses	[%]
a)	Examination-orientated curriculum	113	94
b)	Lack of sufficient ready-made resources to develop LA	93	78
c)	Lack of appropriate training in this area	89	74
d)	Lack of experience in designing tasks for LA	61	51
e)	Teachers do not involve students in making decisions in the classroom	49	41

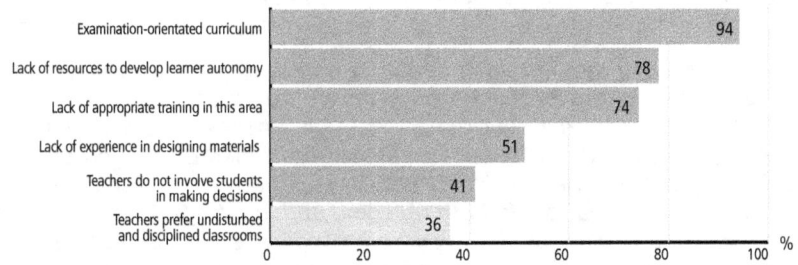

Figure 27. Issues that may prevent the fostering of learner autonomy

There is an additional bar on the chart above. It indicates that there was one more response given by 36 percent of the participants. The last bar represents the option "Other". Forty-three respondents stated that teachers prefer quiet and disciplined students. As the respondents remarked, this may be the reason why their teachers avoid project- and technology-assisted collaborative instruction. The latter, aiming at promoting learner autonomy, adheres to its own rules, and commotion is one of them.

In addition, eight participants elaborated on the issue in question in the following way:

> *I think learner autonomy does not exist in my classroom. We are always told what to do. We practise Matura examination papers all the time. The teacher decides what we do during each lesson and who works with whom. This very pattern is repeated every time we meet. I think my teacher does not have any materials to use in the classroom to develop our autonomy. Possibly, she may not know how to make learner autonomy part of her teaching. For the time being, my teacher is happy with the Matura preparation book, plus the answers book to which she seems to be glued.*

> *My course book does not successfully promote learner autonomy. What is more, my teacher does not design extra tasks. He says our course book is very good and there is no need to supplement it in any way. What is more, we would not even have time for extra activities. He says we hardly have time to do all the activities in the course book and workbooks.*

> *This idea of developing learner autonomy is very interesting, but I think it will not work with my teacher. He is the most important and what he says is the best. He always tells us what to do. We cannot even choose our own partners when we do activities in pairs. He decides who works*

with whom. It is sometimes very difficult to bear. Real life is not like that at all, so how is that supposed to prepare us for future learning or work?

Learner autonomy allows students to negotiate certain things with teachers and make decisions regarding student learning. However, I must admit, I hardly ever experience any of these two. My teacher does not include them in her teaching. She thinks that when she allows students to make decisions about classroom life, these decisions will lead to disturbances in both teaching and learning. She also thinks that we will try to negotiate favourable conditions for ourselves, which means no learning. Well, this may happen from time to time, but not regularly, as we know that the Matura examination is in the wind. By the way, we often have interesting ideas how to make learning more enjoyable.

My teacher does not really help us to become autonomous learners. Well, occasionally he does, but not often, which is a shame. I think he is not very creative. Also, I think he has no experience in designing his own tasks. We always use our course book and workbooks, page by page. The course book is OK, but nothing special. According to our teacher, it is very good. Well, perhaps it is very good, but it is not as interesting as my friends' course book which they use with a different teacher.

My teacher omits a lot of activities in the course book. We practise grammar, vocabulary and the four skills. However, we do not have group discussions, presentations and projects. I think it would be a good opportunity to independently decide what to present/do and how, as well as what skills and talents to show. She says our English is not yet good enough to do these things, but we think otherwise. From time to time we do pair-work activities in the classroom, but only a few minutes, as the teacher says we are too loud and difficult to manage. Perhaps this is the reason why we do not have discussions and projects.

I think the reason is that we do not have enough learner autonomy tasks in the course book. I am sure we would do them if they were part of our course book. We always do almost all activities in the book. Our teacher does not give us tasks from other sources as she says copying is illegal. Rarely does she bring tasks designed by herself.

My teacher does not really know how to help students to become autonomous learners. In general, he is a good teacher. He explains things clearly. The only thing I do not like is that most of the time the students are very passive. We listen to him and do what he says. I think teachers should attend workshops from time to time to be familiarised with new trends in teaching. My private tutor is completely different. We talk a lot and I feel I am part of the teaching-learning process. Also, I think learning should be engaging and fun!

Since the question related to identifying possible problems was used in both questionnaires, it was possible to compare the received responses.

The analysis revealed there were three common responses for both groups of respondents. These responses were: examination-orientated curriculum, lack of sufficient ready-made resources to develop learner autonomy and lack of appropriate training in this area. On closer inspection, an interesting observation was that the first answer the two questionnaires had in common occurred more often in the student questionnaires. In the other two responses, no statistically significant differences were identified. The results are presented in Table 19 and Figure 28.

Table 19. Common responses about problems that prevent the fostering of learner autonomy

	Can you think of any problems that prevent the fostering of learner autonomy in your EFL classroom?	Teachers		Students	
		No of responses	[%]	No of responses	[%]
a)	Examination-orientated curriculum	102	85	113	94
b)	Lack of sufficient ready-made resources to develop learner autonomy	101	84	93	78
c)	Lack of appropriate training in this area	77	64	89	74

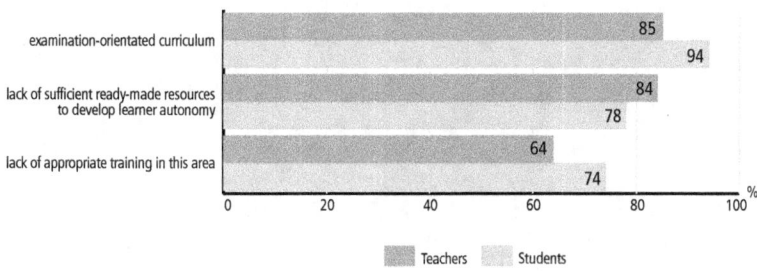

Figure 28. Common responses about problems that prevent the fostering of learner autonomy

5.3 CONCLUSION

The outcomes of the mixed-methods study were deliberately presented in two separate sections: Inquiry 1 and Inquiry 2. This was done to add clarity to the reporting. What is more, such a grouping of the results will be most helpful in responding to the eight research questions posed in Chapter Four. The interpretation of the research outcomes in relation to existing literature will be discussed in the next chapter.

CHAPTER SIX

DISCUSSION OF THE RESEARCH FINDINGS

This chapter discusses the significant findings of the mixed-methods study. The purpose of this study was to obtain a better understanding of various aspects of learner autonomy development in the Polish secondary school EFL classroom. To ensure a smooth discussion, this chapter is divided into four sections. All four sections relate to the eight research questions listed at the beginning of Chapter Four. These sections also correspond to the theoretical framework in Chapter Two and Chapter Three that guided the research project. Thus, the discussion links the empirical and theoretical analyses in this volume, making it a coherent whole. The four sections to be discussed are titled:
1. Importance and Sustainability of Developing Learner Autonomy;
2. Ways of Fostering Learner Autonomy;
3. Involvement of Teachers in Task Development;
4. Obstacles to the Effective Development of Learner Autonomy.

6.1 IMPORTANCE AND SUSTAINABILITY OF DEVELOPING LEARNER AUTONOMY

The findings in the previous chapter revealed that both teachers and students agreed that developing learner autonomy in the classroom is important. Despite the fact that both groups chose exactly the same responses (i.e. *very important*, *important* and *neither important nor unimportant*), it was the student population that expressed a stronger agreement with regard to the importance of developing learner autonomy. The ratio of the collected responses in the student and teacher groups was 70 (58%) to 16 (13%), respectively. In general, teachers (81%) considered fostering learner autonomy as important. The latter had also been observed in the pilot study (see 4.4).

This belief is in agreement with the various positions presented in the literature review in Chapter Two. For example, one of the central arguments for developing learner autonomy is to help language learners to take responsibility for their own learning (e.g. Dam, 2010; Holec, 1981). Enhancing the capacity for independent thought, critical reflection (see 2.3.2.2), decision-making (see 2.3.2.1), independent action, plus developing a repertoire of learning strategies (see 2.3.1) are also underscored (e.g. Cohen, 2011; Little, 1991; Oxford, 1990). Another reason why learner autonomy should be fostered in language education involves the concept of risk-taking. Accordingly, students should be systematically encouraged to use the target language as the main medium of language learning as a goal to becoming fluent and flexible users of that language (Goh & Burns, 2012; Nation & Newton, 2009; Ur, 2012).

All these arguments appear to have a great impact on the present, but also future lives of language learners. The immediate effect is related to students' academic lives in which they need to know how to learn effectively to succeed. The successful development of learner autonomy also affects students' future lives. For instance, in their professional lives, students will be required to demonstrate the desire for and the capacity to continue learning (Dam, 2010; Errey & Schollaert, 2003). As pointed out in Chapter Two, fostering learner autonomy also contributes to the development of self-esteem in students. The higher the level of self-esteem in students, the more confident they are. The more confident the students are, the more risks they take and the more autonomous behaviours they demonstrate (Macaskill & Denovan, 2013). Self-esteem is essential in both academic and professional lives. Self-esteem helps students to survive in the competitive world of the school or language classroom, but also guarantees survival in an extremely competitive labour market. In a similar fashion, high self-esteem is indispensable for the widespread and constant migration of young people today (Dam, 2010). It aids a peaceful transition and ability to settle down in new places, many of which happen to be replete with hostility towards immigrants.

Another point that needs to be mentioned is that self-esteem is also connected to self-efficacy. The latter is defined as "beliefs in one's capabilities to organise and execute the courses of action required to produce given attainments" (Bandura, 1997, p. 3). Hence, the higher the self-esteem, the better the school performance of students. Self-esteem and self-efficacy are further related to the notion of self-concept, which is responsible for how language learners perceive themselves and how they see others perceive them in the classroom (Zargar & Ganai, 2014). Thus, self-concept appears to be a broader notion. Indeed, it is more complex and consists of cognitive, behavioural and affective elements (Glaus, 1999). Self-esteem, in turn, subsumes its affective components. Self-concept plays an important role in human development and learning. The successful development of a self-concept, as research reveals (e.g. Baumrind, 1991; Tuttle & Tuttle, 2004), requires an environment that provides the freedom not only to explore and experiment, but also to exercise independent action. This, again, calls for an active and sustainable fostering of learner autonomy in schools.

In practice, however, as the present study has shown, the teachers' actions do not reflect the opinions aired in the previous question. This also means that the teachers do not commonly follow the core curriculum which describes lifelong learning as one of the key skills to be nurtured at the secondary level. As the gathered data reveal, sixty-two (52%) respondents admitted to devoting no more than 20 percent of their classroom time to fostering learner autonomy, whereas 48 (40%) allocated between 21 and 40 percent for the same purpose. In turn, the more positive finding is that 36 (30%) percent of the teacher population would like to develop learner autonomy on a regular basis. The discrepancy between what teachers do and what they would like to do in their teaching practice may indicate certain barriers that prevent them from carrying out a systematic development of learner autonomy. If this is the case, there is every likelihood that the answer to this problem will be found in the last section of this chapter (see 6.4).

6.2 WAYS OF FOSTERING LEARNER AUTONOMY

Having answered the first two research questions in the previous section, it is time to focus on the methods, techniques, resources and tasks teachers employ while developing learner autonomy. All these aspects come under research questions 3, 4 and 5.

As the data analysis displayed, teachers used a variety of methods and techniques to foster learner autonomy. For example, pair and group work as well as homework assignments turned out to be the most popular. They were used by all the teachers involved in the study. Dialogues, role-plays, simulations as well as learning strategy instruction were less popular with percentages amounting to 93 and 81, respectively. Presentations, projects and technology-enhanced instruction received less than 35 percent of answers, individually scoring 31, 19 and 15 percent, respectively. Extensive reading, portfolios, self-assessment sessions, syllabus and course content negotiation are hardly ever promoted by language instructors. Extensive listening, reflective learning and literature or discussion clubs were not used by any of the teachers.

It can be inferred that all those methods and techniques that are directly related to the Matura examination preparation are present in the classroom (see 3.3). If something is useful, but not part of the final examination, it may be neglected or even eradicated. It is vital that the attention of teachers be drawn to the importance of the less popular or rejected ways of promoting learner autonomy. Teachers must remember that they prepare students for life, not just the end-of-school examination in English.

With this in mind, it is suggested that presentations and projects be a significant part of learning. They boost cooperative learning (see 2.2.1.4) where students have an opportunity to experience different interaction patterns (see 2.2.1.2). They also enable students to practise and learn various transferable skills such as planning, organising, analysing, investigating, negotiating and persuading (Gravells, 2010). In addition, presentations and projects frequently integrate educational technology (see 2.3.4), and thus stimulate meaningful problem-solving (see 2.2.1.4) and genuine communication, as well as interactive, engaged and student-centred learning.

Also, it is advisable that extensive reading and extensive listening be given more prominence in language teaching (Day & Bamford, 1998; Rost, 2013). These two constructs focus on developing good reading and listening habits, knowledge of vocabulary and structure, as well as encouraging a liking for reading and listening in the target language. Extensive reading or extensive listening programmes employ simplified or graded texts that are available in the classroom library. The latter is more than a simple collection of print or audio-books. It supports literacy instruction, serves as a place for learners to interact with and discuss texts, provides opportunities for autonomous reading or listening, assists readers or listeners in learning about and from texts, and eventually motivates them to learn to read or listen and act independently.

Likewise, the roles of portfolios and self-assessment in language learning are invaluable. Since both concepts have already been described in this volume (see 2.3.2.2), it is useful to relate them to reflective practice – an element of autonomous learning. Both portfolios and self-assessment tasks encourage reflective practice on the part of students. Through such instruments, language learners have an opportunity to look back over their learning experiences. The various factors that affect success and failure can be identified (Komorowska, 2002b; Little, 2011). Portfolios and self-assessment tasks also help learners to improve their performance in the target language. More specifically, language learners use outcomes of reflection to inform future practice. Finally, systematic reflective practice assists learners in shifting from surface (i.e. learning key points by rote) to deep conceptual learning that lasts a lifetime (see 3.2.1).

Now that the discussion of methods and techniques for fostering learner autonomy is complete, it is time to look at the materials that language instructors use in their teaching practice. As the data analysis in the previous chapter revealed, course books are the most popular resource used for developing learner autonomy. This observation can be supported by the data collected through student questionnaires (see 5.2.2). As the student participants (63%) noted, their teachers rarely provide them with non-course-book-based tasks. What is more, only 21 (18%) participants stated that these tasks help them to become more independent learners.

The results seem to suggest that teachers do not supplement course books on a regular basis. This observation is in agreement with the pilot study (see 4.4), but contradicts the findings of Graves (2003) and Botelho (2003). In the former study, teachers supplemented textbooks to facilitate the learning process to make it more interesting and relevant. The latter study revealed that course book supplementation was used to promote personalisation (see 3.1.1.4) as well as student creativity and innovation.

Another interesting finding was that learner autonomy never appeared as a criterion for course book selection. Learner autonomy was not taken into consideration when selecting course books for Year 1 and Year 3. It is the suitable language and content (98%) and the well-prepared teacher's book and test book (95%) in Year 1 course books and the well-prepared teacher's book and test book (100%) and Matura examination practice (100%) in Year 3 course books that are given priority. The same two criteria for Year 1 and Year 3 course books had been recorded in the pilot study. The only difference between the responses in the study proper and the pilot study was that Year 1 course book selection criteria appeared in reverse order.

The fact that teachers prefer to work with course books is justified. The importance of course books is widely discussed in the literature (e.g. Bao, 2015; McGrath, 2013; Richards, 2001; Ur, 1996, 2015). For instance, well-designed books standardise language instruction and provide structure for teaching. They help teachers to keep track of what has been done. They also clearly define items to be learnt and tested. Despite all these advantages, it is advisable that teachers share McGrath's view that "a book should not be a course in the sense that it determines the totality of learning experiences for those using it" (McGrath, 2002, p. 58). Otherwise, teachers may:

> (...) feel that they are no longer educationalists – professional educators – but technicians whose intellectual and creative skills have been incorporated into learning packages, the consumption of which they now only disseminate, manage and assess (Allman, 2001, p. 71).

Harmer (2001), in turn, points out that teachers must understand that course books are not playscripts, and therefore need not to be religiously followed. He quickly adds that course books are *"proposals* for action" and not "instructions for use" (Harmer, 2001, p. 8). Hence, it is the teachers that decide whether:

> *(...) they agree with [a course book], if they want to do things in the way the book suggests, or if, on the contrary, they are going to make changes, replacing things, modifying activities [or] approaching texts differently (Harmer, 2001, p. 8).*

As the data analysis showed, secondary school teachers prefer to use diverse course books in different grades (see 3.3). They use standard course books with Year 1 students. These course books are valued because they have the potential for fostering learner autonomy. More specifically, they promote, among other things, cooperative learning (see 2.2.1.4), learning strategies (see 2.3.1) and critical thinking. Year 3 Matura trainers, however, are designed to prepare students for the Matura examination. They are reported to be effective in encouraging cooperative learning and learning strategies. In general, as the data disclose, there are a number of areas that call for improvement in modern course books. There is a particular need for self-assessment sections, educational-technology-related tasks and collaborative projects. For a brief summary of EFL course book analysis see Chapter Three.

It is good to see that a number of teachers acknowledged using other materials along with compulsory course books. The additional items used for fostering learner autonomy include resource packs (26%), authentic texts (19%) and technology-based materials (15%). Unsurprisingly, the poor usage of technology-orientated resources closely corresponds to the previous question, which noted that in course books there was a lack of integration of educational technology into the teaching-learning process. Similar associations were also observed in relation to self-assessment materials and the use of audio-books in the classroom.

In the next section, an attempt will be made to answer research questions 6 and 7. The discussion focuses on the extent to which teachers are involved in developing pedagogical tasks.

6.3 INVOLVEMENT OF TEACHERS IN TASK DEVELOPMENT

According to the data analysis presented in Chapter Five, teachers are not systematically involved in designing pedagogical tasks. Over 50 percent of the teacher population admitted to rarely developing tasks, whilst 29 percent stated that they are involved in task design (see 7.1) from time to time. The low result in the quantitative part of Inquiry 1 can be supported with observations recorded in the teacher journals. For instance, two teachers wrote:

> *I rarely design tasks for my students. The course book I use provides numerous activities; students have a lot of work already.*
>
> *I design my own tasks only from time to time. I have ready-made resources in the staff room.*

These results run counter to Nunan's (1988) findings. In his investigation, teachers used their own activities on a regular basis. What is more, 50 percent of his population did not use commercially-produced materials in their teaching practice.

Knowing that teachers are not keen on designing tasks in general, the teachers were then asked specifically about developing learner autonomy tasks for their students. The statistics showed that 75 percent of the research population never design their own tasks to ensure successful learner autonomy development. Slightly more positive findings were recorded in the pilot study (see 4.4).

Such a state of affairs would be easier to understand if the low results referred to designing technology-based tasks. To design such tasks, programming knowledge (e.g. developing 3D materials) and considerable time are required (Fan, 2011; Korsvold & Rüschoff, 1997). Since teachers hardly ever have any of the two, they do not produce, for example, educational websites. It is specifically the technical knowledge that makes the production of technology-based materials and tasks complex for teachers. Nevertheless, some teachers appear to evaluate the effectiveness of such materials in their teaching practice. As various reports describe (e.g. Fan, 2011), current technology-based materials have flaws. For example, they present too much information, which often confuses students. Also, they tend not to follow any principled approaches to materials development.

Unfortunately, the unsystematic involvement of teachers in task design is not limited to technology-based instruction only. In general, teachers do not design pedagogical tasks. There are probable reasons why teachers do not engage in task design. For example, they may not have the skills nor know how to design tasks (Li, 1998). Some of the teachers may think that they do not have the authority to produce pedagogical tasks. Another reason may be related to the common belief that tasks in published materials are superior to self-designed ones (Ramirez Salas, 2004) because they are "elaborated by people who really know". Thus, such materials become the so-called "bibles" that must be dutifully followed (Ramirez Salas, 2004, p. 3). The existing circumstances can be dealt with by offering training in designing tasks. This issue is discussed later in this chapter (see 6.4), and additionally in Chapter Seven.

It is essential that language teachers realise that the process of designing complex tasks requires a number of criteria, features and principles to be followed. Numerous text selection criteria (see 3.1.1) and task features (see 3.2) have already been discussed in this volume. To succeed in designing high quality learner autonomy tasks, it is advisable that teachers make additional use of two sets of principles: SLA-related and constructivist-language-teaching-orientated. The former pertain to various theories and models of second language learning with which language teachers need to be familiar (Ortega, 2009; Saville-Troike, 2006). The latter emerge from the philosophy of social constructivism presented in Chapter Two (see 2.2).

As a result, it is vital that effective pedagogical tasks which are intended to foster learner autonomy enable learners to:
- engage in social interaction and purposeful communication;
- personalise and individualise their learning experiences;
- respond intellectually, emotionally and aesthetically to texts they receive;
- experience authenticity in terms of input and tasks;
- carefully plan, critically reflect and self-assess their learning;

- develop learning skills, facilitate self-investment and provide feedback;
- bolster their motivation, confidence and self-esteem;
- increase their risk-taking, critical thinking and collaboration skills;
- develop different learning styles; and
- incorporate both print, digital and audio texts into their classrooms.

The positive thing is that teachers know what type of learner autonomy tasks should be included in modern course books. Not being directly involved in the process of designing tasks, as the study disclosed, teachers impose specific requirements on materials writers and expect modern course books to include, among other things: self-assessment tasks (see Task 7 in 7.3), tasks with the use of educational technology (see Task 1 in 7.3), tasks with integrated language skills (see Task 3 in 7.3), reflecting on learning tasks (see Task 9 in 7.3) and, last but not least, learning strategy identification tasks (see Task 5 in 7.3). This observation fully concurs with the findings recorded in my journal (see 3.3).

All the tasks mentioned above are extremely important. Their educational value has been discussed in the literature on a number of occasions. For example, self-assessment tasks are advocated by Buttner (2007). More specifically, she encourages teachers to use weekly rubrics for target language activities. Such rubrics help students to monitor and keep a record of their own participation in classroom activities. Student participation can then be discussed either with individual students or their parents. In a similar fashion, Walstad (2006) promotes self-graded quizzes. Through these tasks, language students have a chance to reflect on their learning and assess how much they have learnt over a particular period of time, both language- and content-wise.

Similarly, technology-based projects are expected to be integrated into the overall goal and structure of language courses. The former are vital as they increase student motivation (see 3.2.1), enhance student linguistic and computing skills and encourage diverse interaction patterns (e.g. Beckett, 2005; Fang & Warschauer, 2004). The latter offer authentic language exemplars and target language-culture elements such as accents and dialects. Such tasks, for example, as presenting an episode or performing a sitcom in class, require that students deal with paralinguistic clues to understand texts, but also use visual and auditory stimuli for predictions and deductions (Hirata & Hirata, 2009; Sherman, 2003; Widodo & Cirocki, 2015). As mentioned earlier in this book, video-based teaching also offers students a range of sensory experiences involving sight, smell, touch, sound and taste (see 3.1.1.3).

The importance of authentic language use (see 3.2.1) and cultural representations in language teaching materials is also considered by McGrath (2013). He states that course book writers are not following recent research findings. This criticism is related to such areas as indirect speech (Barbieri & Eckhardt, 2007), differences between spoken and written grammar (Cullen & Kuo, 2007) or conversation strategies (McCarten & McCarthy, 2010). Also, he goes on to say that "coursebooks perpetuate gender and other stereotypes and misrepresent reality – for instance, by excluding minorities and by depicting a world that is free of problems and sanitized" (McGrath, 2013, p. 12).

The last type of tasks to be discussed focuses on the development and practice of various learning strategies (see 2.3.1). According to the discussion in Chapter Two, learning strategy instruction is vital for a number of reasons. In brief, such training enhances students' awareness of learning strategies and encourages them to try new strategies in practice. Students are also stimulated to use a larger number of strategies to make their own learning more effective. This, in turn, leads language learners to enhance their performance in the target language and guides them to autonomous learning. There is a wide range of tasks that can be used in the language classroom to promote different types of learning strategies (e.g. Cohen, 2011; O'Maley & Chamot, 1990; Oxford, 2011). These include: asking students to reflect (either orally or in writing) about their learning strategies (see Task 4 and Task 5 in 7.3), learning strategy discussions and individual or group learning strategy interviews.

The next section addresses research question 8. It focuses on a number of obstacles that prevent the fostering of learner autonomy.

6.4 OBSTACLES TO THE EFFECTIVE DEVELOPMENT OF LEARNER AUTONOMY

The last research question pertained to problems which prevent the fostering of learner autonomy. According to the collected data, eight obstacles were identified. Above all else, teachers (93%) made it clear that they do not develop learner autonomy in their teaching practice due to a lack of time. This finding can be interpreted in two ways. Firstly, teachers do not seem to consider learner autonomy development as an integral part of the regular teaching-learning process. This line of reasoning may reflect the common belief that learner autonomy is a teaching method (Martinez, 2008). Teachers think they need to allocate extra time to it and develop it separately. Secondly, the lack of time may also be understood as a mental shortcut; teachers do not promote learner autonomy in their teaching practice as they have no time to design complex tasks to supplement course books (see 3.3). Likewise, workload issues have been reported in the Malaysian context. Segumpan and Bahari (2006) conclude that Malaysian teachers have excessive teaching loads and too many roles to play at school. Both factors, as they further point out, are a major source of stress for teachers. A similar observation about numerous responsibilities has also been made among Hong Kong teachers of Mathematics (Taplin, 2002).

The next three obstacles included: examination-orientated curriculum, insufficient resources for developing learner autonomy and a lack of training for the teaching staff. All these possible hindrances were listed by both teachers and students. For instance, the examination-orientated EFL instruction in Poland has been mentioned on a number of occasions in this volume. EFL instruction in Year 3 is a good example. A two-semester training course in examination strategies is not a principal objective of language instruction at this level. What is needed is high-quality instruction that increases language learner engagement (see 3.2.1), the development of numerous transferable skills (see 6.2) and preparation for entering a multicultural world. The problem of examination-orientated education is not new. Examinations were strongly condemned two decades ago (e.g. Orange 2002; Tzuriel, 2001; Zhou, 2008). They were considered to be stumbling blocks that impeded growth and success. Hence, it is advisable that they be reduced to a minimum.

The impact of high-stakes language tests or compulsory end-of-school language examinations on materials development is reflected in the publication of test or examination preparation materials in many contexts (e.g. Bailey & Masuhara, 2013). The same phenomenon is observed in Poland. What should be remembered, though, is that such books are designed and published for language examination courses. Of course, they can be used in traditional EFL courses, but only occasionally. When this is the case, teachers are encouraged to take Bailey and Masuhara's (2013, pp. 309-310) advice that such materials represent the most recent version of the examination, address all the constructs measured by the examination, go beyond examination strategies and promote language development, provide opportunity for interaction, support good teaching and explain the scoring criteria associated with the examination.

In the present study, insufficient resources for fostering learner autonomy turned out to be another problem that teachers face. This is partially true as there is a shortage of activity packs or activity books devoted specifically to learner autonomy. However, a very useful guide was published by Scharle and Szabo in 2000. The main problem is that teachers do not seem to be willing to supplement course books. Were it not for that, teachers would be able to find interesting learner autonomy tasks in other sources. Another option would be that with imagination and creativity; teachers could design their own learner autonomy tasks that ideally match teaching approaches and students' expectations and needs (Block, 1991; McGrath, 2002; Richards, 2001). For a more detailed discussion on how to design pedagogical tasks see Chapter Seven (see 7.1).

The issue of teacher creativity in producing instructional materials has also been raised by Islam and Mares (2003) and Bell and Gower (2011). It is highlighted that there is a need for teachers to partake in the creative dialogue with materials in order to offer what is interesting, exciting and effective. Such an approach is widely recommended by the Asian English Language Teachers' Creative Writing Group. The group was established to engage English language teachers in developing and publishing instructional materials. During the meetings, teachers write poems and stories which are later included in an edited volume and published. These gatherings are unique and contribute to teachers' personal, social and professional development. Some of the teachers' outputs include: *Writing for Ourselves: Poems and Short Stories for Young Learners of English* or *Life in Words and Words in Life. Poems and Stories for Asian Students*.

The next problem that the study showed was that teachers and students ascribe the poor level of learner autonomy development to a lack of available training on learner autonomy for teachers. This scenario would appear to be rather serious, and in fact, this may be the case. During the years I was involved in teacher education courses in Poland, materials development modules in BA or MA TEFL courses were never offered. Professional development courses in materials development or task design for learner autonomy were not available, either. Such a state of affairs convincingly explains why both pre- and in-service teachers prefer to use ready-made activities. Course books or resource packs available in the staff room are the customary sources for these teachers.

The lack of teacher training in materials development in Poland does not seem to be an isolated case. Similar voices were expressed in Ghana (Opoku-Amankwa, 2010). Another study that calls for improvement in the area of teacher training was carried out in Saudi Arabia. Al-Yousef (2007) emphasises that Saudi teachers need training in communicative language teaching methodology. Teachers in Madagascar expect to be given more alternatives materials-wise and training on how to effectively use materials while teaching (Ravelonanahary, 2007).

The situation in the Polish context seems to mirror the observations made by Canniveng and Martinez (2003). These two authors highlight that teacher training courses do not encourage teachers to apply their knowledge and teaching experience to materials writing. Similarly, teacher training courses do not devote enough attention to the area of task development (van der Branden, 2006). Materials writing in general or task design in particular are usually a small component of such courses, as opposed to classroom management, lesson planning or teaching language skills. For this reason, it is recommended that closer attention be paid to how teachers can develop personal specific criteria to suit their teaching practice and the educational context in which they teach.

It is advocated that materials or task development programmes be made widely available for language teachers (Masuhara, 2006; McGrath, 2013; Richards, 2001; Tomlinson, 2014). There are a number of reasons why it is important for teachers to take part in these programmes. Firstly, the programmes contribute to a close scrutiny of the beliefs and theories related to teaching and learning processes. Secondly, taking part in such programmes encourages teachers to consider lesson principles as well as task design principles (see 7.1). Additionally, teachers' awareness of learners' individual needs would be improved. It goes without saying that such courses support and enhance the professional development of language practitioners (Masuhara, 2006; Richards, 2001; Tomlinson, 2014).

It is Masuhara (2006) who notes that engaging teachers in materials design is an effective way of helping teachers to develop professionally. Properly designed materials development courses make teachers more aware, critical, creative, effective, reflective and autonomous in their teaching practice. Procedures and a flexible framework for such courses have been provided by Tomlinson (2013b). In turn, interesting accounts of student-teacher involvement in materials writing have been offered by Tan (2006).

While teacher training in materials development and task design is important, teacher training with regard to fostering learner autonomy must also be brought to the forefront. As the empirical data showed, the latter can be assumed to occur more commonly than the former. Still, it is important that the concept of learner autonomy and its successful development in the classroom is regularly discussed by teachers. Teachers need to understand that learner autonomy is an interrelational concept. This means that its successful development depends on the capacities of both teachers and students (La Ganza, 2008). Given this evidence, it must be inferred that learner autonomy is constantly negotiated in the classroom (see 2.3.2.1) within a "dynamic interrelational space" between teachers and students (La Ganza, 2008, p. 65). The fostering of learner autonomy rests on how teachers and learners communicate and liaise with each other in all aspects of the learning experience.

With this in mind, it is vital that teachers realise that the notion of teacher autonomy is reciprocally linked to learner autonomy. The former is as complex as the latter and needs to be perceived in terms of La Ganza's (2008, pp. 71-72) four dimensions:

- autonomy in relation to the teacher's own internal dialectics with teachers, mentors or other important authority figures who might or might not support a teacher's freedom to foster the autonomy of learners;
- autonomy in relation to learners, who might support the teacher's freedom to be creative as a teacher and the teacher's attempts to encourage their learners' autonomy;
- autonomy in relation to those, in the institution in which the teacher is teaching, who could potentially make decisions influencing the teacher's freedom to be creative, to develop and practise ideas and to pursue his or her goals; and
- autonomy in relation to those, in the institutions and bureaucracies of society at large, who could potentially make decisions influencing the teacher's freedom to be creative as a teacher, to develop and practise ideas, and to pursue his or her goals.

The interconnection between learner and teacher autonomy has also been raised by Sinclair (2000) and Martinez (2008). Both authors state that effective learner autonomy development is determined by the teacher's level of knowledge of this construct as well as by the teacher's awareness of the consequences that their decisions may have for their learners' academic, personal and social functioning and achievements. Breen and Mann (1997) take this approach one step further. According to them, teachers who wish to successfully foster learner autonomy must have a deep awareness of themselves as learners. In other words, apart from recognising their beliefs about the teaching-learning process, teachers must also be conscious of how their own learning and teaching experiences guide their classroom practice.

Two other issues that are believed to prevent the fostering of learner autonomy were mentioned only by the teacher participants. These were: restricted number of classes per week and classroom discipline issues provoked by learner autonomy methodology. In general, teachers seem to believe that the time they have at their disposal with individual groups per week is only sufficient for Matura examination practice. This implies that the number of hours per group should be increased. Such a decision would be very problematic for some schools because the workload of the teachers is already hardly manageable, as mentioned above.

As far as the other problem is concerned, 26 percent of the teacher population stated that they do not promote learner autonomy in their classrooms because this process requires specific methodology and different types of classroom work, including projects or presentations. These forms of classroom work are reported to cause a lot of commotion and a lack of discipline among language learners. This observation must be a common phenomenon because 36 percent of the student population added this answer to the last question under the "Other" option. One of the student participants commented that:

> We do pair-work activities in the classroom from time to time, but only a few minutes, because our teacher says we are too loud and difficult to manage. This must be the reason why we do not do discussions and projects.

As can be seen, teachers prefer teacher-centred to students-centred instruction. Lecture-type lessons enable teachers to clearly see all their students, and consequently, maintain control in the classroom. Classroom discipline issues where group work is involved was also reported by Tsui (2003).

On the other hand, Kramer (2005) says that teachers *should* expect noise during group work and projects because students are social creatures and share knowledge and views through interaction (see 2.2.1.2). Hence, reasonably noisy behaviour in the classroom should not surprise teachers at all. If teachers prefer silence in the classroom most of the time, they "need a reality check" (Kramer, 2005, p. 39). A more optimistic view on classroom management issues is expressed by Tinker Sachs and Ho (2007). They note that such problems tend to occur in transitional moments in teaching, that is, while moving, for example, from individual work to group work. Therefore, it is essential that teachers ensure that in those transitional points, momentum in teaching is not lost. Otherwise, learning time is wasted and undesirable interruptions in the flow of the lesson take place. By contrast, Charles (2002) and Reinke, Herman and Sprick (2011) report that student misbehaviour is generally an ongoing issue that seriously affects teaching and learning. For this reason, teachers should not feel discouraged from developing learner autonomy in the classroom. What is more, if class-management issues happen to occur in the classroom, for whatever reason, there are effective ways of dealing with them. For example, Belvel (2010) offers useful strategies for dealing with and quickly solving challenging classroom situations before the teaching-learning process is disrupted.

A lack of experience in designing tasks for learner autonomy on the part of teachers and a lack of involvement from language learners in the decision-making processes in the classroom were the two issues found on the student questionnaire. The first issue is closely related or can even be a consequence of the lack of proper training discussed above. Teachers may not have relevant experience in designing tasks because they have never been shown how to do it. For this reason, a model for developing learner autonomy will be presented in Chapter Seven.

The last aspect to be discussed in this section is learner involvement or lack of involvement in decision-making processes in the classroom (see 2.3.2.1). As the data in the previous chapter revealed, language learners are motivated to collaborate with teachers to make decisions about the teaching-learning process. For example, they wish to independently choose partners for class tasks as well as decide about class content and diverse forms of class work.

As the discussion in Chapter Two illustrates, inviting students to share in decision-making processes in the classroom is a good practice. While making decisions about class content and the tasks to be used, or various aspects of classroom management, language learners express their opinions and needs, identify primary issues, reach goals together, actively listen to other members of the class community and monitor each other's work and conduct (Edwards, 2011; Kreisberg, 1992; Styles, 2001). All these activities expand students' awareness of interpersonal relationships. Students also learn to develop leadership and organisational skills.

The discussion on the negotiated syllabus (see 2.3.2.1) would not be complete without referring to Breen and Littlejohn (2000). In their opinion, it is vital that classroom reality be negotiated with learners (see 2.2.1.2). Their concept of negotiation is closely akin to the Russian doll model. The set consists of *procedural negotiation* (i.e. the outer doll), *interactive negotiation* (i.e. the middle doll) and *personal negotiation* (i.e. the inner doll). The first one is about arriving at an agreement regarding the things that will be done in the classroom, including the means and the time of their completion. The second one deals with the notion of social interaction and its assistance in coming to those decisions. The last one is related to reflections, understandings and decisions at the individual level and their contribution to collective negotiation.

6.5 CONCLUSION

The purpose of this chapter has been to discuss the findings which have emerged from the mixed-methods study. As the discussion shows, learner autonomy appears to be present in the Polish secondary school EFL classroom in varying intensities and scope. Various weaknesses have been identified and discussed with a view to improving the current situation. For example, the study discloses that teachers lack experience in designing pedagogical tasks. To resolve this problem, a model for developing learner autonomy tasks will be presented in Chapter Seven. The model is presented to encourage teachers to engage in writing high-quality pedagogical tasks to be able to supplement modern course books. A general conclusion and implications for teacher education and materials writers follow in Chapter Eight.

CHAPTER SEVEN

DESIGNING PEDAGOGICAL TASKS FOR LEARNER AUTONOMY

Materials development in ELT and teachers' involvement in TESOL materials writing have recently become key topics in language education (Harwood, 2010, 2014; McGrath, 2013; Tomlinson, 2013b, 2013c, 2014; Cirocki & Tomlinson, 2015). The discussion results from the general observation that materials or tasks teachers use in their teaching practice do not always reflect the reality of the classroom with regard to students' wants, needs, interests or language proficiency. There is a need to bridge the gap between what the current market offers in terms of instructional materials and what is needed by learners to succeed in their language learning journey. For this reason, it is essential that teachers engage in designing pedagogical tasks. This new experience will help them to effectively supplement the existing materials, adapt the available activities or produce brand new tasks.

The question that arises is: *Do TESOL teachers design pedagogical tasks to enhance their students' learning?* A thorough investigation needs to be conducted to answer this question in global terms. In the Polish teaching context, the research findings in the previous chapter revealed that much more could be done in this respect. For this reason, a model for developing pedagogical tasks for learner autonomy will now be offered. The stages of the model will be discussed to make teachers aware of what the process of task design entails and what associated roles or responsibilities teachers are expected to assume to succeed. The second part of this chapter includes a collection of learner autonomy tasks and a rationale for their use. The point is not only to demonstrate what kinds of tasks can be used to promote learner autonomy, but also to stimulate teachers into further experimentation and discovery.

7.1 DESIGNING PEDAGOGICAL TASKS: THE MODEL

The relevance of task-based language pedagogy has been emphasised on a number of occasions in the field of language education (East, 2012; Ellis & Shintani, 2013; Hallet & Legutke, 2013; Masuhara, 2015). This concern is directly related to the contemporary view of language learning. As shown by SLA and psychological research (e.g. Eckerth & Siekmann, 2008; Garcia-Mayo, 2007; Ellis & Shintani, 2013), language learning is a developmental process that follows its own agenda. This means that learners do not learn English in a carefully organised way as presented in high-quality course books nor is the target language learnt in an organised way delivered by well-prepared teachers. Likewise, teaching is not about presenting the target language in ready-to-digest chunks. Neither is it based on the assumption that language is best presented in the classroom through a structural syllabus.

Consequently, according to recent developments in language pedagogy, language learners should be given tasks to transact, as opposed to structures or chunks of language to learn. As demonstrated in Chapter Three (see 3.2), the integration of tasks into instructional materials is vital. It is advisable that pedagogical tasks be widely promoted in current materials, for it is through active involvement in meaningful tasks that interlanguage develops. Complex tasks are regarded as extremely useful in this respect (see 3.2.2). Such tasks contribute to developing learners' communicative competence (see 3.1.1.2) by involving language learners in meaning-driven communication via task performance (e.g. Nunan, 2004). Opportunities are also provided for learners to employ various capabilities, including the cognitive, social-interactive and discursive (Hallet & Legutke, 2013). It can therefore be inferred that the more complex the tasks, the more effective and successful the learning process.

In order to complete the discussion of pedagogical tasks for learner autonomy in Chapter Three, a comprehensive five-stage model is now suggested (see Figure 29). This model is inspired by Tomlinson's writings on materials development. It incorporates three crucial concepts of modern language pedagogy: social constructivism, language learning and reflective teaching into one framework. Various aspects of the first two concepts have been discussed on a number of occasions in this volume. The concept of reflective teaching, in turn, presumes that language teachers should critically review their practice, seeking improvements, turning to appropriate literature and research for innovative insights (Cirocki, Tennekoon, & Peña Calvo, 2014; Cirocki & Farrelly, 2016; Farrell, 2007, 2015; General Teaching Council for Scotland, 2002) and applying these to classroom procedures and task development. Reflection aims to deepen understanding of various bonds between theory and practice of both language teaching and the designing of tasks (Fleming & Stevens, 2004; King, 2010; Korthagen, 2001).

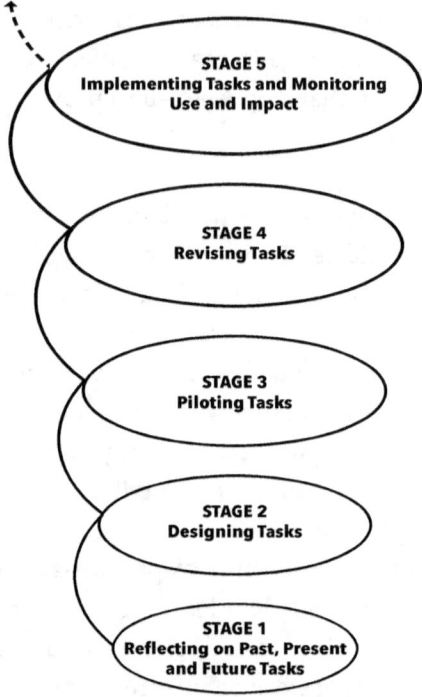

Figure 29. Developing pedagogical tasks for learner autonomy

This model has also been created with language teacher communities of practice in mind (McLaughlin & Talbert, 2006). Such communities are frequently described as groups in which teachers "share a concern, a set of problems, or a passion about a topic, and who deepen their understanding and knowledge of this area by interacting on an ongoing basis" (Wenger, McDermott, Snyder, 2002, p. 4). In this particular case, the various concerns, problems and passions are related to developing tasks for learner autonomy.

Communities of practice have leaders who coordinate their groups. These groups are called the followers. The leaders build and sustain the community by flagging significant issues to be tackled, facilitating member engagement, driving action and structuring interactions within these groups. In the present model, leadership is assumed by language educators. Language educators are teachers of teachers who are involved in professional training of future practitioners. They work at the tertiary level and promote current, applied linguistic and educational theory and research while training language teachers. The followers, in turn, are in-service language practitioners who work with L2 students. The immersion of the model for developing learner autonomy tasks in the community-of-practice framework aims to build bridges between academics and school teachers by engaging them in collaborative work. One purpose of such work is to guide teachers in fostering learner autonomy through complex tasks. Another purpose is to offer in-service teachers ongoing professional development in the areas of learner autonomy and task design. It is also hoped that such communities of practice will minimise the academic/practitioner divide, closing the gap between research and practice.

Being intrinsically coherent with each stage supporting the next, this five-stage model provides language educators and classroom practitioners with hands-on guidelines to produce effective tasks for fostering learner autonomy. The stages of the model are:
1. Reflecting on past and present tasks and thinking about future tasks;
2. Designing tasks;
3. Piloting tasks;
4. Revising tasks;
5. Implementing tasks and monitoring their use and impact.

The model of developing pedagogical tasks for learner autonomy takes the form of a helix. This shape has been deliberately chosen as its spiral structure guarantees continuity and smooth transitions from one stage of the model to the next. As Figure 29 shows, the helix grows upwards. The upwards direction emphasises that a teacher's knowledge and experiences grow with time. Once the teacher completes the entire process, guided by language educators from Stage One to Stage Five, they develop a repository of underpinning knowledge which can be reiteratively utilised when engaging in or analysing new experiences in task design (see 7.1) or adaptation (see 3.3.1).

Additionally, the upwards-growing helix implies that teacher reflections become more meaningful with time as they build on prior knowledge and experiences. To succeed in improving language education or instructional materials and tasks, teachers are expected to apply their reflections to classroom processes. It is essential that classroom processes are always linked to theory, practice and research. These are the various aspects language educators elaborate upon in communities of practice. Finally, the helix shape seeks to portray teachers as lifelong learners. While teaching and developing pedagogical tasks, teachers are not only involved in a dynamic, developmental and ongoing process, but also are encouraged and empowered to:

> acquire all the knowledge, values, skills and understanding they will require throughout their [teaching careers] and to apply them with confidence, creativity and enjoyment in all [teaching] roles, circumstances and environments (Longworth & Davies, 1996, p. 22).

The present model encompasses the key issues of social constructivism (see 2.2). Learning is characterised as a developmental, meaningful and social process of knowledge construction. The concept of reflective thinking and practice is in agreement with Vygotsky's theory. Following his view, reflective thinking is an active process of inquiry and discovery, resting on a firm grasp of one's own learning (Vygotsky, 1978). Apart from Vygotsky, the present model makes reference to Feuerstein's concept of *structural cognitive modifiability*. According to Feuerstein (1990), human cognitive structures can be endlessly modified. As a result, human cognitive capacity can be developed at any point, turning people into lifelong learners.

For the sake of clarity and precision, all the stages of the present model are discussed in separate sections below.

7.1.1 REFLECTING ON PAST AND PRESENT TASKS AND THINKING ABOUT FUTURE TASKS

In Stage One, language educators help teachers in the communities of practice to collaboratively reflect on the tasks the teachers used in the past or are presently using in their teaching practice. This reflection involves analysing the strengths and weaknesses of tasks to single out distinctive features. This type of reflection is what the twelve teachers relied on when agreeing to analyse EFL course books in their journals in Inquiry 1 (see 3.3). Knowing what the target audience enjoyed in the past or what their present preferences are can inform teachers on how new tasks are supposed to look. In addition, teachers should be systematically encouraged to study professional literature and SLA research outcomes to be up-to-date with the latest theories and their implications for task design.

Stage One underscores the important role of reflection in language teaching, with the aim of prompting teachers to continuously analyse and evaluate their own teaching practice (Farrell, 2015; Pollard, 2005). The three processes require that teachers activate reflective thinking at three levels: *technical, contextual* and *dialectical* (Taggart & Wilson, 2005). The first level centres on methodological issues and appropriate selection and implementation of pedagogical tasks to achieve objectives. The second level examines classroom pedagogy from a theory-practice angle. At this level, teachers analyse the theory that underpins their classroom practices. Alternative procedures that could be utilised to satisfy students' needs and wants are examined. At the dialectical level, reflection connects with the wider context of society; various moral, ethical and sociopolitical issues regarding teaching are taken into account (Farrell, 2004).

These three levels of reflective thinking also underpin the *Framework for Reflecting on Practice* developed by Farrell (2015). Farrell's framework comprises five levels of reflection labelled as *Philosophy, Principles,*

Theory, *Practice* and *Beyond Practice*. The Philosophy level is related to reflecting on the "teacher-as-person" (Farrell, 2015, p. 35). In this phase, teachers develop their awareness of who they are as practitioners and how their philosophies are central to their teaching. The Principles level focuses on reflection related to teacher assumptions, beliefs and concepts of the teaching-learning process. The Theory level promotes reflection on theories teachers hold about their own practice. The Practice level centres on reflection about what happens in the classroom while teaching. Due to this type of reflection, teachers acquire a fuller understanding of students, the teaching-learning process and themselves as practitioners. The last level of reflection – Beyond Practice – is intended to encourage teachers to link their own teaching experiences to various social, cultural and structural contexts while bringing to life formerly unquestioned behaviours or norms, for example, classroom- or school-wise (Farrell, 2015).

As shown above, the concept of reflective teaching conceptualises instruction as a developmental and highly complex activity. Teachers critically look at what they do in the classroom, how they do it, why they do it and whether the applied procedures bring the desired outcomes. Through reflection, teachers continuously explore their own teaching and the beliefs that guide it, question the assumptions that sustain their actions, critically evaluate the tasks they employ as well as develop practitioner knowledge and competence, thus enhancing their professional development (Cirocki, Tennekoon & Peña Calvo, 2014; Cirocki & Farrelly, 2016; Farrell, 2007, 2015; Pollard, 2005; Richards & Lockhart, 1994).

7.1.2 DESIGNING TASKS

Intensive reflection and thinking about past, present and future tasks pave the way for Stage Two. This stage is called *Designing Tasks*. In this phase, teachers in their communities of practice are guided in the collaborative production of their own tasks or in the adaptation of published resources. In the creation or adaptation process, language educators draw teachers' attention to such aspects as *task goals, input, task procedures, teacher roles, classroom setting* and *feedback*. Before all these specifications are given individual attention, it must be made clear that the processes of writing or adapting tasks never begin without analysing learner needs (Botha & Coetzee, 2007; Nation & Macalister, 2010).

Learner needs, thoroughly discussed in the literature (e.g. Brindley, 1989; Hutchinson & Waters, 1987; Jordan, 2006), constitute the starting point for developing pedagogical tasks (see 3.2). Generally speaking, the purpose of the process of analysing learner needs is to provide detailed information about "what exactly it is that students have to do through the medium of English" (Robinson, 1991, p. 3). In reality, the process is a bit more complex as different types of needs must be taken into account. For example, *learning needs* are related to what language learners need to do in order to learn. *Target needs* refer to what language learners are expected to do in the target situation (Hutchinson & Waters, 1987). There is another division of needs: *objective* and *subjective needs*. The former are described as factual information about learner current proficiency and difficulties in the target language. The latter, in turn, refer to both cognitive and affective needs of learners, linked to learners' personalities, attitudes and expectations (Brindley, 1989).

The identification of learner needs can be carried out through various instruments (Yalden, 1987). The learner's knowledge, skills and performance can be assessed against a set of standards using these instruments. For example, teachers can collect initial information via checklists, questionnaires or interviews. Subsequent discussions, negotiations or observations may be added. Apart from the great variety of available tools, the most important thing to remember is that needs analysis should be carried out as an ongoing process and systematically contributes to making core decisions about the form of learning tasks (Dudley-Evans & St John, 1998).

In the sections that follow, the six characteristic features of learning tasks are individually discussed.

7.1.2.1 GOALS

Goals are usually defined as "general intentions" which seek to describe what learners will achieve by accomplishing given tasks (Nunan, 2004,

p. 41). They may refer to general outcomes, learner behaviour, the target language or other aspects of the teaching-learning process. For this reason, it is difficult to imagine a clear one-to-one correspondence between goals and tasks. Normally, tasks have more than one goal. It is advisable that teachers ensure that tasks they design help learners to realise both short- and long-term goals (Anderson & Lawrence, 2007). Both types of goals specify various competences language learners are obliged to develop in the course of their study but in different time frames. Another thing teachers should remember is that the most effective goals are invariably related to students and articulated with respect to observable performance (e.g. to practise the ability to write letters/emails asking for advice).

The notion of goals may be clarified by presenting their typology. For example, the *Australian Language Levels* project discussed by Clark (1987) lists four types of goals: *communicative, socio-cultural, learning how to learn* and *language and cultural awareness*. This classification has been deliberately selected for the present discussion as all the goals can be utilised in successful learner autonomy development. An example of the first goal would be encouraging learners to discuss in groups the topic of summer jobs. The discussion should be based on the source text and students should relate the text to their own experiences. An example of a socio-cultural goal would be to encourage learners to discuss the similarities and differences between Christmas customs and present the outcome with the use of educational technology. Examples of the last two goals could be negotiating and planning Prezi presentations, plus setting their submission deadline and encouraging learners to write formal letters of complaint, email them to the assigned classmates and respond accordingly.

As can be seen, goals are not only essential elements of learning tasks; they also indicate a distinct direction for the language curriculum in general (Nunan, 2004). The ultimate goals for learning are externally endorsed and teachers must acknowledge them. However, teachers may make their voices heard when intermediate goals come into play. Intermediate goals, to which task goals belong, function as an effective route to reaching the ultimate goals. For this reason, in the literature, they are more often than not referred to as a means to an end.

The aim of the next section is to discuss the notion of input.

7.1.2.2 INPUT

Input is frequently defined as all the verbal and non-verbal (e.g. graphs, images, maps) information that is provided by the task (Nunan, 1989). Task input may represent different sources (e.g. newspapers, radio scripts, weather forecasts, extracts from film scripts, letters), and therefore take textual or graphic forms. Yet, as mentioned earlier in this volume, it is real-world resources that are the most effective (see 2.3.3.2). There are a number of reasons why such resources should be systematically incorporated into the task design. Such resources contain natural language, offer meaningful messages, enable learners to utilise non-linguistic hints and show the instantaneous relevance of what is done in the classroom and what is needed in the outside world (Brosnan, Brown, & Hood, 1984).

Nunan's (1989) concept of input is popular in language education because of its simplicity. However, it is advisable that input be perceived as a much broader concept. Input must be linked to various cognitive aspects that come into play when it is comprehended and integrated into a learner's interlanguage (Ellis, 2003; Gilabert, Baron, & Llanes, 2009). The more complex the input, the more laborious its processing. Some of the cognitive aspects include: attention, decoding, different types of knowledge (e.g. background, linguistic, lexical), phonology, syntax and semantics. Text-based tasks are a good example. According to Kintsch and van Dijk (1983, p. 337), comprehension of textual input is created in learners' minds through different levels of representation. Therefore, if learners "are unable to imagine a situation in which certain individuals have the properties or relations indicated by the [textual input], [they] fail to understand the text itself".

Kintsch and van Dijk (1983) also emphasise that learners engaged in processing input in text-based tasks construct three mental representations of the texts used, namely: *surface/verbatim representation*, *textbase/propositional representation* and *situational representation*. The first reflects images of the surface structure of texts, the second puts the propositional content of texts into focus, where propositions are related to states or events possessing a truth value with reference to real or imaginary worlds. The third representation only comes into existence through the combination of information from the propositional representation and learners' prior knowledge stored in the memory.

Another important point to remember is that there are two types of input: *finely-tuned input* and *roughly-tuned input*. The former is vital when elements of natural language are introduced to students. Krashen (1982) states that finely-tuned input is represented by texts in which the target language has been carefully selected so as not to be higher than a student's current level of language proficiency. Finely-tuned input is appropriate for tasks promoting conscious learning. Krashen argues that *roughly-tuned input*, also referred to as the $i + 1$ formula (see 2.2.1.1), is also indispensable in the learning process and should follow the presentation of new language items. The value of tasks with roughly-tuned input is that such tasks contain elements language learners are not yet ready to learn. Roughly-tuned input is challenging for learners. It extends the boundaries of their current knowledge and encourages them to use various strategies (see 2.3.1) to understand the conveyed meaning. In this respect, Krashen is in agreement with Vygotsky, whose concept of ZPD is analogous to the $i + 1$ formula.

It should therefore be clear from what has been said so far that input invites learners to a meaning-making process in which they have various options to explore tasks. At the same time, input appears to contribute to creating a unique learning environment where learners make sense of their learning experience.

Additionally, input can be a criterion for task classification (see 3.2). Since this book promotes the fostering of learner autonomy, two types of tasks need to be distinguished: *content-related* and *learning-related* (see 7.3). The former includes tasks related to the content/theme of a particular lesson or course book unit. Such tasks may focus on the development of reading or writing skills. They may aim at promoting vocabulary or practising a specific language structure. An additional aim of these tasks may be related to the promotion of various aspects of learner autonomy, for example, critical thinking, negotiation, collaboration and problem-solving.

Learning-related tasks, on the other hand, centre on the learning process itself. They are essential for the process of fostering learner autonomy. As indicated in Chapter Two, learner autonomy training aims at increasing learner awareness of independence, decision-making, responsibility and reflection in language learning (see 2.3.1). Hence, learning-related tasks mainly focus on learning strategies, reflection and assessment of one's own or others' performance. The most important thing, however, is that teachers regularly employ both types of tasks in their practice. Only then can high-quality provision be ensured.

The discussion of input would not be complete without mentioning the importance of instructional materials discussed in Chapter Three. These materials provide the input that undergoes extensive exploration in the classroom. As mentioned above, materials include textbooks, newspapers, CDs/DVDs and handouts. These materials promote input in various modalities (see 3.1). What is more, it is common to see different modalities in one task. The main reason for this is that multiple modalities enhance language acquisition (Paivio, 2007; Sueyoshi & Hardison, 2005). For example, it is suggested that written input be supported with images while learning vocabulary (Sydorenko, 2010). However, task input should not include too many modalities, for this may lead to cognitive overload in learners. For example, using audio, video and captions simultaneously while practising L2 listening may be overwhelming for L2 learners. The three different types of stimuli require a lot of attention on the part of the learners. As a result, it is very likely that in tasks with audio, video and captions learners will not pay attention to the auditory input because of the available captions (Vanderplank, 1988).

That being said, it is vital that language educators demonstrate to in-service teachers in communities of practice the type of input, materials and tools the teachers could incorporate into their own tasks. For this purpose, I will use Task 2 included in the bank of tasks (see 7.3) in Chapter Seven. This task focuses on designing an online newsletter. It consists of a number of stages and requires different types of materials and tools. These include: a fill-in table to be put on the board, examples of school newsletters, computers, Internet and colour printers.

The title of the task discloses that Task 2 is part of a unit with the theme SCHOOL. First of all, it is important that teachers prepare the task instruction (see Figure 30) and the stimulus material (see Figure 31) that will form the task. The instruction must be as clear and as concise as possible. On the other hand, the stimulus material needs to link the task to the theme of the unit and the input material already covered in the class. To contextualise the task, teachers could use various images (see Figure 31). This link is crucial because it activates student background knowledge (see 3.1.1.1) and helps them to prepare for the brainstorming activity in which the students think about ideas, facts and information that can be included in school newsletters.

You are going to design an online newsletter about your school for your partner school in England.

1. With your partner, brainstorm ideas and think about facts and information that should be included in a newsletter.

2. Share your ideas with your class and write interesting points on the board (e.g. history, courses, admission procedures, final exams, staff, school trips, home town, etc.).

3. In groups of four, decide on the design of the newsletter and its sections. Choose graphics and visuals to be used.

4. Within each group, decide who is responsible for different elements of the project. At the same time, collaborate and assess the work of your partners.

5. Make sure the initial draft of the project is ready by the end of the class.

6. Finish the project at home.

7. Present your newsletter during the next class period.

8. Comment on the newsletters of your classmates.

Figure 30. Task instruction

Figure 31. Task stimulus material

Next, the instruction and the images must be put together, and different colours and font sizes must be employed. The task should please and attract a student's eye. It is advisable that the task have a number and a title. All these elements must be properly laid out so that the material is reasonably easy to process (see Task 2 in 7.3).

Additionally, Task 2 requires two other elements that should be available as photocopiables in the teacher's book. One of the elements is a table with pre-defined categories for students to fill in (see Figure 32).

Courses			

Figure 32. Task table with pre-defined categories

The table can be displayed on the board by an overhead projector so that everyone can see it well. Teachers need to design the table, but provide only some of its categories. The students supply other categories after they have shared opinions with their classmates. The completed table then serves as input for the next stage in the present task.

The other element of the task input is the various templates of school newsletters (see Figure 33). Teachers either design templates of such newsletters or use ready-made examples available online. It is necessary that these templates are shown to the class before they start designing their own newsletters. Students then have a general idea of the layout and graphics they could use. Those templates are likely to generate new ideas among students with regard to their final product – the newsletter.

Figure 33. Newsletter templates

As can be seen, input determines the degree of the task's success. The more attractive the input, the more engaging the task. Teachers can either prepare the input themselves or use ready-made sources available both in print and online. The ready-made sources need to be carefully chosen. Therefore, it is vital that language practitioners follow the various selection criteria presented in Chapter Three (see 3.1.1). It is important that the language (see 3.1.1.2) and the content (see 3.1.1.3) of the stimulus newsletters fall within the ZPD (see 2.2.1.1) of the students. Otherwise, they will not be able to use them. Also, teachers must make sure their tasks are not too demanding (see 3.2.2). Tasks which are too demanding may impede the promotion of both classroom and real-world discourses. Clearly, a teacher's creativity is the key to success, no matter whether they develop new or adapt existing sources. On no account should creativity be regarded as an inherited disposition. Creativity can be taught and is needed in the classroom to trigger language learners' self-esteem, motivation and attainment (Downing, 1997).

7.1.2.3 PROCEDURES

Task procedures can be defined as guidelines or directives for task performance (Ellis, 2003; Nunan, 2004). The latter is nothing less than a process that begins with a task explanation and ends with a task execution (Thomas & Reinders, 2010). It is the time when language learners process the task in terms of their own frames, knowledge and experience (Breen, 1989). The task is completed through active involvement in meaning and content negotiation as well as input comprehension and output production.

Task completion rests on various procedures. These procedures must be well-defined because they not only serve to structure the task, but also guarantee its successful completion. Task procedures may be approached by learners in different ways. Some prefer to follow the prescribed procedure, whereas others may choose a different route to complete a task. The choice depends on the learning styles and experiences of the students (see 3.1.1.4).

With this in mind, while designing tasks, teachers need to decide how a particular task will be performed in the classroom. For example, the following question must be asked: *Will students be working individually, in pairs or in groups while performing a given task?* Well-designed tasks boost learner participation in a variety of ways. For example, participation can be encouraged by arranging seating to promote different types of work, creating opportunities for collaborative learning (see 2.2.1.4), assigning roles to students and setting expectations for participation (Dalglish, Evans, & Lawson, 2011; Hativa, 2000). Secondly, if a task is a mini-project, it is recommended that it clearly specifies how many stages there are, what the stages individually involve, which sections follow, who is responsible for what in each stage and so on. Thirdly, it is vital that tasks specify whether they focus on obtaining skills or using skills. For instance, the goal of some tasks can be helping students to learn new skills (e.g. social expressiveness), whereas other tasks may be concerned with encouraging students to make use of skills they already possess (e.g. assessing their learning). Fourthly, tasks may focus on developing either fluency or accuracy, which, contrary to a common belief, are complimentary. It is Brumfit (1984, p. 51) that details the fluency-accuracy contradiction in his *Communicative Methodology in Language Teaching*:

> (...) the demand to produce work for display to the teacher in order that evaluation and feedback could be supplied conflicted directly with the demand to perform adequately in the kind of natural circumstances for which teaching was presumably a preparation. Language display for evaluation tended to lead to a concern for accuracy, monitoring, reference rules, possibly explicit knowledge, problem-solving and evidence of skill getting. In contrast, language use requires fluency, expression rules, a reliance on implicit knowledge and automatic performance. It will on occasion also require monitoring and problem-solving strategies, but these will not be the most prominent features as they tend to be in the conventional model where the student produces, the teacher corrects, and the student tries again.

Lastly, it is important that tasks detail what kind of educational technology (see 2.3.4), if any, is to be used, for what purposes and how it contributes to the final product (Krajka, 2007). As can be seen, all these procedures are of primary importance as they provide guidelines for effective classroom performance. Clarity, structure and, to a large degree, the success of a learning task can thus be warranted.

7.1.2.4 TEACHER ROLES

The complex process of developing pedagogical tasks for learner autonomy necessitates a brief discussion of the many roles teachers play in the classroom (e.g. McGrath, 2013; Müller-Hartmann & Schocker-von-Ditfurth, 2011; Renandya, 2012; Willis & Willis, 2007). In this section, the main focus will be on those roles which are directly related to designing and later administering learner autonomy tasks. As pointed out in the previous chapter, it is advisable that teachers involve students in task design (see also 7.2). Teacher and learner roles can then affect each other mutually, causing new relationships and channels of communication to arise. The intensity of these relationships depends on the extent to which teachers involve students in task design. Therefore, the discussion will also indicate which of the following teacher roles could be supported or even taken over by students.

First of all, teachers are expected to be proficient users of the target language. The foreign language competence of the teachers must be close to that of a native speaker. Teachers must be able to provide high quality input (see 7.1.2.2) and a good model to be followed in the use of learner autonomy tasks by the classroom community.

Also, it is essential that teachers ensure that the task features (see 3.2), text selection criteria (3.1.1) and elements of social constructivist pedagogy (see 2.2.1) discussed earlier in this volume are all incorporated in the process of task design. Only such tasks stand a good chance of promoting learner autonomy effectively.

According to van Avermaet, Colpin, van Gorp, Bogaert and van der Branden (2006, p. 175), teachers are responsible for "motivating the learner to invest intensive mental energy in task completion" and to ensure that such processes as "the negotiation of meaning and content, the comprehension of rich input, the production of output and focus on form" are activated. In task-driven instruction, teacher roles are strictly linked to the task planning, the task performance and the post-task assessment phases (van Avermaet, Colpin, van Gorp, Bogaert, & van der Branden, 2006; Willis, 2009). The planning phase, for example, includes both mental and physical actions that teachers perform while preparing tasks. At this stage, teachers need to ask themselves about the types of tasks they intend to prepare. Teachers also need to show that their tasks have the potential to stimulate meaningful action in the classroom and that the tasks affect both cognitive and interactional processes in students. If such a clarification is not made, deep conceptual learning (see 3.2.1) will not occur. In the performance stage, teachers must ensure that cognitive and interactional processes take place smoothly in the classroom. The potential of the task must also be fully exploited by learners. In the last stage, the focus of the teacher's action is twofold: assessing students' engagement in the tasks and evaluating task effectiveness (van Avermaet, Colpin, van Gorp, Bogaert, & van der Branden, 2006).

It is important, furthermore, that language educators clarify to teachers that the approach to designing learner autonomy tasks must be creative. In such an approach, as Breen (1987, p. 43) describes, teachers:

> (...) enter into a 'dialogue' with language learners for whom the tasks are being planned. Such a dialogue (...) [is to contribute to the production of] a careful cycle of [learner autonomy] tasks concerning the learners' own purposes in learning the language, learners' background knowledge, their own preferred ways of working, their views on the 'best' uses to which the classroom can be put, and their interests, motivations and attitudes in relation to learning the language. This cycle [should also involve] learners in the evaluation of [these] tasks.

Additionally, it is necessary that teachers adopt the roles of picture consultants, media consultants, graphic designers, piloting invigilators and editors. For example, the picture consultant selects illustrations to go with the textual material in complex tasks. The media consultant selects different types of media to be used in task design. The graphic designer works on the layout of the tasks. The piloting invigilator is responsible for collecting data about the effectiveness of the designed tasks from both teachers and students. This stage seeks to provide feedback on whether or not the tasks actually work in the classroom (Davison, 1998). The editor eventually reviews the created tasks and prepares the final draft to be either photocopied and distributed among the teachers at school or sent for publication.

If students are involved in the process of designing tasks (see 7.2), they can offer support at the picture consultation, media consultation and graphic design stages. The picture consultation stage could even be entirely handed over to students. Students design a bank of images to be used in tasks. The other two stages are a little more complex, requiring that both teachers and students work together. Both perspectives are equally important and guarantee the success of new tasks.

The aim of the next section is to discuss the notion of classroom setting.

7.1.2.5 CLASSROOM SETTING

This feature is linked to classroom arrangements either specified or implied by the learning task. The classroom setting decides whether or not particular tasks can be successfully carried out in the classroom. It is fundamental that tasks promote different working patterns. According to Hue (2007), tasks should promote the following three aspects of classroom management: *physical* (e.g. seating layouts), *instructional* (e.g. teaching strategies or assessment practices) and *socio-affective* (e.g. collaboration, removal of communication barriers). All of them are inextricably connected and, when well-orchestrated, contribute to creating a positive climate that impacts student learning (Belvel, 2010).

It should also be noted that more and more importance has recently been attached to learning outside the classroom. The influx of technological devices that support modern language instruction and the popularity of collaborative learning (see 2.2.1.4) have replaced traditional classrooms with computer labs or multimedia centres (e.g. Cennamo, Ross, & Ertmer, 2010; Erben & Sarieva, 2008). One may argue, though, that the concept of *classroom* has taken on a new meaning. The issue is not which viewpoint is better or should be preferred. The essence lies in the learning environment itself and its diversity. The more varied the learning environment, the more enhanced the cognitive, personal and social growth of the learners (Ming-tak & Wai-shing, 2008).

The discussion of learning environments would not be complete without mentioning Legutke's (1998) metaphors for a task-orientated language classroom. The main reason why these metaphors are discussed here is that they all harmonise with the concepts discussed in this book. In other words, these metaphors reflect social constructivist pedagogy (see 2.2), of which learner autonomy is a significant part. According to Legutke (1998), the language classroom can be described by means of six metaphors. First of all, the language classroom is a *project room* or a *workshop*, where the teaching-learning processes are based on knowledge construction through tasks. Secondly, the language classroom is a *training centre*, where meaningful and lifelong learning is promoted via innovative pedagogy and interactive tutorials. Thirdly, the language classroom is described as an *observatory*. In such an observatory, language learners are surrounded by authentic tasks (see 3.2.1) and authentic texts (see 2.3.3.2). Regular exposure to language in use encourages students to interact with real-life discourse and to reflect on authentic contexts in which the target language occurs. Fourthly, the language classroom is a *communication centre* in which meaningful and purposeful communication is stimulated (see 3.2.3). In such a classroom, communication is broadly understood and includes educational technology (see 2.3.4). Thus, *synchronous* (i.e. immediate) and *asynchronous* (i.e. delayed) communication is taken into account. Finally, the language classroom is a *teaching centre* with a well defined and developed curriculum. Students are provided with ample opportunities to enhance their knowledge and skills. The *teaching centre* also supports the students as they learn and prepares them for the challenges of real life outside the school walls.

Legutke's metaphors are very interesting and precisely specify various roles the language classroom plays in the teaching-learning process. It is, therefore, recommended that language educators draw the attention of in-service teachers to these six metaphors. The complete clarity with which Legutke conceptualises the language classroom tempts me to discard my own *language classroom* metaphor that squeezes together all the notions presented above, resulting in a less reader-friendly framework.

In order to remain consistent with the social constructivist tradition, I tend to compare the language classroom to a *mountain trekking expedition*. The task of learning English is nothing less than climbing a mountain in terms of the challenge that learners face. For some, the language classroom is like a mountain range – a frightening place for students who are unsure of what or who they may find there. Others are curious to explore it as they perceive the language classroom as a place full of surprises, the unknown and the unexpected. One day can be fun, whereas the next day may be full of stress and exertion. Of course, a trekking expedition always requires a guide (i.e. a teacher), who is sometimes more and sometimes less experienced. The guide provides trekkers (i.e. language learners) with engaging stories and objects (e.g. realia) and supports and takes care of them during the journey (i.e. learning process). The mountain range across which the group travels can be compared to the role of knowledge. The elements involved in knowledge can be found at various locations on the knowledge landscape. Thus, the climbers must be attentive in order not to miss any aspects of the new experience. Since trekking in the mountains is very challenging, it requires the use of prior knowledge to construct new information and the ability to solve problems encountered in the unexplored land. Knowledge construction is supported by guide books (i.e. course books and dictionaries) that the trekkers carry with them to feel more confident and secure. The climbers constantly make plans and decisions, face risks, assess situations, and then cope with the consequences. Trying to make progress, the travellers sometimes work independently. Sometimes they are required to work in pairs or in groups. They are always supported and monitored by the guide as well. The trekkers use technology during their adventures, but since it is not always possible, they have to resort to other communication strategies at times. As a result, communication takes different forms, and is often determined by situations travellers find themselves in. It is the duty of the guide to safely shift the travellers across the mountains and encourage them to pick up relevant elements before reaching their destination (i.e. task completion and tests). At this stage, the guide checks how well the group remembers their discussions and how well the group is able to successfully demonstrate some of the skills learnt during the complex travel. If the outcome is satisfactory, the guide invites the group to join the next and more demanding part of their expedition. Before this happens, however, the guide must carefully plan the next stage, analysing both the situation and the travellers' needs (see 7.1.2).

7.1.2.6 FEEDBACK

The last parameter to be discussed is feedback. Feedback refers to the process of assessment of learners' work invested into a task (Candlin, 1987). It may have different addressees (e.g. peers or the teacher), may be delivered in different forms (e.g. oral, written, non-verbal) and may be submitted at different points in time (e.g. immediate feedback or delayed feedback). Since feedback is an integral part of the learning-teaching-assessment cycle, it is vital that tasks either implicitly or explicitly state who is in charge of giving feedback, when and how it is related to the content (see 7.1.2.2) or the process of a given task (see 7.1.2.3). Effective feedback addresses crucial tenets of the learning process, providing advice for improvement in a clear, direct, descriptive, constructive, realistic, ongoing and timely way (Black & Wiliam, 1998; Heritage, 2007; Tuttle, 2009).

7.1.3 PILOTING TASKS

Once all the variables in Stage Two have been taken into consideration, the tasks must be made ready for pilot testing – Stage Three of the present model.

The purpose of the pilot stage is to conduct the following two processes: *analysis* and *evaluation*. The former concentrates on tasks and carries out their objective examination (Tomlinson, 2003c). This process aims to answer the following questions: *What kind of challenge do the tasks pose? What extra scaffolding should be provided, if any? Do they correspond to learner needs and interests?* Evaluation, on the other hand, centres on the users of learning tasks; it reports on various effects tasks exert on learners (Tomlinson, 2003c). Both processes are vital as they provide teachers with useful information about their products (Amrani, 2011). Additionally, teacher feedback and student feedback show how both groups perceive and use the newly produced tasks.

Although many sources mix analysis and evaluation (e.g. Cunningsworth, 1984; Mariani, 1983), it is advisable that these two processes be separated and one used before the other. For example, analysis of tasks could precede evaluation (Tomlinson, 2003c). Littlejohn's (2011) model of evaluation, slightly adapted for the purposes of the current discussion, consists of the following four phases: *analysis of the target situation of use, task analysis, match and evaluation* (determining the appropriacy of the tasks to the target situation of use) and *action*. The first phase focuses on such aspects as the cultural context, the institution, the course, the teacher and the learner. The second stage begins with an objective account of facts about the context, and then moves to a subjective examination of expectations and needs and "inferences about the appropriateness and value of particular methodologies and content" (Littlejohn, 2011, p. 202). The third phase seeks to relate the appropriateness of various aspects of design and publication to the target situation in which particular tasks are used. Lastly, the action phase requires that evaluators decide whether the tasks under investigation should be accepted, adapted, supplemented or rejected.

In practice, in the evaluation process which is thoroughly discussed in the literature (e.g. Brown, 1997; Donovan, 1998; Littlejohn, 2011), teachers distribute new tasks among small groups of students and teachers to be reviewed and constructively criticised. In order to conduct valid and reliable evaluation of learning tasks, it is essential that the entire process is based on the various criteria discussed in Chapter Three (see 3.2). Also, it is important that the value of the tasks is measured while they are being used and while they are observed being used. Hence, it is advisable that tasks be evaluated by both students and teachers. Checklists or questionnaires are instruments that can be employed in the evaluation process (McGrath, 2002). Following Tomlinson's (2003c) concept of whilst-use evaluation, the following tenets can be taken into consideration: clarity of instructions, clarity of layout, comprehensibility of texts, credibility of tasks, achievability of tasks, achievement of performance objectives, potential for localisation, practicality, teachability, flexibility, appeal, motivating power, impact and effectiveness in facilitating learning.

Likewise, it is strongly recommended that students and teachers be actively involved in the post-use evaluation (Tomlinson, 2003c). The purpose of this type of evaluation is to measure the outcomes of task utilisation. This stage allows for making key decisions about task application, adaptation or rejection. Some tools that can be used to measure task outcomes are: can-do tests, questionnaires, interviews or post-lesson reports. For more information on post-use evaluation instruments, see Cunningsworth (1995) and Tomlinson (2003c). Additionally, teacher-student and teacher-teacher collaboration (see 2.2.1.4), promoted at this stage, invariably leads to intensive reflection (see 7.1.1), critical analysis and to an ongoing cycle of questions. All of these factors are very likely to enhance the quality of new tasks (DuFour, 2004; Merrill, Tennyson, & Posey, 1992).

7.1.4 REVISING TASKS

In Stage Four, teachers analyse the feedback they received in the previous phase. This useful information, more often than not, presents different perspectives on task design. The reviewers not only come from different backgrounds and bring diverse learning and teaching experiences, but also have individual needs, wants and expectations. Therefore, it is essential that language educators encourage teachers to look critically at the developed tasks and adapt them (see 3.3.1) with regard to the valuable observations of others. Such an approach enables teachers to include McDonough and Shaw's (1993) principles of localisation and personalisation in task design. The former refers to acknowledging the need for contextual relevance, whereas the latter is related to addressing learner interests and satisfying their individual needs, for example, academic, educational or professional (see 3.1.1.4). The adaptation process (see 3.3.1) should take form and content into account. As far as form is concerned, alterations can refer to colour (e.g. intensity), typeface (e.g. bold) as well as text rearrangement and visual distribution of certain items. Modifications of content, on the other hand, may involve replacing difficult words with their simpler equivalents or clarifying confusing concepts.

7.1.5 IMPLEMENTING TASKS AND MONITORING THEIR USE AND IMPACT

In the last stage, language educators guide teachers in putting the revised tasks into effect. Teachers are encouraged to regularly monitor use, effectiveness and the impact of the tasks. The latter, attracting learner inquisitiveness, imagination and attention, can be measured by learner opinions about task novelty, variety, appealing content and presentation and, last but not least, achievable challenge (Tomlinson, 2011b). Regular vigilance and close observation of tasks allow teachers to see how tasks work in the classroom. The monitoring stage may take a number of forms, including observations, feedback sessions, written reports or reviews (Richards, 2001). Of course, students differ in their attitudes, motivation and learning styles (see 3.1.1.4), and therefore what works in one classroom context does not necessarily work in another. Such a situation obliges teachers to adapt what already exists (see 3.3.1) or developing completely new tasks. It is imperative that learners' needs be satisfied (see 7.1.2). Naturally, the processes of task adaptation or production are invariably preceded by reflection (see 7.1.1), which begins a new cycle in the spiral model.

7.2 FINAL REMARKS ON THE MODEL

The present model presents a number of procedures that teachers are strongly advised to incorporate into the process of developing their own tasks. Even though the model under discussion has been designed with ELT communities of practice in mind, it provides plenty of room for students to be involved in the process of task design. In fact, with the teacher's consent, the student participation is possible at each of the five stages of the model. In this way, students can contribute to task development, task evaluation or task revision. This advantage closely coincides with McGrath's (2013, p. 21) views on the relationship between learners and materials. He points out that learners should:

- be involved in textbook evaluation and selection or decisions about which parts of a textbook should be studied;
- be shown how to make independent use of both classroom materials and out-of-class resources;
- be encouraged to interact critically with the content of textbooks and other materials;
- provide supplementary materials to be used in class; and
- generate materials that can be used by other learners.

The idea of engaging students in choosing, producing and evaluating class materials has also been raised by Assinder (1991), Campbell and Kryszewska (1992), Tudor (1993) and McGrath (2013).

Why is it important to encourage language learners to take part in designing pedagogical tasks? The answer is simple. Involving learners in the designing of tasks has clear benefits. For instance, apart from using the target language spontaneously and creatively, they develop and practise various skills and learning strategies (see 2.3.1). The process of developing tasks engages learners in collaborative work and problem-solving (see 2.2.1.4). They then have a chance to make use of their own creativitity, talents and diverse experiences (see 3.1.1.4). They also become part of a meaningful activity, playing the role of the knowers. Additionally, learners make choices as well as give opinions about the significance and attractiveness of their products.

As far as teachers are concerned, learner involvement in task production provides the teachers with feedback (see 7.1.2.6) on their students' current state of knowledge. Besides this, teachers have an opportunity to observe their class in a different situation. The teachers become familiar with the students' needs, wants and preferences not only for instructional materials and tasks, but for classroom work as well. Finally, teachers gain more information about their learners and the process of learning.

Having specified some of the benefits of involving learners in producing pedagogical tasks, it seems fitting to present an exemplary product developed by my students. The following task was designed in the secondary school where I began my teaching career in 1996. I used to regularly invite my students to materials or task development workshops, which were run in this school as extra-curricular activities. Some of the workshops were theme-based, whereas others were either teacher-guided or student-led. The purpose of these workshops was fourfold:
- to encourage learners to produce and take ownership of materials/tasks used in the classroom;
- to involve students in the decision-making process regarding teaching and learning;
- to promote collaborative learning and authentic communication in the target language;
- to stimulate students to make use of their imagination, creativity, talents and skills to contribute to the bank of classroom materials/tasks.

The workshops were attended by students who represented individual learning styles, diverse learning experiences and different levels of target language proficiency. All these factors greatly contributed to generating interesting tasks, an example of which is displayed below (see Figure 34).

This task was produced by a group of upper-intermediate (CERF B2) students. They based their task on a self-designed questionnaire. More specifically, they wanted to involve their classmates in a discussion on listening skills. To personalise the task, these upper-intermediate students listed six questions, all of which started with *I*. This task was to encourage their classmates to reflect on their own learning, and in meaningful conversation related to a relevant topic.

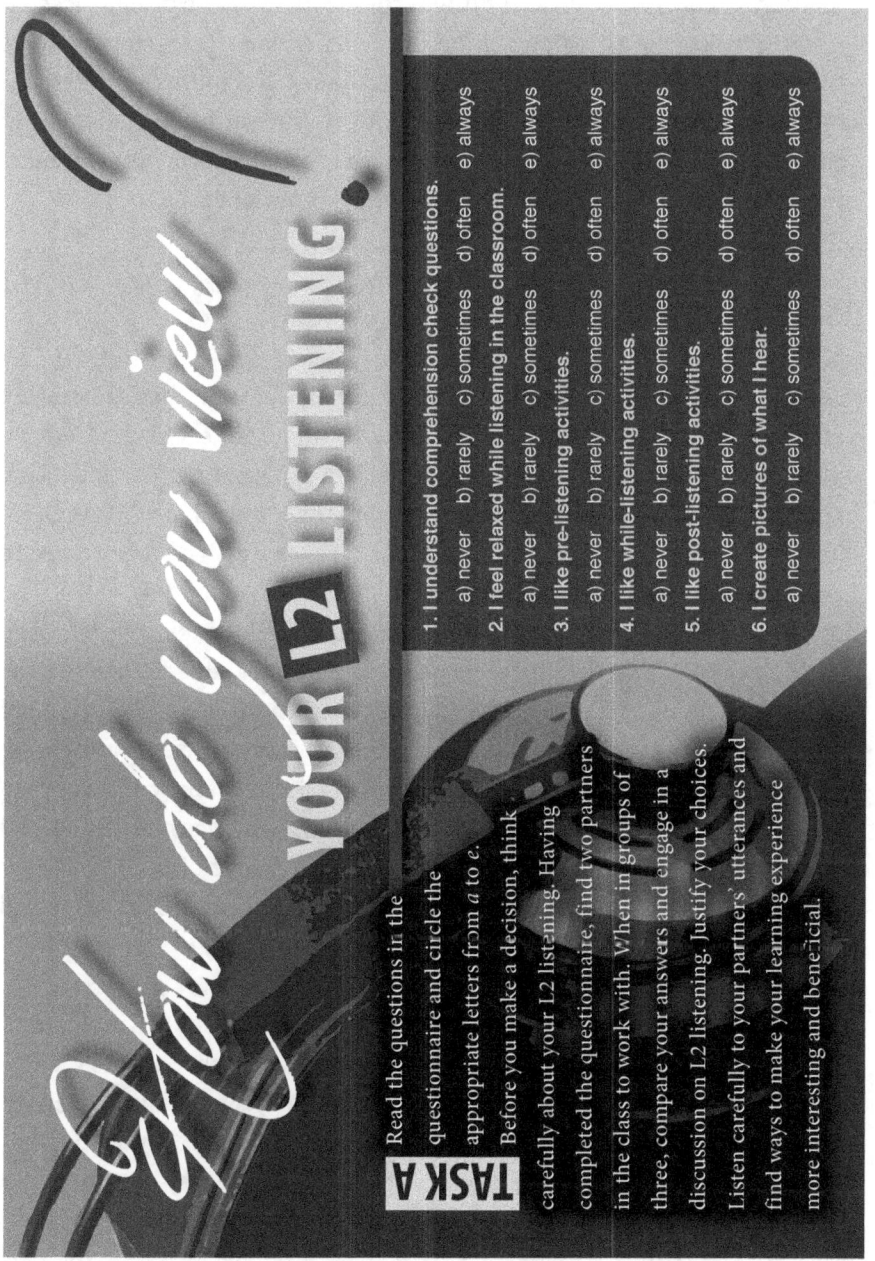

Figure 34. Task A: Foreign language listening questionnaire

By and large, it is advisable that learners be regularly engaged in developing tasks. Only in this way can learners determine or negotiate the content of their course as well as highlight their concerns and preferences for learning tasks (see 2.3.2.1). Additionally, learners bring a variety of skills and talents to the process, which allows them to include their personal voice in the final product. In turn, employing student-generated tasks in the classroom highlights not only their own usefulness, but also the value of the learner's personal and (inter)cultural experiences.

7.3 A BANK OF TASKS FOR FOSTERING LEARNER AUTONOMY

Having presented the significance of engaging learners in the creation process of the task, it is now appropriate to turn the teachers' attention to the ready-made tasks for developing learner autonomy. The collection consists of ten tasks which match the previously introduced content-related and learning-related task divisions (see 7.1.2.2). The former group is composed of tasks 1-3, whereas the latter consists of tasks 4-10. The design of these tasks is supported by recent applied linguistic research and social constructivist language pedagogy, both of which underpin the line of argument in this volume. These tasks stimulate negotiations of meaning through which ample comprehensible input is offered and learners are pushed to produce messages. These tasks also engage learners in constructing the activities, to which process they bring their individual motives and goals. This bank also offers a wide range of practical ideas and provides teachers with useful information. The aims of the tasks and suggested timings are included.

Additionally, it should be clarified that both types of tasks are important. Their focus, complexity and nature are distinct, though. For this reason, both of the task types take different places on a task continuum. Considering the focus of this book, it is the learning-related tasks that take priority because their main objective is to boost learner autonomy development. The following collection of learning-related tasks aims at identifying and practising learning strategies; assessing one's knowledge, skills and performance in the target language and reflecting on learning experiences.

task 01

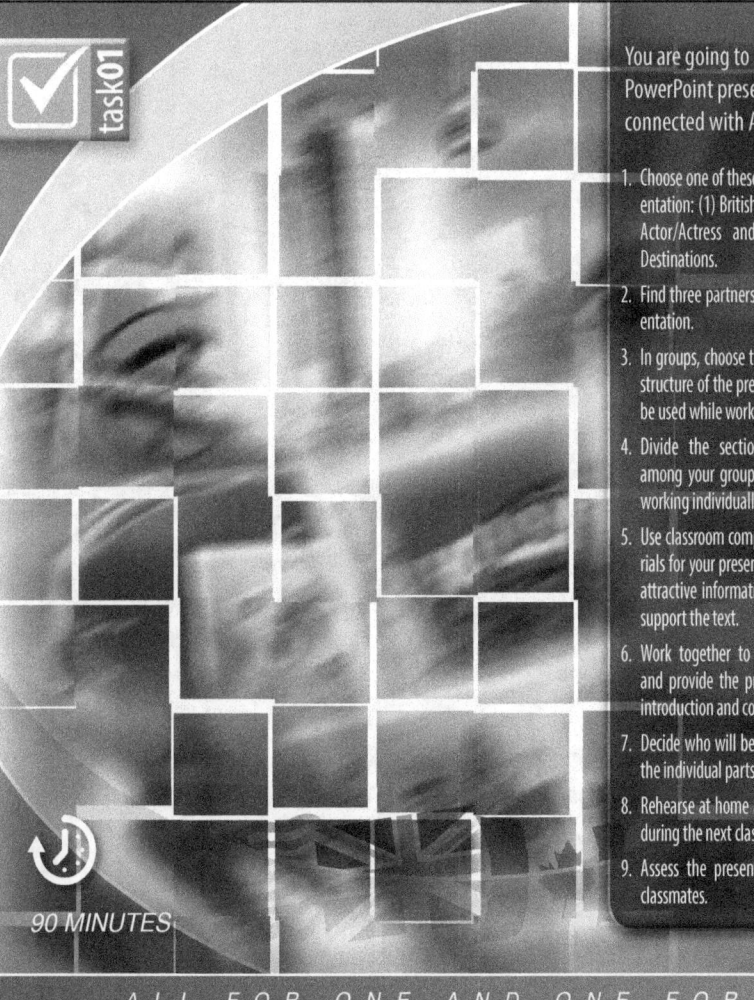

You are going to prepare a 15-minute PowerPoint presentation on a topic connected with Anglophone culture.

1. Choose one of these three topics for your presentation: (1) British Pub Culture, (2) American Actor/Actress and (3) Australian Holiday Destinations.
2. Find three partners to work with on the presentation.
3. In groups, choose the topic and decide on the structure of the presentation and strategies to be used while working on the project.
4. Divide the sections of your presentation among your group members, and then start working individually on your section.
5. Use classroom computers to find online materials for your presentation. Select relevant and attractive information, plus visual material to support the text.
6. Work together to combine all the sections and provide the presentation with a concise introduction and conclusion.
7. Decide who will be responsible for presenting the individual parts to the class.
8. Rehearse at home and give your presentation during the next class period.
9. Assess the presentations delivered by your classmates.

90 MINUTES

ALL FOR ONE AND ONE FOR ALL

ANGLOPHONE CULTURE

TEACHER'S NOTES
Level. Intermediate and above
Aims:
1. to prompt peer collaboration, negotiation, self-/peer-assessment and decision-making.
2. to implement computer technology in L2 learning and practise computer skills.
3. to practise delivering presentations in L2.
4. to integrate and practise all the four language skills.

RATIONALE
According to Green and Brown (2002), classroom projects are highly desirable in the modern teaching-learning process. They incorporate the philosophy of *all for one and one for all*. Students collaborate with one another and take responsibility for the final product. In other words, classroom projects, being a cooperative effort, provide students with opportunities to combine their language skills with numerous learning strategies, various individual talents and different computer technologies.

School Events

 Task02

You are going to design an online newsletter about your school for your partner school in England.

1. With your partner, brainstorm ideas and think about facts and information that should be included in a newsletter.

2. Share your ideas with your class and write interesting points on the board (*e.g. history, courses, admission procedures, final exams, staff, school trips, home town, etc.*).

3. In groups of four, decide on the design of the newsletter and its sections. Choose graphics and visuals to be used.

4. Within each group, decide who is responsible for different elements of the project. At the same time, collaborate and assess the work of your partners.

5. Make sure the initial draft of the project is ready by the end of the class.

6. Finish the project at home.

7. Present your newsletter during the next class period.

8. Comment on the newsletters of your classmates.

TEACHER'S NOTES

Rationale: As the literature demonstrates (Barron, Orwig, Ivers, & Lilavois, 2002; Green & Brown, 2002), classroom projects involve students in creating and communicating meaning in various ways. Many opportunities are provided by the technological tools students use in these collaborative endeavours. Students interact with the rich linguistic environment which, supported by images, graphics and animations, simplifies difficult and abstract notions.

Level: Intermediate and above

Aims:
1. to prompt peer collaboration, negotiation, self-/peer-assessment and decision-making.
2. to implement computer technology in L2 learning and practise computer skills.
3. to practise delivering presentations in L2.
4. to integrate and practise all the four language skills.

90 MINS.

HORROR FILMS

You are going to work on a ten-stage horror film project:

Task 03

01 Listen to some sound effects from a horror film. Look at the provided images and guess which of them matches the material presented on the CD.

02 Find a partner to discuss your choice. Talk about your feelings and emotions towards the CD material. Use your imagination to anticipate what the film is about.

03 Listen to an interview with Mr Wilson, who directed the film. While listening, look at the handout with three horror film synopses. Choose the right summary of the film, thinking about the CD material and the three images provided earlier. Find a partner and compare your choices.

04 Read a short version of the filmed story. Work in groups of four and discuss the following

▶ Can you divide the text into parts? If so, how many?

▶ Can you label them?

▶ Can you see any words/phrases which describe/suggest any emotions (e.g. shock, fear, etc.)?

▶ Is there anything in the text that involves the senses?

▶ What parts of the text create an atmosphere of mystery or suspense?

▶ What tenses are used?

05 Write your own horror story (300-400 words). Continue working in groups of four. Decide on the following elements:

▶ PERIOD (e.g. when there is a harvest moon)

▶ LOCATION (e.g. a luxurious hotel, a medieval castle)

▶ CHARACTERS (e.g. a honeymoon couple)

▶ EVENTS (e.g. bride disappears)

06 Decide on the story title, the plot (order of events), plus how to set the scene in the beginning part and how to dramatically end the story.

07 Decide who is going to be responsible for

▶ Writing the beginning of the story (S1)

▶ Writing the main body (S2+S3)

▶ Writing the ending of the story (S4)

08 Combine the three parts into one text. Work in pairs and read the text in terms of

▶ Coherence and cohesion (pair 1)

▶ Adequate title and proper use of dramatic words/phrases (pair 2)

09 Critically assess your story and make any necessary changes. Next, save your story as a Word document. Support the text with images or drawings taken from the Internet.

10 Email your story to the teacher for correction.

90 MINS

TEACHER'S NOTES

Level: Intermediate and above.

Aims: ▶1 to integrate and practise all the four language skills. ▶2 to engage students in creative writing. ▶3 to prompt peer collaboration negotiation, self-/peer-assessment and decision-making.

Rationale: According to recent academic debates (e.g. Burkhardt, 2006; Schlepphege, 2009), creative writing classroom projects are highly desirable in the modern teaching-learning process. By being involved in creative writing projects, L2 learners not only practise all the four language skills, but also participate in L2 literacy development in general. Creative writing projects also stimulate a student's imagination, critical thinking and artistic expression in the target language.

task 04

You are going to complete a self-reflection sheet on your reading in English. Read through the sentences carefully and tick any of the statements which are true about you. Next, find a partner to compare and discuss the selected points. When you have finished, actively participate in the class discussion about how you view your reading in English.

How do You View Your L2 Reading?

01 I read and understand
a) texts concerned with contemporary problems. ☐
b) contemporary literary prose (e.g. short stories). ☐

02 I find supporting information for main ideas in texts. ☐

03 I read for different purposes (e.g. to search for simple information, to integrate information or to learn from texts). ☐

04 I like looking up all new words/phrases in a dictionary. ☐

05 I list new words/phrases in my notebook, and then learn them. ☐

06 I think it is important to understand all the words in the texts. ☐

07 I think it is important to translate L2 texts into my native language. ☐

08 I like the following types of reading activities:
a) multiple choice ☐
b) matching titles with paragraphs ☐
c) .... ☐
d) .... ☐

09 I dislike the following types of reading activities:
a) jumbled-texts – putting paragraphs in order ☐
b) cloze tests ☐
c) .... ☐
d) .... ☐

10 I think my reading speed is good. ☐

25 MINS

TEACHER'S NOTES

Intermediate and above

Aims: ▶1 To reflect on L2 learning skills. ▶2 To practise reading, speaking and interactive listening.

Rationale: According to the literature (Doyle, 2008; Suskie, 2009), activities that encourage reflection on learning are essential. Reflection, being a blend of both *"intellectual and affective activities in which [students] engage to explore [their] experiences"* (Doyle, 2008, p. 81), stimulate metacognition and synthesis. The former refers to learning how to learn, whereas the latter is the capacity to put together what has been learnt and *"see the big picture"* (Suskie, 2009, p. 185). In consequence, reflecting on reading tasks prompts students to raise questions about their L2 reading and stimulates the assessment of the skill in question.

task 05

STRATEGIES DO YOU USE WHILE READING IN ENGLISH?

▶ You are going to do a questionnaire on L2 reading strategies. ▶ Think about the strategies you use while reading in English. ▶ Complete the questionnaire provided by circling one letter from **a** to **e**. ▶ Next, share your reading experience with your partner. ▶ Finally, actively participate in the class discussion about reading strategies. Listen carefully to your classmates' experiences so that you know how to become a better and more effective reader.

01 I set purposes for reading.

a) never   d) often
b) rarely   e) always
c) sometimes

02 I preview texts.

a) never   d) often
b) rarely   e) always
c) sometimes

03 I pay attention to text structure.

a) never   d) often
b) rarely   e) always
c) sometimes

04 I am able to predict the content of texts.

a) never   d) often
b) rarely   e) always
c) sometimes

05 I pose questions about texts.

a) never   d) often
b) rarely   e) always
c) sometimes

06 I draw conclusions and make judgements about texts.

a) never   d) often
b) rarely   e) always
c) sometimes

07 I retell and summarise texts.

a) never   d) often
b) rarely   e) always
c) sometimes

08 I identify difficulties.

a) never   d) often
b) rarely   e) always
c) sometimes

09 I critique texts.

a) never   d) often
b) rarely   e) always
c) sometimes

10 I think of what I have learnt from texts.

a) never   d) often
b) rarely   e) always
c) sometimes

11 I make connections between texts and my background knowledge.

a) never   d) often
b) rarely   e) always
c) sometimes

12 I discriminate what is important from what is not.

a) never   d) often
b) rarely   e) always
c) sometimes

13 I make inferences from texts.

a) never   d) often
b) rarely   e) always
c) sometimes

14 I guess meanings of new words/phrases from context.

a) never   d) often
b) rarely   e) always
c) sometimes

15 I check comprehension.

a) never   d) often
b) rarely   e) always
c) sometimes

TEACHER'S NOTES

Level: Intermediate and above

Aims: ▶1 To reflect on L2 reading skills. ▶2 To practise reading, speaking and interactive listening.

Rationale: According to the literature (Kern, 2000; Grabe & Stoller, 2002), reading is a dynamic process. Readers, while reading, are involved in creating meaning through interacting with the texts. According to numerous researchers (Kern, 2000; Grabe, 2009), this process can be facilitated by various reading strategies. For instance, observations of good readers indicate that the more strategies the readers use, the more effective and the more fluent the readers they are (Carrasquillo, Kucer & Abrams, 2004). Thus it is essential that students are provided with tasks that help them to identify their own reading strategies and encourage them to use new ones.

25 MINS

DESCRIBING AN EVENT: *a Plan*

task06

You are going to complete a chart about describing an event. In pairs, look at all the sections of the chart. Decide on the event you wish to describe and fill the chart in. Next, swap charts with a pair sitting next to you and peer-correct their work. Then, work in groups of four and discuss the charts. Finally, in pairs again, describe the previously selected event and give your text to the teacher for feedback.

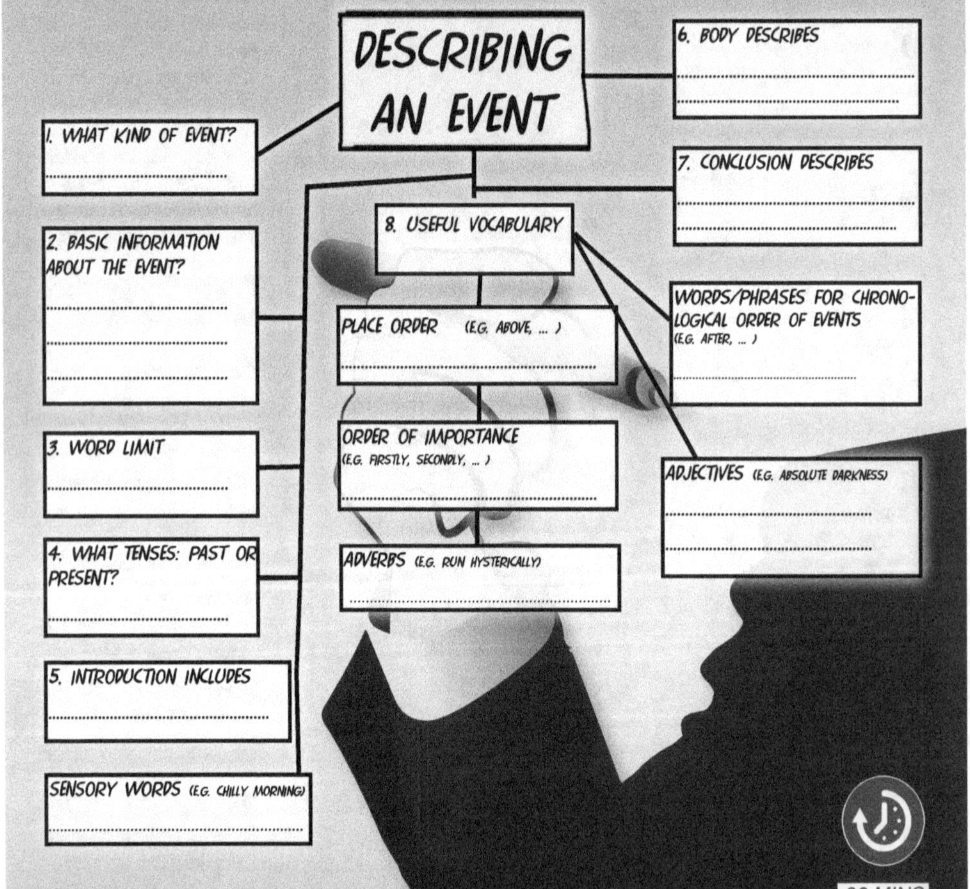

DESCRIBING AN EVENT

1. WHAT KIND OF EVENT?
....

2. BASIC INFORMATION ABOUT THE EVENT?
....
....
....

3. WORD LIMIT
....

4. WHAT TENSES: PAST OR PRESENT?
....

5. INTRODUCTION INCLUDES
....

SENSORY WORDS (E.G. CHILLY MORNING)
....

6. BODY DESCRIBES
....
....

7. CONCLUSION DESCRIBES
....
....

8. USEFUL VOCABULARY

PLACE ORDER (E.G. ABOVE, ...)
....

ORDER OF IMPORTANCE (E.G. FIRSTLY, SECONDLY, ...)
....

ADVERBS (E.G. RUN HYSTERICALLY)
....

WORDS/PHRASES FOR CHRONOLOGICAL ORDER OF EVENTS (E.G. AFTER, ...)
....

ADJECTIVES (E.G. ABSOLUTE DARKNESS)
....

90 MINS

TEACHER'S NOTES

Level: Pre-intermediate and above

Aims: ▶ 1 To plan a written text in detail.
▶ 2 To practise L2 writing.

Rationale: According to the literature (Doyle, 2008; Suskie, 2009), activities that encourage reflection on learning are essential. Reflection, being a blend of both "intellectual and affective activities in which [students] engage to explore [their] experiences" (Doyle, 2008, p. 81), stimulate metacognition and synthesis. The former refers to learning how to learn, whereas the latter is the capacity to put together what has been learnt and "see the big picture" (Suskie, 2009, p. 185). In consequence, reflecting on reading tasks prompts students to raise questions about their L2 reading and stimulates the assessment of the skill in question.

Oral PRESENTATION SELF-ASSESSMENT

task07

YOU ARE GOING TO COMPLETE A SELF-ASSESSMENT CHART ON YOUR PRESENTATION. ASSESS YOUR PERFORMANCE. USE THE CRITERIA AND RATING SCALE PROVIDED. NEXT, DISCUSS THE COMPLETED FORM WITH YOUR TEACHER DURING YOUR TEACHER'S OFFICE HOURS.

PERFORMANCE CRITERIA	RATING SCALE
ORGANISATION	
I clearly structured the presentation (introduction, body and conclusion).	
I properly organised all the ideas.	
I clearly explained all the ideas.	
CONTENT	
I clearly defined and elaborated on the topic of the presentation.	
I was well-informed about the topic and used diverse arguments to support my position.	
I used original and creative ideas in the presentation.	
I included personal opinions and experiences in the presentation.	
LANGUAGE	
I used accurate grammar.	
I used accurate pronunciation, intonation and spelling.	
I used appropriate and interesting vocabulary/phrases.	
DELIVERY	
I spoke loudly, distinctly and with an appropriate pace.	
I kept eye-contact with the audience.	
I interacted with the audience.	
I was confident and enthusiastic about the topic.	
MATERIALS AND EQUIPMENT	
I used diverse materials to support my argument (e.g. images, tables, charts, realia, etc.).	
I used different technologies (e.g. laptop, OHP, interactive board, etc.).	
I prepared a concise handout for my classmates.	
LIKES	
What I liked about the presentation is ...	
CHANGES	
What I would change next time is ...	

The rating scale is:
1 — FAIL
2 — POOR
3 — SATISFACTORY
4 — GOOD
5 — VERY GOOD
6 — EXCELLENT

TEACHER'S NOTES

Level: Pre-intermediate and above

Aims: ▶1 To self-assess an oral presentation. ▶2 To practise reading, speaking and interactive listening. ▶3 To justify one's opinions/beliefs through logical arguments.

Rationale: According to Berry's (2008) theoretical considerations, self-assessment should be an integral part of language education. Therefore, oral presentations self-assessment sheets are an interesting idea. They help learners to monitor oral performance in the target language, indicating their strengths and weaknesses. Also, thanks to these sheets, students can gain skills in estimating the quality of their work.

10 MINS

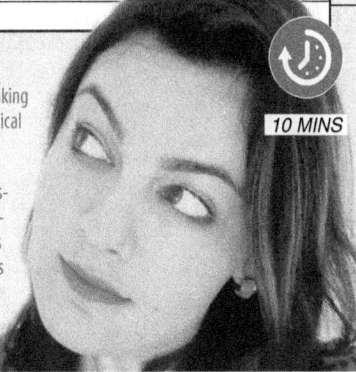

End of Unit Self-Assessment: HOW GOOD ARE YOU?

15 MINS

1 – FAIL   2 – POOR   3 – SATISFACTORY   4 – GOOD   5 – VERY GOOD   6 – EXCELLENT.

task 08

LEARNING OUTCOMES AND GAINED SKILLS	1	2	3	4	5	6
1. I can discuss the topic of the unit.						
2. I can use the vocabulary from the unit.						
3. I can write a coherent text summary.						
4. I can describe an event in writing.						
5. I can produce emphatic sentences.						
6. I can accurately use English tenses.						
7. I can fluently read the texts in the unit.						
8. I can comprehend the recorded texts.						
9. I can give arguments and negotiate positions in class discussions.						
10. I can confidently express my opinions.						
11. I can use exam strategies *						

* (e.g. oral presentations, writing a summary or describing an event).

LEARNING HABITS	1	2	3	4	5	6
1. I attentively listened to my teacher.						
2. I attentively listened to my classmates.						
3. I carefully planned my work.						
4. I clearly presented my work.						
5. I tried to do the tasks independently.						
6. I successfully collaborated with my classmates.						
7. I challenged my classmates' points of view.						
8. I was creative and innovative.						
9. I looked for extra information in other sources.						
10. I used different types of technologies (e.g. laptop, OHP, etc.)						
11. I attended all the classes systematically and punctually.						

MY TARGETS FOR FUTURE WORK

I intend to . . .

▶ You are going to complete an end-of-unit chart. Read all the items very carefully and apply the appropriate rating scale. Next, work in groups of three and discuss your charts. At the end of the class, leave your chart on your teacher's desk.

TEACHER'S NOTES

Level: Pre-intermediate and above

Aims: ▶ 1 To assess learning outcomes and habits, as well as gained skills in a particular course book unit. ▶ 2 To practise reading, speaking and interactive listening.

Rationale: Following Neary (2000, p. 124), self-assessment should play a vital role in L2 learning. Students should be encouraged to complete end of unit self-assessment charts on a regular basis. The charts help learners to better understand their learning experiences, allow for a great deal of feedback and develop student confidence and autonomy.

What TYPE of LEARNER are YOU

You are going to find out what type of learner you are. Read through the sentences carefully and tick any of the statements which are true about you. Find a partner to compare and discuss the selected points. Next, actively participate in the class discussion about different types of learners

01 I enjoy learning by doing things and experiencing the world around me.

02 I must see my teacher, his/her facial expressions and body language in order to clearly understand the lesson.

03 I like working with illustrated texts, charts and handouts.

04 I like listening to lectures and learning by reading my notes aloud. Written information is not important for me.

05 I dislike sitting and listening to lectures for more than 15 minutes.

VISUAL	KINAESTHETIC	AUDITORY
See it	Do it	Hear it

10-15 MINUTES

TEACHER'S NOTES

Aims: 1. To identify learner types. ▶ **2.** To practise reading, speaking and interactive listening.

Rationale: Numerous texts (e.g. Rogers, 2002; Davis, 2009) in the field demonstrate that since students differ from one another, they consequently collect, interpret and organise information in various ways. Therefore, it is vital to involve students in doing activities which will help them to identify their own learning styles. Having identified them, students are more likely to create better learning environments and develop new learning approaches.

 task10

You are going to complete a self-assessment sheet on the project you completed during the previous class. First, individually, think about your group work experience. Next, with your project partner, complete each section of the sheet in detail. Decide which of you will present the completed sheet to the class.

WORK SELF-ASSESSMENT

Student's Name:	
Working With:	
Title of the Project:	
Materials:	

List any problems that you encountered while working on the project. How did you solve them?

_____
_____
_____

Advantages of collaborating with other students

_____
_____
_____

Disadvantages of collaborating with other students

_____
_____
_____

Suggestions for the future

_____
_____
_____

30 MINS

TEACHER'S NOTES

Aims: ►1 To practise assessing one's work, identifying problems, finding solutions to the problems and thinking about improving future work. ►2 To practise L2 writing.

Level: Pre-intermediate and above

Rationale: According to Tan (2008), self-assessment should be widely applied in the classroom context. Hence, self-assessment sheets seem to be a good idea. They assist learners not only in controlling their learning and identifying their strengths and weaknesses, but also in judging the quality of their own performance.

CHAPTER EIGHT

CONCLUSION, IMPLICATIONS AND FUTURE RESEARCH

This book has been inspired by major developments in the area of fostering learner autonomy in the language classroom. It subscribes to the tenet that it is vital to develop a more complete picture than is currently available on fostering learner autonomy in the language classroom. The concept in question can then be more effectively handled in practice. In the past three decades, extensive research has been conducted on the various ways of fostering learner autonomy (e.g. Benson, 2007, 2011; Lamb & Reinders, 2008; Little, 1991, 2008). For this reason, this volume marries two concepts that have seldom been described together in the literature. These concepts are: learner autonomy and task design for the successful development of learner autonomy. The marriage of the two notions has been deliberately chosen to ensure an original and significant contribution to the field.

More specifically, this volume consists of eight chapters. The introductory chapter sets the scene for this volume. The reader has been introduced to the topic of the book and the crucial aspects of each chapter have been briefly synthesised.

Chapter Two has provided a general theoretical background to further discussion by defining the notion of learner autonomy, constructing a profile of an autonomous learner, plus discussing the psychological, educational and philosophical roots of learner autonomy. It is important that the reader knows what the concept of learner autonomy entails and what factors contribute to its complexity. Then, four approaches to developing learner autonomy have been detailed; the focus of this presentation has been both practical and empirical in nature. The scope of these approaches is related to the learner, the classroom, teaching resources and educational technology, respectively.

In Chapter Three, however, the discussion shifts to the second concept – developing pedagogical tasks. Various criteria for text selection and features of pedagogical tasks are carefully examined. This examination has been supported by the theory and research concerning the philosophy of social constructivism, SLA and educational psychology. All these perspectives have enriched the discussion and informed the reader about recent developments and their influence on language education. To design high-quality tasks that aim at developing learner autonomy, the presented criteria and features must be taken into account. It is argued that complex tasks, also referred to as competence-orientated tasks (Hallet & Legutke, 2013), need to be promoted as they "initiate complex interactions and negotiation processes along the lines of challenging lifeworld situations" (Hallet & Legutke, 2013, p. 147). Through these situations, language learners are afforded opportunities to take part in "real cultural discourses and social processes" (Hallet & Legutke, 2013, p. 147).

Chapter Two and Chapter Three have formed the literature review for the present volume. It is important to point out that this theoretical framework, immersed in the philosophy of social constructivism, provides a foundation on which the empirical project is based. Such a structure makes the volume a logical and coherent whole.

It should be emphasised that the research project presented in this volume has sought answers to the issues that have not been given sufficient attention in the Polish teaching context as well as in the literature in general. A thorough analysis has been made of the research outcomes. Interesting conclusions have been drawn in the hopes of contributing to the improvement of learner autonomy development. The implementation of high-quality pedagogical tasks would be one of the best means for such improvement.

The empirical part has commenced with a discussion of the research methodology adopted in the study. More specifically, Chapter Four has listed eight research questions and explained why a mixed-methods framework was adopted for the study reported. The purpose and description of the pilot study have also been presented. Finally, the research population, research tools, research procedures, ethical issues and limitations of the study have been described.

With this information, the reader has been invited to the next stage of the project in Chapter Five. Here, a detailed analysis of the research outcomes has been presented. All the data gathered in the study, both quantitative and qualitative, have been analysed and, whenever possible, displayed in tables and graphs. Interesting comparisons between the data collected through different instruments have also been made.

The discussion of the research findings in Chapter Six is a logical extension of what has been presented in Chapter Five. The research outcomes have been discussed and links to appropriate literature have been made. The purpose of this discussion has been to connect the mixed-methods study with the literature review. This has been done to not only relate the current project to existing literature and research, but also to share the new and unique contributions of the study and the knowledge of learner autonomy development as well as task design.

The study has demonstrated that teachers consider developing learner autonomy important. They are generally aware of the various ways for its effective development, yet in practice, they do very little to promote it. Another finding is that teachers are hardly ever involved in supplementing instructional materials and designing learner autonomy tasks.

Such a state of affairs has made Chapter Seven an urgent necessity. The model for developing learner autonomy tasks was created to familiarise in-service teachers with the complex process of designing pedagogical tasks. The model was also meant to prompt these teachers to put the process of designing pedagogical tasks into practice in their communities of practice. Teachers are encouraged to produce, either with other fellow teachers or with students, cognitively challenging tasks to supplement modern course books. Of course, the initial work of designing tasks needs to be guided by language educators who have relevant subject matter knowledge and experience. It should also be pointed out that the presentation of the model and the literature review discussed at the beginning of the book integrate a number of crucial elements of modern language pedagogy, including social constructivism and applied linguistic research.

The final phase of this research project is to suggest implications (see 8.1) and future research directions (see 8.2) in the area of learner autonomy and task design for learner autonomy development. These two areas are discussed in separate sections below.

8.1 IMPLICATIONS FOR TEACHER EDUCATION AND MATERIALS WRITING

This section focuses on the various implications this research has. Since the focus of these suggestions is twofold, implications for teacher education are discussed first, and implications for materials developers follow.

8.1.1 IMPLICATIONS FOR TEACHER EDUCATION

The mixed-methods study reveals that teachers are, in general, aware of the concept of learner autonomy and its importance in language education. However, a number of weaknesses have been observed, and consequently need to be addressed. The weaknesses must be discussed at both the macro and micro levels. Only when these two perspectives are addressed can the current situation be improved.

The macro-level issues are related to teacher education. First of all, considerable attention should be devoted to the effective use of diverse methods and techniques for developing learner autonomy. For example, during BA or MA courses in TESOL or professional development courses/workshops for in-service language instructors, teachers should be involved in theoretical and research-based discussions, practical implementation and reflective evaluation of projects, educational technology, extensive reading, extensive listening, literature or discussion clubs, self-assessment or reflecting-on-learning sessions. Enhanced awareness of the place and role of the above in successful learner autonomy development will enable teachers to produce more autonomous learners.

It is important that teacher training for learner autonomy is practical in nature. Korthagen's (1999) model of reflection is a good reference to follow. It is a model where trainees are involved in: the action within an authentic learning environment (i.e. a language classroom) and observation of this action, reflection by looking back on the action taken and increasing awareness and understanding of key features of the action on a more abstract level (e.g. teachers link the action with prior experience, theoretical frameworks of language teaching, theories of language learning and SLA research). All of the above suggest new options for future action and trialling these options in real classrooms.

Secondly, task-based pedagogy needs to become a permanent element of teacher education or professional development courses. It is strongly recommended that teachers be trained in effective use, adaptation or design of complex tasks. It is necessary to point out the various ways these tasks differ from standard course book activities. The benefits that well-designed tasks offer students and how the tasks contribute to language learning/acquisition in general must be emphasised.

Thirdly, it is essential that teacher education and professional development courses include the issue of backwash in language teaching. Both the positive and negative aspects should be included. The detrimental effect of backwash in Year Three in Polish secondary schools must be specifically stressed. What is needed at this level is high-quality language instruction which includes Matura examination support, not a whole year of Matura examination strategy training.

The micro-level issues, on the other hand, focus on the actual teaching practice. Successful teaching requires a vast number of resources and a bank of high-quality tasks. It is impossible for course books to completely meet both teachers' and students' expectations. For this reason, it is vital that teachers be encouraged to design their own tasks. Additional use of audio books, authentic texts, educational technology and other aids can be incorporated. Establishing ELT communities of practice would offer teachers opportunities to be familiarised with various intricacies of designing pedagogical tasks. Experience in the actual writing of tasks needs to be provided since the practical element is frequently missing in teacher education courses. Another reason why it is vital that teachers be engaged in designing interesting and creative tasks is that such practitioners appear to be less dependent on course books and find teaching more enjoyable.

8.1.2   IMPLICATIONS FOR MATERIALS WRITERS

The present study also offers interesting implications for materials writers. Firstly, it is vital that modern course books actively promote learner autonomy. This means cognitively challenging learner autonomy tasks are called for in course books. The included tasks should be: self-assessment tasks based on questionnaires; mini-project tasks with the use of educational technology; real-life texts with tasks which aim to develop all language skills; tasks connected with reflecting on learning sheets; tasks based on learning strategy identification sheets and video- or film-based tasks. Such tasks involve learners in active and collaborative language learning. Learners are also encouraged to take responsibility for, monitor and reflect on the process.

Secondly, as this book has highlighted, more sections and tasks based on real-life texts are needed in course books. Authentic texts provide appropriate ways of stimulating foreign language acquisition (Cirocki & Peña Calvo, 2015). These texts offer meaningful contexts for processing and interpreting new language. They also expose learners to different registers, styles and types of language use, at the same time constituting a highly valuable source for developing reading skills. The reading tasks that accompany texts in course books should not only focus on reading comprehension. What is expected is opinion, interpretation, personalised and speculative questions. Language learners will then have a chance to take part in meaningful communication and will be able to make text-to-self, text-to-text and text-to-world connections.

Finally, it is advisable that teacher books that accompany course books contain detailed information on how to adapt or modify certain activities to make learner autonomy happen in the classroom. This information, plus ready-made photocopiable resources placed in the appendix, would be extremely useful for teachers who are at the beginning of their teaching journey or in-service teachers who lack the necessary creativity.

8.2 FUTURE RESEARCH

The literature review and the empirical study suggest a number of important considerations for future research. For example, an exploratory case study could be conducted in order to investigate EFL teacher involvement in designing tasks for learner autonomy development at primary, secondary and tertiary levels in Poland. Such an investigation would shed more light on teachers' beliefs about materials development in general and task design in particular. A better understanding of the intricacies of fostering learner autonomy in the classroom would take place. It is recommended that colleagues from other countries follow suit as this type of investigation has not yet been reported in the literature. Likewise, it would be good to see detailed research focusing on the engagement of students in choosing, producing and evaluating class materials and tasks. Some of these aspects have been theoretically discussed, yet solid empirical evidence is required. Another important undertaking to be sought is the empirical validation of the proposed model for designing learner autonomy tasks in ELT communities of practice. The findings would reveal the extent to which this model meets the expectations of both language educators and in-service teachers. Constructive feedback would contribute to improving the current model to make it more useful for classroom practitioners. Finally, it would be interesting to conduct action research among course book writers. The purpose of this investigation would be threefold: to deepen the writers' knowledge of fostering learner autonomy, to familiarise them with the proposed model for designing learner autonomy tasks and to encourage them to use this model in their practice. Materials writers would then be urged to reflect on their professional practice so that new instructional materials can contribute to the improvement of three domains. These domains are: the improvement of learner autonomy development practice, an improvement in the understanding of the practice by language teachers and the improvement of the situation in which learner autonomy development practice occurs.

REFERENCES

Aggarwal, J. C. (2009). *Teaching of social studies. A practical approach* (4th ed.) New Delhi: Vikas Publishing House.

Ahmadi, R. (2012). Readiness for self-access language learning. A case study of Iranian students. *Studies in Self-Access Learning Journal, 3*(3), 254-264.

Ainscow, M. (2009). Foreword. In P. Hick, R. Kershner, & P. T. Farrell (Eds.), *Psychology for inclusive education. New directions in theory and practice* (pp. xi-xii). New York, NY: Routledge.

Alderson, C. J. (2000). *Assessing reading.* Cambridge: Cambridge University Press.

Allman, P. (2001). *Revolutionary social transformation: Democratic hopes, political possibilities and critical education.* Westport, CT: Bergin and Garvey.

Allwright, D., & Hanks, J. (2009). *The developing language learner. An introduction to exploratory practice.* Basingstoke: Palgrave Macmillan.

Allwright, R. L. (1981). What do we want teaching materials for? *English Language Teaching Journal, 36*(1), 5-18.

Alsup, J. (Ed.). (2010). *Young adult literature and adolescent identity across cultures and classrooms.* New York, NY: Routledge.

Al-Yousef, H. (2007). An evaluation of the third grade intermediate English coursebook in Saudi Arabia (Unpublished master's dissertation). King Saud University, Riyadh, Saudi Arabia.

Amrani, F. (2011). The process of evaluation: A publisher's view. In B. Tomlinson (Ed.), *Materials development in language teaching* (pp. 267-295). Cambridge: Cambridge University Press.

Anderson, A., & Lynch, T. (1988). *Listening.* Oxford: Oxford University Press.

Anderson, W. M., & Lawrence, J. E. (2007). *Integrating music into the elementary classroom.* Belmont, CA: Thomson Schirmer.

Applebee, A. N. (1986). Problems in process approach: Toward a reconceptualization of process instruction. In A. Petrosky & D. Bartholomae (Eds.), *The teaching of writing. Eighty-fifth yearbook of the National Society for the Study of Education* (pp. 95-113). Chicago, IL: University of Chicago Press.

Ariew, R., & Frommer, J. G. (1987). Interaction in the computer age. In W. M. Rivers (Ed.), *Interactive language teaching* (pp. 177-193). Cambridge: Cambridge University Press.

Armstrong, T. (2009). *Multiple intelligences in the classroom.* Alexandria, VA: ASCD.

Assinder, W. (1991). Peer teaching, peer learning: One model. *ELT Journal*, 45(3), 218-229.

Aston, G. (1993). The learner's contribution to the self-access centre. *ELT Journal*, 47(3), 219-227.

Babbie, E. (2013). *The practice of social research* (13th ed.). Belmont, CA: Wadsworth, Cengage Learning.

Bachman, L. (1990). *Fundamental considerations in language teaching.* Oxford: Oxford University Press.

Bachman, L., & Palmer, A. (1996). *Language testing in practice.* Oxford: Oxford University Press.

Bailey, K. M. (1990). The use of diary studies in teacher education programs. In J. C. Richards & D. Nunan (Eds.), *Second language teacher education* (pp. 215-226). Cambridge: Cambridge University Press.

Bailey, K. M., & Masuhara, H. (2013). Language testing washback: The role of materials. In B. Tomlinson (Ed.), *Applied Linguistics and materials development* (pp. 303-318). London: Bloomsbury Academic.

Bandura, A. (1997). *Self efficacy: The exercise of control.* New York, NY: Worth Publishers.

Bao, D. (2015). Flexibility in second language materials. *The European Journal of Applied Linguistics and TEFL*, 4(2), 37-52.

Barbieri, F., & Eckhardt, S. (2007). Applying corpus-based findings to form-focused instruction: The case of reported speech. *Language Teaching Research*, 11(3), 319-346.

Barron, A. E., Orwig, G. W., Ivers, K. S., & Lilavois, N. (2002). *Technologies for education: A practical guide* (4th ed.). Greenwood Village, CO: Libraries Unlimited.

Barthes, R. (1964). *Elements of semiology.* New York, NY: Hill and Wang.

Barthes, R. (1977). *Image-music-text*. London: Fontana.

Bastable, S. B. (Ed.). (2006). *Essentials of patient education*. Sudbury, MA: Jones and Bartlett Publishers.

Baumrind, D. (1991). The influence of parenting style on adolescent competence and substance abuse. *Journal of Early Adolescence, 11*, 56-94.

Bearne, E. (2002). *Making progress in writing*. New York, NY: Routledge-Falmer.

Bearne, E. (2009). Assessing multimodal texts. In A. Burke & R. F. Hammett (Eds.), *Assessing new literacies: Perspectives from the classroom* (pp. 15-34). New York, NY: Peter Lang.

Beauvois, M. H. (1995). E-talk: Attitudes and motivation in computer-assisted classroom discussion. *Computers and the Humanities, 28*, 177-190.

Beauvois, M. H. (1997). Computer-mediated communication (CMC): Technology for improving speaking and writing. In M. D. Bush & R. M. Terry (Eds.), *Technology-enhanced language learning* (pp. 165-184). Lincolnwood, IL: National Textbook Company.

Beckett, G. H. (2005). Academic language and literacy socialisation through project based instruction: ESL student perspectives and issues. *Journal of Asian Pacific Communication, 15*, 191-206.

Beckett, G. H., & Miller, P. C. (Eds.). (2006). *Project-based second and FL education. Past, present, and future*. Greenwich, CO: Information Age Publishing.

Bell, J., & Gower, R. (2011). Writing course materials for the world: A great compromise. In B. Tomlinson (Ed.), *Materials development in language teaching* (pp. 135-150). Cambridge: Cambridge University Press.

Belvel, P. S. (2010). *Rethinking classroom management. Strategies for prevention, intervention, and problem solving*. Thousand Oaks, CA: Corwin.

Benson, P. (1997). The philosophy and politics of learner autonomy. In P. Benson & P. Voller (Eds.), *Autonomy & independence in language learning* (pp. 18-34). London and New York: Longman.

Benson, P. (2001). *Teaching and researching autonomy in language learning*. Harlow: Pearson Education.

Benson, P. (2011). *Teaching and researching: Autonomy in language learning* (2nd ed.). Harlow: Pearson Education.

Benson, P. (Ed.). (2007). *Learner autonomy 8: Teacher and learner perspectives*. Dublin: Authentik.

Benson, P., & Cooker, L. (2013). The social and the individual in Applied Linguistics research. In P. Benson & L. Cooker (Eds.), *The applied linguistic individual. Sociocultural approaches to identity, agency and autonomy* (pp. 1-16). Sheffield: Equinox.

Berdie, D. R., Anderson, J. F., & Niebuhr, M. A. (1986). *Questionnaire design and use* (2nd ed.). Metuchen, NJ: The Scarecrow Press.

Berg, Z. L. (1999). Interaction in post-secondary web-based learning. *Educational Technology*, 39(1), 5-11.

Berry, R. (2008). *Assessment for learning.* Hong Kong: Hong Kong University Press.

Black, P., & Wiliam, D. (1998). Assessment and classroom learning. *Assessment in Education*, 5(1), 7-74.

Blaxter, L., Hughes, C., & Tight, M. (1996). *How to research.* Buckingham: Open University Press.

Blin, F. (1999). CALL and development of learner autonomy. In R. Debski & M. Levy (Eds.), *World CALL: Global perspectives on computer assisted language learning* (pp. 133-147). Lisse: Swets & Zeitlinger.

Block, D. (1991). Some thoughts on DIY materials design. *ELT Journal*, 45(3), 211-217.

Block, D. (2007). *Second language identities.* London: Continuum.

Bloor, M., & Bloor, T. (1988). Syllabus negotiation: The basis of learner autonomy. In A. Brookes & P. Grundy (Eds.), *Individualization and autonomy in language learning* (pp. 62-74). ELT Documents 131. Modern English Publications and The British Council.

Boekaerts, M. (2010). The crucial role of motivation and emotion in classroom learning. In H. Dumont, D. Istance, & F. Benavides (Eds.), *The nature of learning. Using research to inspire practice* (pp. 91-111). Paris: OECD.

Borg, S. (2003). Teacher cognition in language teaching: A review of research on what language teachers think, know, believe and do. *Language Teaching*, 36(2), 81-109.

Botelho, M. (2003). Multiple intelligence theory in English language teaching: An analysis of current textbooks, materials and teachers' perceptions (Unpublished mater's dissertation). Ohio University, Athens, USA.

Botha, J. A., & Coetzee, M. (2007). Outcomes-based learning programme design. In M. Coetzee (Ed.), *Practising education, training and develop-*

ment in South African organisations (pp. 118-163). Cape Town: Juta & Company Ltd.

Boud, D. (1988). Moving towards autonomy. In D. Boud (Ed.), *Developing student autonomy in learning* (pp. 17-39). London: Kogan.

Boud, D. (1995). *Enhancing learning though self-assessment*. London: Kogan Page.

Bouissac, P. (1976). *Circus and culture: A semiotic approach*. Bloomington, IN: Indiana University Press.

Bredella, L., & Delanoy, W. (Eds.). (1996). *Challenges of literary texts in the foreign language classroom*. Tübingen: Narr.

Breen, M. P. (1987). Learner contributions to task design. In C. Candlin & D. Murphy (Eds.), *Language learning tasks* (pp. 23-46). Englewood Cliffs, NJ: Prentice Hall.

Breen, M. P. (1989). The evaluation cycle for language learning tasks. In R. K. Johnson (Ed.), *The second language curriculum* (pp. 187-206). Cambridge: Cambridge University Press.

Breen, M. P., & Littlejohn, A. (Eds.). (2000). *Classroom decision-making. Negotiation and process syllabuses in practice*. Cambridge: Cambridge University Press.

Breen, M. P., & Mann, S. J. (1997). Shooting arrows at the sun: Perspectives on a pedagogy for autonomy. In P. Benson & P. Voller (Eds.), *Autonomy & independence in language learning* (pp. 132-149). London and New York: Longman.

Breen, M. P., & Waters, A. (1979). Communicative materials design: Some basic principles. *RELC Journal*, 10(2), 1-13.

Brindley, G. (1984). Needs analysis and objective setting in the adult migrant education program (Report of the New South Wales Adult Migrant Education Program for the Joint Commonwealth/States Committee). Sydney: N. S. W. Adult Migrant Education Service.

Brindley, G. (1989). The role of needs analysis in adult ESL programme design. In R. K. Johnson (Ed.), *The second language curriculum* (pp. 63-78). Cambridge: Cambridge University Press.

British Educational Research Association. (2011). *Ethical guidelines for educational research*. London: BERA.

Brooks, L., & Swain, M. (2009). Languaging in collaborative writing: Creation of and response to expertise. In A. Mackey & C. Polio (Eds.),

Multiple perspectives on interaction: Second language research in honor of Susan M. Gass (pp. 58-89). New York, NY: Routledge.

Brosnan, D., Brown, K., & Hood, S. (1984). *Reading in context*. Adelaide: National Curriculum Resource Centre.

Brown, J. B. (1997). Textbook evaluation form. *The Language Teacher*, 21(10), 15-21.

Brown, J. D. (2014). *Mixed methods research for TESOL*. Edinburgh: Edinburgh University Press.

Brumfit, C. (1984). *Communicative methodology in language teaching*. Cambridge: Cambridge University Press.

Bruner, J. S. (1978). The role of dialogue in language acquisition. In A. Sinclair, R. J. Jarvelle, & W. J. M. Levelt (Eds.), *The child's conception of language* (pp. 241-256). New York, NY: Springer-Verlag.

Bruner, J. S. (1986). *Actual minds, possible worlds*. Cambridge, MA: Harvard University Press.

Bruner, J. S. (1990). *Acts of meaning*. Cambridge, MA: Harvard University Press.

Bullen, M., & Janes, D. P. (2007). *Making the transition to E-learning. Strategies and issues*. Hershey, PA: Information Science Publishing.

Burbules, N. C. (2006). Self-educating communities. Collaboration and learning through the Internet. In Z. Bekerman, N. C. Burbules, & D. Silberman-Keller (Eds.), *Learning in places: The informal educational reader* (pp. 273-284). New York, NY: Peter Lang.

Burkhardt, R. M. (2006). *Using poetry in the classroom: Engaging students in learning*. Lenham, MD: Rowman & Littlefield Education.

Burwitz-Melzer, E. (2000). *Literatur (nicht nur) für Kinder* [Literature (not only) for children]. Koblenz: Universität Koblenz-Landau.

Burwitz-Melzer, E. (2007). Literarische Texte für junge Fremdsprachenlernende [Literary texts for young adults learning foreign languages]. In W. Hallet and A. Nünning (Eds.), *Neue Ansätze und Konzepte der Literatur- und Kulturdidaktik* [New guidelines and concepts for teaching literature and culture] (pp. 219-237). Trier: Wissenschaftlicher Verlag Trier.

Buttner, A. (2007). *Activities, games and assessment strategies for the foreign language classroom*. New York, NY: Taylor and Francis.

Bygate, M., Skehan, P., & Swain, M. (Eds.). (2001). *Researching pedagogic tasks: Second language learning, teaching and testing*. London: Longman.

Cameron, L. (2001). *Teaching languages to young learners.* Cambridge: Cambridge University Press.

Campbell, A. P. (2003). Weblogs for use with ESL classes. *The Internet TESL Journal,* 9(2). Retrieved from http://iteslj.org/Techniques/Campbell-Weblogs.html

Campbell, C., & Kryszewska, H. (1992). *Learner-based teaching.* Oxford: Oxford University Press.

Campbell, J. R., Donahue, P. L., Reese, C. M., & Phillips, G. W. (1996). *NAEP 1994 reading report card for the nation and the states. Findings from the National Assessment of Educational Progress and Trial State Assessment.* Washington, DC: National Library of Education.

Candlin, C. N. (1987). Towards task-based language learning. In C. N. Candlin & D. F. Murphy (Eds.), *Language learning tasks* (pp. 5–22). Lancaster: Prentice Hall International.

Candy, P. C. (1991). *Self-direction for lifelong learning: A comprehensive guide to theory and practice.* San Francisco and Oxford: Jossey-Bass Publishers.

Canniveng, C., & Martinez, M. (2003). Materials development and teacher training. In B. Tomlinson (Eds.), *Developing materials for language teaching* (pp. 479–489). London: Continuum.

Capel, S., Leask, M., & Turner, T. (Eds.). (2013). *Learning to teach in the secondary school. A companion to school experience* (6th ed.). London and New York: Routledge.

Carpenter, C. (1996). Peer teaching: A new approach to advanced level language teaching. In E. Broady & M-M. Kenning (Eds.), *Promoting learner autonomy in university language teaching* (pp. 23–38). London: Association for French Language Studies/CILT.

Carrasquillo, A., Kucer, S. B., & Abrams, R. (2004). *Beyond the beginnings: Literacy interventions for upper elementary English language learners.* Clevedon: Mulilingual Matters.

Carter, R., & Long, M. N. (1991). *Teaching literature.* London: Longman.

Cazden, C. (1983). Adult assistance to language development: Scaffolds, models and direct instruction. In R. P. Parker & F. A. Davies (Eds.), *Developing literacy* (pp. 3–18). Delaware: International Reading Association.

Cennamo, K. S., Ross, J. D., & Ertmer, P. A. (2010). *Technology integration for meaningful classroom use. A standards-based approach.* Belmont, CA: Wadsworth, Cengage Learning.

Charles, C. M. (2002). *Essential elements of effective discipline*. Boston, MA: Allyn and Bacon.

Chen, N., Hsieh, S., & Kinshuk, K. (2008). The effects of short-term memory and content representation type on mobile language learning. *Journal of Learning and Technology, 12*, 93-113.

Chik, A. (2011). Learner autonomy development through digital gameplay. *Digital Culture and Education, 3*(1), 50-64.

Chiu, H. L. W. (2012). Supporting the development of autonomous learning skills in reading and writing in an independent language learning centre. *Studies in Self-Access Learning Journal, 3*(3), 266-290.

Cirocki, A. (2009). The place and role of literary texts in language education: A historical overview. In A. Cirocki (Ed.), *Extensive reading in English language teaching* (pp. 157-170). München: Lincom.

Cirocki, A. (2011). Age is only a number: Evaluating and modernising dated EFL materials. *Folio, 14*(2), 12-16.

Cirocki, A. (2012). Establishing a club of readers in the EFL classroom. *Modern English Teacher, 21*(4), 53-57.

Cirocki, A. (2013a). Literature in the EFL classroom: A social constructivist perspective. *The European Journal of Applied Linguistics and TEFL, 2*(1), 69-88.

Cirocki, A. (2013b). Teaching English in use: Bridging the gap between a sentence and the native speaker's meaning. *Teresian Journal of English Studies, 5*(1), 1-21.

Cirocki, A. (2013c). The reading portfolio: A tool for learning and assessment in the secondary school EFL classroom. *The International Journal of Innovation in English Language Teaching and Research, 2*(2), 223-240.

Cirocki, A., & Arceusz, A. (2016/forthcoming). Research methods in foreign/second language didactics. *TEANGA, Journal of the Irish Association for Applied Linguistics, 24*.

Cirocki, A., & Farrelly, R. (2016/forthcoming). Research and reflective practice in the EFL classroom: Voices from Armenia. *Eurasian Journal of Applied Eurasian Journal of Applied Linguistics, 2*(1).

Cirocki, A., & Peña Calvo, A. (2015). *In a strange land. Short stories for creative learning*. Pforzheim: LinguaBooks.

Cirocki, A., & Tomlinson, B. (Eds.). (2015). Materials in the ELT classroom: Development, use and evaluation [Special issue]. *The European Journal of Applied Linguistics and TEFL, 4*(2).

Cirocki, A., Tennekoon, S., & Peña Calvo, A. (2014). Research and reflective practice in the ESL classroom: Voices from Sri Lanka. *The Australian Journal of Teacher Education*, 39(4). Retrieved from http://ro.ecu.edu.au/ajte/vol39/iss4/2/

Clare, B. (2007). Promoting deep learning: A teaching, learning, assessment endeavour. *Social Work Education*, 26(5), 433-446.

Clark, J. L. (1987). *Curriculum renewal in school foreign language learning*. Oxford: Oxford University Press.

Claus, A., Grau, M., Legutke, M. K., & Rau, N. (2008). *Pädagogische Leistungskultur: Englisch als erste Fremdsprache* [A culture of pedagogic achievement: English as a first foreign language]. Frankfurt: Grundschulverband.

Cohen, A. D. (1998). *Strategies in learning and using a second language*. Harlow: Addison Wesley.

Cohen, A. D. (2008). Speaking strategies for independent learning: A focus on pragmatic performance. In S. Hurd & T. Lewis (Eds.), *Language learning strategies in independent settings* (pp. 119-140). Bristol: Multilingual Matters.

Cohen, A. D. (2011). *Strategies in learning and using a second language* (2nd ed.). Harlow: Longman/Pearson Education.

Cook, G. (1992). *The discourse of advertising*. London: Routledge.

Cooker, L. (2002). Towards independence in the management of one's own learning. *The Journal of Konda University of International Studies*, 13, 13-21.

Cope, B., & Kalantzis, M. (2009). 'Multiliteracies': New literacies, new learning. *Pedagogies: An International Journal*, 4, 164-195.

Cotterall, S., & Reinders, H. (2001). Fortress or bridge? Learners' perceptions and practice in self-access language learning. *TESOLANZ*, 8, 23-38.

Council of Europe. (2001). *The common European framework of reference for languages: Learning, teaching, assessment*. Cambridge: Cambridge University Press.

Crabbe, D. (1993). Fostering autonomy from within the classroom: The teacher's responsibility. *System*, 21(4), 443-452.

Crafton, L. K., Silvers, P., & Brennan, M. (2009). Creating critical multiliteracies curriculum: Repositioning in the early childhood classroom. In M. Narey (Ed.), *Making meaning. Constructing multimodal perspectives of language, literacy and learning through arts based early childhood education* (pp. 31-51). Pittsburgh, PA: Springer.

Craik, F. I. M., & Lockhart, R. S. (1972). Levels of processing. A framework for memory research. *Journal of Verbal Learning and Verbal Behaviour*, 11, 671-684.

Cram, B. (1995). Self-assessment: From theory to practice. Developing a workshop guide for teachers. In G. Brindley (Ed.), *Language assessment in action* (pp. 271-306). Sydney: Macquarie University, NCELTR.

Crittenden, B. (1978). Autonomy as an aim of education. In K. A. Strike & K. Egan (Eds.), *Ethics and educational policy* (pp. 105-126). London: Routledge & Kegan Paul.

Cullen, R., & Kuo, I. (2007). Spoken grammar and ELT course materials. A missing link? *TESOL Quarterly*, 41(2), 361-386.

Cunningsworth, A. (1984). *Evaluating and selecting EFL teaching materials*. London: Heinemann.

Cunningsworth, A. (1995). *Choosing your coursebook*. Oxford: Heinemann.

Cutrim Schmid, E. (2008). Interactive whiteboards and the normalisation of CALL. In R. de Cassia Veiga Morriott & P. L. Torres (Eds.), *Handbook of research on E-learning methodologies for language acquisition* (pp. 69-83). Hershey, PA: IGI Global.

Cutrim Schmidt, E. (2009). The pedagogical potential of interactive whiteboards 2.0. In M. Thomas (Ed.), *Handbook of research on Web 2.0 and second language learning* (pp. 491-505). Hershey, PA: IGI Global.

Dalglish, C., Evans, P., & Lawson, L. (2011). *Learning in the global classroom. A guide for students in the multicultural university*. Cheltenham: Edward Elgar Publishing Limited.

Dam, L. (2010). Developing learner autonomy with adult immigrants. In B. O'Rourke & L. Carson (Eds.), *Language learner autonomy: Policy, curriculum, classroom* (pp. 79-102). Bern: Peter Lang.

Danielson, C. (2007). *Enhancing professional practice: A framework for teaching* (2nd ed.). Alexandria, VA: ASCD.

Davis, B. (2009). *Tools for teaching* (2nd ed.). San Francisco, CA: John Wiley & Sons.

Davison, C. (Ed.). (2005). *Information technology and innovation in language education*. Hong Kong: Hong Kong University Press.

Davison, P. (1998). Piloting - A publisher's view. In B. Tomlinson (Ed.), *Materials development in language teaching* (pp. 149-189). Cambridge: Cambridge University Press.

Day, R., & Bamford, J. (1998). *Extensive reading in the second language classroom*. Cambridge: Cambridge University Press.
de Beaugrande, R., & Dressler, W. (1981). *An introduction to text linguistics*. London: Longman.
Deci, E. L., & Flaste, R. (1996). *Why we do what we do: Understanding self-motivation*. New York, NY: Penguin Books.
Denscombe, M. (2007). *The good research guide for small-scale social research projects* (3rd ed.). Maidenhead: Open University Press.
Denzin, N. K. (1978). *Sociological methods: A sourcebook* (2nd ed.). New York, NY: McGraw-Hill.
Denzin, N. K., & Lincoln, Y. S. (Eds.). (1994). *Handbook of qualitative research*. Thousand Oaks, CA: Sage.
de Vos, A. S. (2002). Intervention research. In A. S. de Vos, H. Strydom, C. B. Fouche, & C. S. L. Delport (Eds.), *Research at grass roots: For the social sciences and human service professions* (pp. 394-418). Pretoria: Van Schaik Publishers.
Dewey, J. (1944). *Democracy and education: An introduction to the philosophy of education*. New York, NY: The Free Press.
Dickinson, L. (1987). *Self-instruction in language learning*. Cambridge: Cambridge University Press.
Díez, M. P., Place, R., & Fernández, O. (Eds.). (2012). *Plurilingualism. Promoting co-operation between communities, people and nations*. Bilbao: University of Deusto.
Donato, R. (2000). Sociocultural contributions to understanding the foreign and second language classroom. In J. P. Lantolf (Ed.), *Sociocultural theory and second language learning* (pp. 27-50). Oxford: Oxford University Press.
Donovan, C. A., & Smolkin, L. B. (2001). Genre and other factors influencing teachers' book selections for Science instruction. *Reading Research Quarterly*, 36, 412-440.
Donovan, P. (1998). Piloting - A publisher's view. In B. Tomlinson (Ed.), *Materials development in language teaching* (pp. 149-189). Cambridge: Cambridge University Press.
Dörnyei, Z. (2001). *Teaching and researching motivation*. Harlow: Longman.
Dörnyei, Z. (2002). The motivational basis of language learning tasks. In P. Robinson (Ed.), *Individual differences in second language acquisition* (pp. 137-158). Amsterdam: John Benjamins.

Dörnyei, Z. (2005). *The psychology of the language learner*. Mahwah, NJ: Lawrence Erlbaum Associates.

Doughty, C., & Long, M. H. (2003). Optimal psycholinguistic environments for distance foreign language learning. *Language Learning and Teaching, 7*, 50-80.

Downing, J. P. (1997). *Creative teaching. Ideas to boost student interest*. Englewood, CO: Teacher Ideas Press.

Doyle, T. (2008). *Helping students learn in a learner-centered environment: A guide to facilitating learning in higher education*. Sterling, VA: Stylus Publishing, LLC.

Driscoll, M., & Carliner, S. (2005). *Advanced web-based training strategies: Unlocking instructionally sound online learning*. San Francisco, CA: John Wiley & Sons.

Droździał-Szelest, K. (2008). Trening strategiczny na lekcji języka obcego – mit czy rzeczywistość? [Strategic training during a foreign language lesson – a myth or reality?] In M. Pawlak (Ed.), *Autonomia w nauce języka angielskiego – co osiągnęliśmy i dokąd zmierzamy?* [Autonomy in English language learning – what have we achieved and where are we heading?] (pp. 405-415). Poznań, Kalisz, Poznań: Universytet A. Mickiewicza w Poznaniu, Wydział Pedagogiczno-Artystyczny UAM w Kaliszu i Wydawnictwo Państwowej Wyższej Szkoły Zawodowej w Koninie.

Dudley-Evans, T., & St John, M. J. (1998). *Developments in English for specific purposes: A multi-disciplinary approach*. Cambridge: Cambridge University Press.

DuFour, R. (2004). What is a professional learning community? *Educational Leadership, 61*(8), 6-11.

Dunford, N. (2004). *How do teachers interpret the need for the adaptation and supplementation of coursebooks, with specific reference to data collected by questionnaire from Shane English Schools Japan?* (Unpublished master's dissertation). University of Nottingham, Nottigham, UK.

Duran, G., & Ramaut, G. (2006). Tasks for absolute beginners and beyond: Developing and sequencing tasks at basic proficiency levels. In K. van den Branden (Ed.), *Task-based language education: From theory to practice* (pp. 47-75). Cambridge: Cambridge University Press.

East, M. (2012). *Task-based language teaching from the teacher's perspective: Insights from New Zealand*. Amsterdam: John Benjamins.

Ebersbach, A., Glaser, M., Heigl, R., & Warta, A. (2008). *Wiki web collaboration* (2nd ed.). Berlin and Heidelberg: Springer-Verlag.

Eckerth, J., & Siekmann, S. (2008). *Task-based language learning and teaching. Theoretical, methodological and pedagogical perspectives.* Frankfurt & New York: Peter Lang.

Edwards, C. H. (2011). *Democratic discipline in learning communities. Theory and practice.* Lenham, MD: Rowman and Littlefield Education.

Ellis, R. (1999). *Learning a second language through interaction.* Amsterdam: John Benjamins.

Ellis, R. (2003). *Task-based language teaching and learning.* Oxford: Oxford University Press.

Ellis, R. (Ed.). (2001). *Form-focused instruction and second language learning.* Oxford: Blackwell.

Ellis, R., & Shintani, N. (2013). *Exploring language pedagogy through second language acquisition research.* Abingdon: Routledge.

Ellis, R., Basturkmen, H., & Loewen, S. (2002). Doing focus on form. *System, 30*(4), 419–432.

Eom, M. (2006). *An investigation of operationalized constructs of second language listening tests.* Ann Arbor, MI: ProQuest Information and Learning Company.

Erben, T., & Sarieva, L. (Eds.). (2008). *CALLing all foreign language teachers. Computer-assisted language learning in the classroom.* Larchmont, NY: Eye On Education.

Erikson, E. H. (1963). *Childhood and society* (2nd ed.). New York, NY: Norton.

Errey, L., & Schollaert, R. (Eds.). (2003). *Whose learning is it anyway? Developing learner autonomy through task-based learning.* Antwerp/Apeldoorn: Garant.

Esch, E. M. (1997). Learner training for autonomous language learning. In P. Benson & P. Voller (Eds.), *Autonomy & independence in language learning* (pp. 164–175). London and New York: Longman.

Everhard, C. J., & Murphy, L. (Eds.). (2015). *Assessment and autonomy in language learning.* Basingstoke: Palgrave Macmillan.

Fan, J. (2011). Constructing web-based learning environment for college English teaching. In W. Yanwen (Ed.), *Computing and intelligent systems* (Part III) (pp. 515–522). Berlin and Heidelberg: Springer.

Fang, X., & Warschauer, M. (2004). Technology and curricular reform in China: A case study. *TESOL Quarterly, 38*(2), 301–323.

Farrell, T. S. C. (2004). *Reflective practice in action. 80 reflection break for busy teachers.* Thousand Oaks, CA: Corwin Press.

Farrell, T. S. C. (2007). *Reflective language teaching: From research to practice.* London: Continuum.

Farrell, T. S. C. (2015). *Promoting teacher reflection in second language education. A framework for TESOL professionals.* New York, NY: Routledge.

Farrell, T. S. C., & Jacobs, G. M. (2010). *Essentials for successful English language teaching.* London: Continuum.

Fenner, A-B. (2001). *Cultural awareness and language awareness based on dialogic interaction with texts in foreign language learning.* Strasbourg: Council of Europe.

Fernández-Toro, M., & Jones, F. R. (1996). Going solo: Learners' experiences of self-instruction and self-instruction training. In E. Broady & M-M. Kenning (Eds.), *Promoting learner autonomy in university language teaching* (pp. 185–214). London: CILT.

Feuerstein, R. (1990). The theory of structural cognitive modifiability. In B. Presseisen (Ed.), *Learning and thinking styles: Classroom applications* (pp. 68–134). Washington, DC: National Education Association.

Feuerstein, R., Klein, P. S., & Tannenbaum, A. (Eds.). (1991). *Mediated learning experience (MLE).* London: Freund.

Feuerstein, R., Rand, Y., Hoffman, M., & Miller, R. (1980). *Instrumental enrichment.* Glenview, IL: Scott Foresman.

Feuersten, R., Rand, Y., & Rynders, J. E. (1988). *Don't accept me as I am – Helping "retarded" people to excel.* New York, NY: Plenum Press.

Finkbeiner, C. (2002). Foreign language practice and cooperative learning. In C. Finkbeiner (Ed.), *Wholeheartedly English: A life of learning* (pp. 109–122). Berlin: Cornelsen.

Finkbeiner, C., & Knierim, M. (2008). Developing L2 strategic competence online. In F. Zhang & B. Barber (Eds.), *Handbook of research on computer-enhanced language acquisition and learning* (pp. 377–402). Hershey, PA: IGI Global.

Fleming, M., & Stevens, D. (2004). *English teaching in the secondary school: Linking theory and practice* (2nd ed.). London: David Fulton Publishers.

Freire, P. (1970). *Pedagogy of the oppressed.* New York, NY: Herder & Herder.

Fujii, A., & Mackey, A. (2009). Interactional feedback in learner-learner interactions in a task-based output EFL classroom. *International Review of Applied Linguistics in Language Teaching, 47*(3/4), 267-301.

Gao, X. (2007). A tale of Blue Rain Café: A study on the online narrative construction about a community of English learners on the Chinese mainland. *System, 35*(2), 259-270.

Gao, X. (2009). English corner as an out-of-class learning activity. *English Language Teaching Journal, 63*(1), 60-67.

Garcia-Mayo, M. P. (Ed.). (2007). *Investigating tasks in formal language learning*. Clevedon: Multilingual Matters.

Gardner, D., & Miller, L. (1999). *Establishing self-access: From theory to practice*. Cambridge: Cambridge University Press.

Gardner, D., & Miller, L. (Eds.). (1996). *Tasks for independent language learning*. Washington, DC: TESOL.

Gass, S. (1997). *Input, interaction and the second language learner*. Mahwah, NJ: Lawrence Erlbaum Associates.

Gass, S., & Varonis, E. (1985). Task variation and non-native/non-native negotiation of meaning. In S. Gass & C. Madden (Eds.), *Input in second language acquisition* (pp. 149-161). Rowley, MA: Newbury House.

Geddes, M., & Sturtridge, G. (Eds.). (1982). *Individualisation*. London: Modern English Publications.

General Teaching Council for Scotland (GTCS). (2002). *Code of practice on teacher competence*. Retrieved from http://gtcs.org.uk/Professional-Conduct/Competence.asp

Geva-Grofman, D. (2008). *Development from repetition to symbolization in the first six years of life and its mirroring in children's books*. Ann Arbor, MI: ProQuest LLC.

Gibbons, P. (2015). *Scaffolding language, scaffolding learning: Teaching English language learners in the mainstream classroom* (2nd ed.). Portsmouth, NH: Heinemann.

Gilabert, R., Baron, J., & Llanes, A. (2009). Manipulating cognitive complexity across task types and its impact on learners' interaction during oral performance. *International Review of Applied Linguistics in Language Teaching, 47*(3/4), 367-395.

Glaus, K. (1999). Measuring self-esteem. In C. J. Carlock (Ed.), *Enhancing self-esteem* (pp. 457-476). New York, NY: Routledge.

Godwin-Jones, B. (2003). Blogs and wikis: Environments for on-line collaboration. *Language Learning & Technology*, 5(3), 7-12.

Godwin-Jones, B. (2005). Skype and podcasting: Disruptive technologies for language learning. *Language Learning & Technology*, 9(3), 9-12.

Goh, C. C. M., & Burns, A. (2012). *Teaching speaking: A holistic approach.* Cambridge: Cambridge University Press.

Goodman, K., Bird, L., & Goodman, Y. (Eds.). (1991). *The whole language catalogue.* Santa Rosa, CA: American School Publishers.

Gottfried, A. E. (2008). Home environment and academic intrinsic motivation. In N. Salkind (Ed.), *Ecyclopedia of Educational Psychology* (pp. 485-490). Thousand Oaks, CA: Sage Publications.

Gowans, S. (2012). *EFL communication strategies in second life. An exploratory study.* Pforzheim: LinguaBooks.

Grabe, W. (2009). *Reading in a second language: Moving from theory to practice.* Cambridge: Cambridge University Press.

Grabe, W., & F. L. Stoller. (2002). *Teaching and researching reading.* Harlow: Longman.

Gravells, A. (2010). *Delivering employability skills in the lifelong learning sector.* Exeter: Learning Matters.

Graves, K. (2003). Coursebooks. In D. Nunan (Ed.), *Practical English language teaching* (pp. 225-246). New York, NY: McGraw Hill.

Green, T. D., & Brown, A. (2002). *Multimedia projects in the classroom: A guide to development and evaluation.* Thousand Oaks, CA: Corwin Press.

Gregory, A., Yeomans, L., & Powell, J. (2003). Peer assessment and enhancing student learning. In R. Kaye & D. Hawkridge (Eds.), *Learning and teaching for business: Case studies in successful innovation* (pp. 108-123). London: Kogan Page.

Grotjahn, R. (1987). On the methodological basis of introspective methods. In C. Faerch & G. Kasper (Eds.), *Introspection in second language research* (pp. 54-81). Clevedon: Multilingual Matters.

Gruba, P. (2004). Computer assisted language learning (CALL). In A. Davies & C. Elder (Eds.), *The handbook of Applied Linguistics* (pp. 623-648). Oxford: Blackwell Publishing.

Gu, P. (2008). *Listening strategies of upper primary school pupils in Singapore.* Paper presented at the conference of the International Association for Applied Linguistics, Essen.

Guskey, T. R., & Anderman, E. M. (2008). Students at bat. *Educational Leadership*, 66(3), 8-14.

Guzdial, M., & Turns, J. (2000). Effective discussion through a computer mediated anchored forum. *Journal of the Learning Sciences*, 9(4), 437-469.

Hadley, G. (2014). Global textbooks in local contexts: An empirical investigation of effectiveness. In N. Harwood (Ed.), *English language teaching textbooks. Content, consumption, production* (pp. 205-238). New York, NY: Palgrave Macmillan.

Hallet, W. (2011). Visual images of space, movement and modality in the multimodal novel. In R. Brosch (Ed.), *Moving images – Mobile viewers. 20th century visuality* (pp. 227-248). Berlin: LIT Verlag.

Hallet, W., & Legutke, M. K. (2013). Task-approaches revisited: New orientations, new perspectives. *The European Journal of Applied Linguistics and TEFL*, 2(2), 139-158.

Hallet, W., & Nünning, A. (Eds.). (2007). *Neue Ansätze und Konzepte der Literatur und Kulturdidaktik. WVT-Handbücher zur Literatur- und Kulturdidaktik, Band 1* [New guidelines and concepts for teaching literature and culture. WVT textbooks for teaching literature and culture]. Trier: WVT.

Halliday, M. A. K., & Hasan, R. (1976). *Cohesion in English*. London: Longman.

Harmer, J. (2001). Coursebooks: A human, cultural and linguistic disaster. *Modern English Teacher*, 10(3), 5-10.

Harris, A. J., & Sipay, E. R. (1990). *How to increase reading ability: A guide to developmental and remedial methods* (9th ed.) White Plains, NY: Longman.

Harris, V., & Noyau, G. (1990). Collaborative learning: Taking the first steps. In I. Gathercole (Ed.), *Autonomy in language learning* (pp. 54-64). London: CILT.

Harsch, C., & Schröder, K. (2008). Schülerkompetenzen im Englischen: Textrekonstruktion: C-Test [Learner competences in an English lesson: Text reconstruction: Test C]. In DESI-Konsortium (Ed.), *Ergebnisse der DESI-Studie* [DESI research findings] (pp. 149-156). Weinheim: Beltz.

Harwood, N. (2014). *English language teaching textbooks. Content, consumption, production*. New York, NY: Palgrave Macmillan.

Harwood, N. (Ed.). (2010). *English language teaching materials. Theory and practice*. Cambridge: Cambridge University Press.

Hassett, D. D., & Curwood, J. S. (2009). Theories and practices of multimodal education: The instructional dynamics of picture books and primary classrooms. *The Reading Teacher, 63*(4), 270-282.

Hativa, N. (2000). *Teaching for effective learning in higher education.* Dordrecht: Kluwer Academic Publishers.

Hawkins, M. R. (2005). Becoming a student: Identity work and academic literacies in early schooling. *TESOL Quarterly, 39*(1), 59-82.

Hedge, T. (2000). *Teaching and learning in the language classroom.* Oxford: Oxford University Press.

Hellerman, J. (2008). *Social actions for classroom language classroom.* Clevedon: Multilingual Matters.

Heritage, M. (2007). Formative assessment: What do teachers need to know and do? *Phi Delta Kappan, 89,* 140-145.

Hewson, C. (2007). Qualitative approaches and possibilities for mixed methods research. In A. Johnson, K. McKenna, T. Postmes, & U-D. Reips (Eds.), *The Oxford handbook of Internet psychology* (pp. 405-428). Oxford: Oxford University Press.

Hill, S. E., & Nichols, S. (2013). Early literacy: Towards a semiotic approach. In O. N. Saracho & B. Spodek (Eds.), *Handbook of research on the education of young children* (pp. 147-156). New York, NY: Taylor & Francis.

Hirata, Y., & Hirata, Y. (2009). Development of visuaLexs for hybrid language learning. In F. Lee Wang, J. Fong, L. Zhang, & V. S. K. Lee (Eds.), *Hybrid learning and education. Proceedings of Second International Conference* (pp. 55-65). Berlin: Springer.

Hirumi, A. (2006). Analysing and designing E-learning interactions. In C. Juwah (Ed.), *Interactions in online education* (pp. 46-71). New York, NY: Routledge.

Hofstede, G. (1980). *Culture consequences: International differences in work-related values.* London: Sage Publications.

Hofstede, G. (2001). *Culture's consequences: Comparing values, behaviours, institutions, and organizations across nations.* Thousand Oaks, CA: Sage.

Holec, H. (1981). *Autonomy in foreign language learning.* Oxford: Pergamon.

Holec, H. (1996). Self-directed learning: An alternative form of training. In H. Holec, D. Little, & R. Richterich (Eds.), *Strategies in language learning and use* (pp. 75-124). Strasbourg: Council of Europe.

Holec, H. (Ed.). (1988). *Autonomy and self-directed learning: Present fields of application*. Strasbourg: Council of Europe.

Howatt, A. P. R. (1984). *A history of English language teaching*. Oxford: Oxford University Press.

Howe, K. R., & Berv, J. (2000). Constructing constructivism, epistemological and pedagogical. In D. C. Phillips (Ed.), *Constructivism in education: Opinions and second opinions on controversial issues* (pp. 19-40). Chicago, IL: The University of Chicago Press.

Hsu, Y-C., & Ching, Y-H. (2013). Mobile computer-supported collaborative learning: A review of experimental research. *British Journal of Educational Technology, 44* (5), E111-E114.

Huat, C. M., & Kerry, T. (2008). *International perspectives on education*. London: Continuum.

Hue, M. T. (2007). Classroom management for children with diverse learning needs. In S. N. Phillipson (Ed.), *Learning diversity in the Chinese classroom contexts and practice for students with special needs* (pp. 459-486). Hong Kong: Hong Kong University Press.

Hutchinson, T., & Waters, A. (1987). *English for specific purposes: A learning-centered approach*. Cambridge: Cambridge University Press.

Hutz, M., & Kolb, A. (2007). *Gummybears and *Handshoes. Zur Entstehung von Fehlern [*Gummybears and *Handshoes. The emergence of errors]. *The Primary English Magazine 3,* 6-8.

Hyland, K. (2003). Genre-based pedagogies. A social response to process. *Journal of Second Language Writing, 12,* 17-29.

Hyland, K. (2007). Genre pedagogy: Language literacy and L2 writing instruction. *Journal of Second Language Writing, 16,* 148-164.

Illich, I. (1971). *Deschooling society*. London: Calder & Boyars.

Irie, K., & Stewart, A. (Eds.). (2012). *Realizing autonomy. Practice and reflection in language education contexts*. New York, NY: Palgrave Macmillan.

Islam, C., & Mares, C. (2003). Adapting classroom materials. In B. Tomlinson (Ed.), *Developing materials for language teaching* (pp. 86-100). London: Continuum.

Jarvis, H., & Achilleos, M. (2013). From computer assisted language learning (CALL) to mobile assisted language use. *TESL-EJ, 16*(4). Retrieved from http://www.tesl-ej.org/wordpress/issues/volume16/ej64/ej64a2/

Jarvis, H., & Krashen, S. (2014). Is CALL obsolete? Language acquisition and language learning revisited in a digital age. *TESL-EJ*, 17(4). Retrieved from http://www.tesl-ej.org/wordpress/issues/volume17/ej68/ej68a1/

Jenkins, J. (2007). *English as a lingua franca: Attitude and identity*. Oxford: Oxford University Press.

Jenkins, J. (2012). English as a lingua franca from the classroom to the classroom. *ELT Journal*, 66(44), 86-494.

Jennex, M. E. (Ed.). (2011). *Global aspects and cultural perspectives on knowledge management. Emerging dimensions*. Hershey, PA: Information Science Reference.

Jensen, B. K. (2002). The qualitative research process. In K. B. Jensen (Ed.), *A handbook of media and communication research. Qualitative and quantitative methodologies* (pp. 235-253). London: Routledge.

Johns, A. M. (Ed.). (2002). *Genre in the classroom: Multiple perspectives*. Mahwah, NJ: Lawrence Erlbaum Associates.

Johnson, D. W., & Johnson, R. T. (1996). Conflict resolution and peer mediation programs in elementary and secondary schools: A review of the research. *Review of Educational Research*, 66(4), 459-506.

Johnson, K. (2013). *An introduction to foreign language learning and teaching* (2nd ed.). New York, NY: Routledge.

Jonassen, D. H. (1991). Objectivism vs. constructivism: Do we need a new paradigm? *Educational Technology: Research and Development*, 39(3), 5-14.

Jonassen, D. H. (1994). Thinking technology. *Educational Technology*, 34(4), 34-37.

Jones, J. (1995). Self-access and culture. *ELT Journal*, 49(3), 228-234.

Jordan, R. R. (2006). *English for academic purposes. A guide and resource book for teachers*. Cambridge: Cambridge University Press.

Kaptelinin, V., & Cole, M. (2001). Individual and collective activities in educational computer game playing. In T. Koschmann, R. Nelson, & N. Miyake (Eds.), *CSCL 2: Carrying forward the conversation* (pp. 303-315). Mahwah, NJ: Lawrence Erlbaum.

Kaupmann, K. (2012). Suggestions for the effective use of reading logs in the ninth grade. In P. Lennon (Ed.), *Learner autonomy in the English classroom. Empirical studies and ideas for teachers* (pp. 123-146). Frankfurt: Peter Lang.

Keene, E., & Zimmerman, S. (1997). *Mosaic of thought: Teaching comprehension in a reader's workshop*. Portsmouth, NH: Heinemann.

Kehrwald, J. (2013). A social-ecological exploration of autonomy, beliefs and identity. In P. Benson & L. Cooker (Eds.), *The applied linguistic individual. Sociocultural approaches to identity, agency and autonomy* (pp. 90-103). Sheffield: Equinox.

Kenny, B. (1993). For more autonomy. *System, 21*(4), 431-442.

Kern, R. (2000). *Literacy and language teaching*. Oxford: Oxford University Press.

Kilpatrick, W. H. (1925). *Foundations of method*. New York, NY: Macmillan.

Kim, Y., & McDonough, K. (2008). The effect of interlocutor proficiency on the collaborative dialogue between Korean as a second language learners. *Language Teaching Research, 12*, 211-234.

King, S. (2010). Reflecting critically on practice. In C. Brooks (Ed.), *Studying PGCE Geography at M level. Reflection, research and writing for professional development* (pp. 36-50). New York, NY: Routledge.

Kintsch, W., & van Dijk, T. A. (1983). *Strategies of discourse comprehension*. New York, NY: Academic Press.

Kirkpatrick, A. (2007). *World Englishes. Implications for international communication and English language teaching*. Cambridge: Cambridge University Press.

Kohonen, V. (1992). Experiential language learning: Second language learning as cooperative learner education. In D. Nunan (Ed.), *Collaborative language learning and teaching* (pp. 14-39). Cambridge: Cambridge University Press.

Kolb, A. (2007). *Portfolioarbeit. Wie Grundschulkinder ihr Sprachenlernen reflektieren* [Working with a portfolio. What do primary school pupils think about learning languages?]. Tübingen: Narr.

Komorowska, H. (2002a). *Metodyka nauczania języków obcych* [Foreign language teaching methodology]. Warszawa: Fraszka Edukacyjna.

Komorowska, H. (2002b). *Sprawdzanie umiejętności w nauce języka obcego: Kontrola, Ocena, Testowanie* [Examining: Control, assessment, testing in foreign language learning]. Warszawa: Fraszka Edukacyjna.

Korsvold, A-K., & Rüschoff, B. (Eds.). (1997). *New technologies in language learning and teaching*. Strasbourg: Council of Europe.

Korthagen, F. A. J. (1999). Linking reflection and technical competence: The logbook as an instrument in teacher education. *European Journal of Teacher Education, 22,* 2(3), 191-207.

Korthagen, F. A. J. (2001). *Linking practice and theory. The pedagogy of realistic teacher education.* Mahwah, NJ: Lawrence Erlbaum Associates.

Kost, C. R. (2008). Use of communication strategies in a synchronous CMC environment. In S. Sieloff Magnan (Ed.), *Mediating discourse online* (pp. 153-190). Amsterdam: John Benjamins.

Kötter, M. (2002). *Tandem learning on the Internet: Learner interactions in virtual online environments (MOOs).* Frankfurt: Lang.

Kötter, M. (2003). Negotiations of meaning and codeswitching in online tandems. *Language Learning & Technology, 7*(2), 145-172.

Krajka, J. (2007). *English language teaching in the Internet-assisted environment. Issues in the use of the web as a teaching medium.* Lublin: Maria Curie-Skłodowska University Press.

Kramer, P. A. (2005). *The ABC's of classroom management.* Indianapolis, IN: Kappa DeltaPi.

Kramsch, C. (1998). *Language and culture.* Oxford: Oxford University Press.

Krashen, S. (1980). The input hypothesis. In J. Alatis (Ed.), *Current issues in bilingual education* (pp. 168-180). Washington, DC: Georgetown University Press.

Krashen, S. (1982). *Principles and practice in second language acquisition.* Oxford: Pergamon.

Krashen, S. (1989). We acquire vocabulary and spelling by reading: Additional evidence for the input hypothesis. *The Modern Language Journal, 73,* 440-464.

Kreisberg, S. (1992). *Transforming power. Domination, empowerment and education.* Albany, NY: State University of New York Press.

Kress, G. (1999). Genre and the changing contexts for English language arts. *Language Arts, 76*(6), 461-469.

Kress, G., & van Leeuwen, T. (1996). *Reading image. The grammar of visual design.* London: Routledge.

Kumaravadivelu, B. (2006). *Understanding language teaching: From method to postmethod.* Mahwah, NJ: Lawrence Erlbaum.

La Ganza, W. (2008). Learner autonomy – teacher autonomy. Interrelating and the will to empower. In T. Lamb & H. Reinders (Eds.), *Learner* and teacher autonomy. Concepts, realities and responses (pp. 63-79). Amsterdam: John Benjamins.

Lamb, M. (2013). The struggle to belong: Individual language learners in situated learning theory. In P. Benson & L. Cooker (Eds.), *The applied linguistic individual. Sociocultural approaches to identity, agency and autonomy* (pp. 32-45). Sheffield: Equinox.

Lamb, T., & Reinders, H. (Eds.). (2008). *Learner and teacher autonomy. Concepts, realities and responses* (6th ed.). Amsterdam: John Benjamins.

Lan, R. (2008). *Language learning strategies of young Taiwanese learners of EFL*. Paper presented at the conference of the International Association for Applied Linguistics, Essen.

Langner, M., & Prokop, M. (2003). Autonomous students in language learning centres. In G. Bräuer & K. Sanders (Eds.), *New visions in foreign and second language education* (pp. 77-88). San Diego: Larc Press.

Lanham, R. A. (2001). What's next for text? *Education, Communication & Information, 1*(1), 15-36.

Lantolf, J. P. (2008). SLA, I + 1, SCT, the ZPD, and other things. A response to Evensen. *Journal of Applied Linguistics, 5*(2), 215-219.

Lantolf, J. P. (2013). Sociocultural theory and the dialectics of L2 learner autonomy/agency. In P. Benson & L. Cooker (Eds.), *The applied linguistic individual. Sociocultural approaches to identity, agency and autonomy* (pp. 17-31). Sheffield: Equinox.

Lantolf, J. P. (Ed.). (2000). *Sociocultural theory and second language learning*. Oxford: Oxford University Press.

Lantolf, J. P., & Aljaafreh, A. (1995). Second language learning in the zone of proximal development: A revolutionary experience. *International Journal of Educational Research, 23*, 619-632.

Lantolf, J. P., & Pavlenko, A. (2001). Second language activity theory: Understanding second language learners as people. In M. P. Breen (Ed.), *Learner contributions to language learning* (pp. 141-158). Harlow: Longman.

Lantolf, J. P., & Thorne, S. L. (2006). *Sociocultural theory and the genesis of SL development*. Oxford: Oxford University Press.

Law, E. Y. Y. (2011). Evaluating learning gain in a self-access centre. In D. Gardner (Ed.), *Fostering autonomy in language learning* (pp. 199-213). Gaziantep: Zirve University.

Lee, K. R., & Oxford, R. L. (2008). Understanding EFL learners' strategy use and strategy awareness. *Asian EFL Journal*, 10(1), 7-32.

Legutke, M. K. (1998). Handlungsraum Klassenzimmer and Beyond [The classroom and beyond as an action space]. In J-P. Timm (Ed.), *Englisch Lernen and Lehren* [Learning and teaching English] (pp. 93-109). Berlin: Cornelsen.

Legutke, M. K. (1999). Möglichkeiten zur Neugestaltung des Fremdsprachenunterrichts – Vier Praxisberichte (Fallvignetten) [The potential of the new look of an English lesson]. In C. Edelhoff & R. Weskamp (Eds.), *Autonomes Fremdsprachenlernen* [Autonomous learning of foreign languages] (pp. 94-112). Ismaning: Hueber.

Legutke, M. K., & Lortz, W. (Eds). (2002). *Mein Sprachenportfolio* [My language portfolio]. Frankfurt: Diesterweg.

Legutke, M. K., & Thomas, H. (1991). *Process and experience in the language classroom*. Harlow: Pearson Education.

Legutke, M. K., Müller-Hartmann, A., & Schocker-von Dithfurt, M. (2009). *Teaching English in the primary school*. Stuttgart: Klett.

Leinhardt, G., & Steele, M. (2005). Seeing the complexity of standing on the side. *Cognition and Instruction*, 23, 87-163.

Lenz, P. (2003). The European language portfolio – A tool for comprehensive assessment and the promotion of plurilingualism. In G. Bräuer & K. Sanders (Eds.), *New visions in foreign and second language education* (pp. 123-152). San Diego: Larc Press.

Levy, M. (1997). *Computer-assisted language learning: Context and contextualisation*. Oxford: Clarendon Press.

Levy, M., & Kennedy, C. (2005). Learning Italian via mobile SMS. In A. Kukulska-Hulme & J. Traxler (Eds.), *Mobile learning: A handbook for educators and trainers* (pp. 76-83). London: Taylor and Francis.

Li, Y. (2000). Linguistic characteristics of ESL writing in task-based E-mail activities. *System*, 28, 229-245.

Liebenhoff, K. (2004). The very hungry caterpillar. Ein Theaterstück [A play]. *Primary English*, 3, 12-18.

Little, D. (1991). *Learner autonomy 1: Definitions, issues and problems*. Dublin: Authentik.

Little, D. (1997). Responding authentically to authentic texts: A problem for self-access language learning? In P. Benson & P. Voller (Eds.), *Au-*

tonomy & independence in language learning (pp. 225-236). London and New York: Longman.

Little, D. (2008). Learner autonomy in practice: A challenge for university language teaching. In R. Arntz & B. Kühn (Eds.), *Autonomes Fremdsprachenlernen in Hochschule und Erwachsenenbildung* [Autonomous learning of foreign languages at the tertiary level and in adult education] (pp. 47-63). Bochum: AKS-Verlag.

Little, D. (2011). *The European language portfolio: A guide to the planning, implementation and evaluation of whole-school projects*. Strasbourg: Council of Europe.

Little, D. (Ed.). (1989). *Self-access systems for language learning*. Dublin: Authentik/CILT.

Littlejohn, A. (1982). A procedural guide for teacherless language learning groups (Unpublished master's dissertation). University of Lancaster, Lancaster, UK.

Littlejohn, A. (2011). The analysis of language teaching materials: Inside the Trojan horse. In B. Tomlinson (Ed.), *Materials development in language teaching* (pp. 179-211). Cambridge: Cambridge University Press.

Littlejohn, S. W. (1992). *Theories of human communication* (4th ed.). Belmont, CA: Wadsworth.

Littlewood, W. (1997). Self-access: Why do we want it and what can it do? In P. Benson & P. Voller (Eds.), *Autonomy & independence in language learning* (pp. 79-91). London and New York: Longman.

Long, M. H. (1981). Input, interaction, and second language acquisition. *Foreign Language Acquisition: Annals of the New York Academy of Sciences*, 379, 259-278.

Long, M. H. (1985). Input and second language acquisition theory. In S. Gass & C. Madden (Eds.), *Input and second language acquisition* (pp. 377-393). Rowley, MA: Newbury House.

Long, M. H. (1991). Focus on form: A design feature in language teaching methodology. In K. De Bot, R. B. Ginsberg, & C. Kramsch (Eds.), *Foreign language research in crosscultural perspective* (pp. 39-52). Philadelphia, PA: Benjamins.

Long, M. H. (1996). The role of the linguistic environment in second language acquisition. In W. C. Ritchie & T. K. Bhatia (Eds.), *Handbook of second language acquisition* (pp. 413-468). San Diego, CA: Academic Press.

Long, M. H. (2015). *Second language acquisition and task-based language teaching*. Oxford: Wiley-Blackwell.

Long, P. D. (2002). Blogs: A disruptive technology coming of age? Retrieved from http://www.campus-technology.com/article.asp?id=6774

Longworth, N., & Davies, W. K. (1996). *Lifelong learning: New visions, new implications, new roles – for industry, government, education, and the community for the 21st century*. London: Kogan Page.

Lu, M. (2008). Effectiveness of vocabulary learning via mobile phone. *Journal of Computer Assisted Learning, 24*(6), 515–525.

Luria, A. R. (1979). *The making of mind: A personal account of Soviet psychology*. Cambridge, MA: Harvard University Press.

Lynch, L., Fawcett, A. J., & Nicolson, R. I. (2000). Computer-assisted reading intervention in a secondary school: An evaluation study. *British Journal of Educational Technology, 31*(4), 333–348.

Macaskill, A., & Denovan, A. (2013). Developing autonomous learning in first year university students using perspectives from positive psychology. *Studies in Higher Education, 38*(1), 124–142.

Mackey, A., & Gass, S. (2005). *Second language research methodology and design*. Mahwah, NJ: Lawrence Erlbaum.

Maley, A. (2003). Input, processes & outcomes in materials development: Extending the range. *Folio, 8*(1/2), 8–12.

Manheimer, R. (1993). Close the task: Improve the discourse. *Estudios de Linguistica Aplicada, 17*, 18–40.

Mann, B. L. (2006). Testing the validity of post and vote web-based peer assessment. In D. Williams, S. Howell, & M. Hricko (Eds.), *Online assessment, measurement and evaluation: Emerging practices* (pp. 131–152). London: Idea Group.

Mariani, L. (1983). Evaluating and supplementing coursebooks. In S. Holden (Ed.), *Second selections from Modern English Teacher* (pp. 127–130). Harlow: Longman.

Markee, N. (1997). *Managing curricular innovation*. Cambridge: Cambridge University Press.

Martinez, H. (2008). The subjective theories of student teachers. Implications for teacher education and research on learner autonomy. In T. Lamb & H. Reinders (Eds.), *Learner and teacher autonomy. Concepts, realities and responses* (pp. 103–124). Amsterdam: John Benjamins.

Mason, J. (1992). Reading stories to preliterate children: A proposed connection to reading. In P. B. Gough, L. C. Ehri, & R. Treiman (Eds.), *Reading acquisition* (pp. 215-243). Hillsdale, NJ: Erlbaum.

Masuhara, H. (2006). Materials as a teacher development tool. In J. Mukundan (Ed.), *Readings on ELT materials II* (pp. 34-46). Petaling Jaya: Pearson Malaysia.

Masuhara, H. (2015). "Anything goes" in task-based language teaching materials? – The need for principled materials evaluation, adaptation and development. *The European Journal of Applied Linguistics and TEFL, 4*(2), 113-127.

McCarten, J., & McCarthy, M. (2010). Bridging the gap between corpus and course book. The case of conversation strategies. In F. Mishan & A. Chambers (Eds.), *Perspectives on language learning materials development* (pp. 11-32). Bern: Peter Lang.

McDonough, J., & Shaw, C. (1993). *Materials and methods in ELT: A teacher's guide.* London: Blackwell.

McGarry, D. (1995). *Learner autonomy 4: The role of authentic texts.* Dublin: Authentik.

McGrath, I. (2002). *Materials evaluation and design for language teaching.* Edinburgh: Edinburgh University Press.

McGrath, I. (2004). The representation of people in educational materials. *RELC Journal, 35*(3), 351-358.

McGrath, I. (2013). *Teaching materials and the roles of EFL/ESL teachers. Practice and theory.* London: Bloomsbury.

McKay, P. (2006). *Assessing young language learners.* Cambridge: Cambridge University Press.

McLaughlin, M., & Allen, M. B. (2009). *Guided comprehension in grades 3-8* (2nd ed.). Newark, DE: International Reading Association.

McLaughlin, M. W., & Talbert, J. E. (2006). *Building school-based teacher learning communities: Professional strategies to improve student achievement.* New York, NY: Teachers College, Columbia University.

McNabb, D. E. (2010). *Research methods for Political Science: Quantitative and qualitative approaches* (2nd ed.). New York, NY: M. E. Sharpe.

McNamara, T. F. (1996). *Measuring second language performance.* New York, NY: Addison Wesley Longman Limited.

Menezes, V. (2013). Chaos and the complexity of second language acquisition. In P. Benson & L. Cooker (Eds.), *The applied linguistic individual.*

Sociocultural approaches to identity, agency and autonomy (pp. 59-74). Sheffield: Equinox.

Merrill, D., Tennyson, R. D., & Posey, L. O. (1992). *Teaching concepts: An instructional design guide* (2nd ed.). Englewood Cliffs, NJ: Educational Technology Publications.

Mews, M-T., Stute, T., & Uplawski, G. (2009). *Talk! Materialen zur Vorbereitung auf die mündliche Abschlussprüfung Englisch für das einfache und mittlere Niveau (A2/A2+)* [Talk! Examination materials for the final oral examination in English for levels A2/A2+]. Braunschweig: Diesterweg/Westermann.

Michońska-Stadnik, A. (2008). Identyfikacja oraz trening strategii dla rozwoju autonomii [Identification and training in the use of strategies for autonomy development]. In M. Pawlak (Ed.), *Autonomia w nauce języka angielskiego – co osiągnęliśmy i dokąd zmierzamy?* [Autonomy in English language learning – what have we achieved and where are we heading?] (pp. 393-403). Poznań, Kalisz, Poznań: Uniwersytet A. Mickiewicza w Poznaniu, Wydział Pedagogiczno-Artystyczny UAM w Kaliszu i Wydawnictwo Państwowej Wyższej Szkoły Zawodowej w Koninie.

Ming-tak, H., & Wai-shing, L. (2008). *Classroom management. Creating a positive learning environment.* Hong Kong: Hong Kong University Press.

Mishan, F. (2005). *Designing authenticity into language learning materials.* Bristol: Intellect Books.

Mochizuki, N., & Ortega, L. (2008). Ballancing communication and grammar in beginning level foreign language classrooms: A study of guided planning and relativization. *Language Teaching Research, 12,* 11-37.

Moreillon, J. (2007). *Collaborative strategies for teaching reading comprehension: Maximize impact.* Chicago, IL: American Library Association.

Morita, N. (2004). Negotiating participation and identity in second language academic communities. *TESOL Quarterly, 38*(4), 573-603.

Motteram, G. (2011). Developing language learning materials with technology. In B. Tomlinson (Ed.), *Materials development in language teaching* (pp. 303-327). Cambridge: Cambridge University Press.

Mullen, T., Appel, C., & Shanklin, T. (2009). Skype-based tandem language learning and Web 2.0. In M. Thomas (Ed.), *Handbook of research on*

Web 2.0 and second language learning (pp. 101–118). Hershey, PA: Information Science Reference.

Müller-Hartmann, A. (2000). The role of tasks in promoting intercultural learning in electronic learning networks. *Language Learning & Technology*, 4(2), 129–147.

Müller-Hartmann, A., & Schocker-von-Ditfurth, M. (2011). *Teaching English: Task-supported language learning.* Paderborn: Schöningh.

Murawski, W. M. (2010). *Collaborative teaching in elementary schools: Making the co-teaching marriage work!* Thousand Oaks, CA: Corwin.

Nagel, P. S. (1999). E-mail in the virtual ESL/EFL classroom. *The Internet TESL Journal*, 5(7). Retrieved from http://iteslj.org/Articles/Nagel-Email.html

Nah, K. C., White, P., & Sussex, R. (2008). The potential of using a mobile phone to access the Internet for learning EFL listening skills within a Korean context. *ReCALL*, 20(3), 331–347.

Nassaji, H., & Fotos, S. S. (2011). *Teaching grammar in second language classrooms. Integrating form-focused instruction in communicative context.* New York, NY: Routledge.

Nation, I. S. P., & Newton, J. (2009). *Teaching ESL/EFL listening and speaking.* New York, NY: Routledge.

Nation, P., & Macalister, J. (2010). *Language curriculum design.* New York, NY: Routledge.

Neary, M. (2000). *Teaching, assessing and evaluation for clinical competence: A practical guide for practitioners and teachers.* Cheltenham: Stanley Thornes.

Nelson, T. J. (2008). Writing in the wikishop: Constructing knowledge in the electronic classroom. In R. E. Cummings & M. Barton (Eds.), *Wiki writing: Collaborative learning in the college classroom* (pp. 194–203). Ann Arbor, MI: University of Michigan Press.

Newman, F., & Holzman, L. (1993). *Lev Vygotsky: Revolutionary scientist.* New York, NY: Routledge.

Nguyen, L. T. C., & Gu, Y. (2013). Strategy-based instruction: A learner-focused approach to developing learner autonomy. *Language Teaching Research*, 17(1), 9–30.

Niżegorodcew, A. (2007). *Input for instructed L2 learners. The relevance of relevance.* Clevedon: Multilingual Matters.

Norwich, B. (2013). *Addressing tensions and dilemmas in inclusive education. Living with uncertainty.* Abingdon: Routledge.

Nunan, D. (1988). *The learner-centred curriculum.* Cambridge: Cambridge University Press.

Nunan, D. (1989). *Designing tasks for the communicative classroom.* Cambridge: Cambridge University Press.

Nunan, D. (1992). *Research methods in language learning.* Cambridge: Cambridge University Press.

Nunan, D. (1997). Designing and adapting materials to encourage learner autonomy. In P. Benson & P. Voller (Eds.), *Autonomy & independence in language learning* (pp. 192-203). London and New York: Longman.

Nunan, D. (2004). *Task-based language teaching.* New York, NY: Cambridge University Press.

Nunan, D., & Lamb, C. (1996). *The self-directed teacher. Managing the learning process.* Cambridge: Cambridge University Press.

Nuttall, C. (1996). *Teaching reading skills in a foreign language.* Oxford: Macmillan.

O'Malley, J. M., & Chamot, A. U. (1990). *Learning strategies in second language acquisition.* Cambridge: Cambridge University Press.

Opoku-Amankwa, K. (2010). What happens to textbooks in the classroom? Pupils' access to literacy in an urban primary school in Ghana. *Pedagogy, Culture and Society, 18*(2), 159 –172.

Orange, C. (2002). *The quick reference guide to educational innovations. Practices, programs, policies and philosophies.* Thousand Oaks, CA: Corwin Press.

O'Rourke, B., & Carson, L. (Eds.) (2010). *Language learner autonomy. Policy, curriculum, classroom.* Bern: Peter Lang.

Ortega, L. (2009). *Understanding second language acquisition.* London: Hodder Education.

Oxford, R. L. (1989). Use of language learning strategies: A synthesis of studies with implications for strategy training. *System, 17,* 235-247.

Oxford, R. L. (1990). *Language learning strategies: What every teacher should know.* Rowley, MA: Newbury House.

Oxford, R. L. (2001). 'The bleached bones of a story': Constructions of language teachers. In M. P. Breen (Ed.), *Learner contributions to language learning: New directions in research* (pp. 86-111). Harlow: Pearson Education.

Oxford, R. L. (2008). Hero with a thousand faces: Learner autonomy, learning strategies and learning tactics in independent language learning. In S. Hurd & T. Lewis (Eds.), *Language learning strategies in independent settings* (pp. 41-66). Bristol: Multilingual Matters.

Oxford, R. L. (2011). *Teaching and researching language learning strategies.* Harlow: Pearson Longman.

Paivio, A. (2007). *Mind and its evolution: A dual coding theoretical approach.* Mahwah, NJ: Erlbaum Associates.

Paltridge, B. (2006). *Discourse analysis.* London: Continuum.

Pappas, C. C., & Barro Zecker, L. (2001). Summary and ongoing reflections: Struggles and significance in creating collaborative interactions and talk in urban classrooms. In C. C. Pappas & L. Barro Zecker (Eds.), *Teacher inquiries in literacy teaching-learning. Learning to collaborate in elementary urban classrooms* (pp. 241-252). Mahwah, NJ: Lawrence Erlbaum Associates.

Pawlak, M. (2008). Jak rozwijać autonomię przy pomocy europejskiego portfolio językowego dla uczniów szkół ponadgimnazjalnych i studentów [How to develop learner autonomy using the European language portfolio for secondary school and university students]. In M. Pawlak (Ed.), *Autonomia w nauce języka angielskiego – Co osiągnęliśmy i dokąd zmierzamy?* [Autonomy in learning English – What have we achieved and where are we heading?] (pp. 267-280). Poznań, Kalisz, Poznań: Uniwersytet A. Mickiewicza w Poznaniu, Wydział Pedagogiczno-Artystyczny UAM w Kaliszu i Wydawnictwo Państwowej Wyższej Szkoły Zawodowej w Koninie.

Pawlak, M. (2011a). Research into language learning strategies: Taking stock and looking ahead. In J. Arabski & A. Wojtaszek (Eds.), *Individual learner differences in SLA* (pp. 17-37). Bristol: Multilingual Matters.

Pawlak, M. (Ed.). (2004). *Describing and researching interactive processes in the foreign language classroom.* Konin: PWSZ.

Pawlak, M. (Ed.). (2011b). *Autonomia w nauce języka obcego – uczeń a nauczyciel* [Autonomy in foreign language learning – student vs teacher]. Poznań, Kalisz, Konin: Uniwersytet im. Adama Mickiewicza w Poznaniu oraz Wydawnictwo Państwowej Wyższej Szkoły Zawodowej w Koninie.

Pearson, P. D., & Gallagher, G. (1983). The gradual release of responsibility model of instruction. *Contemporary Educational Psychology,* 8, 112-23.

Pennycook, A. (1997). Cultural awareness and autonomy. In P. Benson & P. Voller (Eds.), *Autonomy & independence in language learning* (pp. 35-53). London and New York: Longman.

Peters, O. (1998). *Learning and teaching in distance education. Analysis and interpretations from an international perspective.* London: Kogan Page.

Peterson, K. D. (2000). *Teacher evaluation. A comprehensive guide to new directions and practices* (2nd ed.). Thousand Oaks, CA: Corwin Press.

Phillips, D. C. (2000). An opinionated account of the constructivist landscape. In D. C. Phillips (Ed.), *Constructivism in education: Opinions and second opinions on controversial issues* (pp. 1-18). Chicago, IL: The University of Chicago Press.

Piaget, J. (1952). *The origins of intelligence in children.* New York, NY: International Universities Press.

Piaget, J. (1972). *The psychology of the child.* New York, NY: Appleton-Century Crofts.

Piaget, J. (1978). *Behaviour and evolution.* New York, NY: Random House.

Pica, T. (1988). Interlanguage adjustments as an outcome on NS-NNS negotiated interaction. *Language Learning, 38,* 45-73.

Pica, T. (1994). Research on negotiation: What does it reveal about second language learning conditions, processes and outcomes? *Language Learning, 44,* 493-527.

Plester, B., Wood, C., & Joshi, P. (2009). Exploring the relationship between children's knowledge of text message abbreviations and school literacy outcomes. *British Journal of Developmental Psychology, 27*(1), 145-161.

Pollard, A. (2005). *Reflective teaching* (2nd ed.). London: Continuum.

Poole, D., & Patthey-Chavez, G. G. (1994). Locating assisted performance: A study of instructional activity setting and their effects on the discourse of teaching. *Issues in Applied Linguistics, 5,* 3-35.

Popham, W. J. (2008). The assessment-savvy student. *Educational Leadership, 66*(3), 80-82.

Pritchard, A., & Woollard, J. (2013). *Psychology for the classroom: Constructivism and social learning.* New York, NY: Routledge.

Prodromou, L. (2002). The great ELT textbook debate. *Modern English Teacher, 11*(4), 25-33.

Pulverness, A. (2007). *Reading matters: A guide to using graded readers.* Borgaro Torinese: G. Canale and C. Spa.

Purcell, K., Heaps, A., Buchanan, J., & Friedrich, L. (2013). *How teachers are using technology at home and in their classrooms.* Washington, DC: Pew Research Centre's Internet & American Life Project. Retrieved from http://www.pewinternet.org/files/old-media/Files/Reports/2013/PIP_TeachersandTechnologywithmethodology_PDF.pdf

Purpura, J. E. (2004). *Assessing grammar.* Cambridge: Cambridge University Press.

Rabinowitz, P. J. (1987). *Before reading: Narrative conventions and the politics of interpretation.* Ithaca, NY: Cornell University Press.

Raith, T. (2006). Weblogs in the EFL classroom – A study on the relationship between audience and writing. *NEOS – Journal of New Trends in Education, 3*(30), 3-30.

Raith, T. (2009). The use of weblogs in language education. In M. Thomas (Ed.), *Handbook of research on Web 2.0 and second language learning* (pp. 274-291). London: IGI Global.

Ramirez Salas, M. (2004). English teachers as materials developers. *Revista Electrónica Actualidades Investigativas en Educación, 4*(2). Retrieved from http://www.redalyc.org/pdf/447/44740214.pdf

Ravelonanahary, M. (2007). The use of textbooks and educational media: The Malagasy experience. In M. Horsley & J. McCall (Eds.), *Peace, democratization and educational media. Papers from the Ninth International Conference on Textbooks and Educational Media* (pp. 166-175). Retrieved from www.iartem.no/documents/9thIARTEMConferenceVolume.pdf

Raz, J. (1986). *The morality of freedom.* Oxford: Clarendon.

Reinke, W. M., Herman, K. C., & Sprick, R. (2011). *Motivational interviewing for effective classroom management. The classroom check-up.* New York, NY: The Guildford Press.

Renandya, W. A. (2012). Teacher roles in EIL. *The European Journal of Applied Linguistics and TEFL, 2,* 65-80.

Richards, J. C. (2001). *Curriculum development in language teaching.* Cambridge: Cambridge University Press.

Richards, J. C., & Lockhart, C. (1994). *Reflective teaching in second language classrooms.* Cambridge: Cambridge University Press.

Ritchhart, R., Church, M., & Morrison, K. (2011). *Making thinking visible. How to promote engagement, understanding and independence for all learners.* San Francisco, CA: Jossey-Bass.

Ritchhart, R., Palmer, P., Church, M., & Tishman, S. (2006). *Thinking routines: Establishing patterns of thinking in the classroom*. Paper presented at the American Educational Research Association annual meeting, San Francisco.

Robb, T. N. (1996). E-mail keypals for language fluency. *Foreign Language Notes*, 38(3), 8-10.

Robinson, P. (1991). *ESP today: A practitioner's guide*. London: Prentice Hall.

Robinson, P. (Ed.). (2011). *Second language task complexity. Researching the cognition hypothesis of language learning and performance*. Amsterdam: John Benjamins.

Roehler, L. R., & Cantlon, D. J. (1997). Scaffolding: A powerful tool in social constructivist classrooms. In K. Hogan & M. Pressley (Eds.), *Scaffolding student learning: Instructional approaches and issues* (pp. 6-42). Cambridge, MA: Brookline.

Rogers, A. (2002). The interpersonal relationship in the facilitation of learning. In R. Harrison, F. Reeve, A. Hanson & J. Clarke (Eds.), *Supporting lifelong learning, volume I: Perspectives on learning* (pp. 8-24). London: RoutledgeFalmer.

Rogers, C. R. (1969). *Freedom to learn*. Columbus, OH: Charles Merrill.

Rogers, Y., & Price, S. (2009). How mobile technologies are changing the way children learn. In A. Druin (Ed.), *Mobile technology for children: Designing for interaction and learning* (pp. 3-17). Amsterdam: Elsevier.

Rooke, J. (2015). Using iPads to support peer assessment of writing. *English 4-11*, 55, 7-8.

Rosen, H. (1984). *Stories and meanings*. Sheffield: National Association of the Teaching of English.

Rosenblatt, L. (1978). *The reader, the text, the poem: The transactional theory of the literary work*. Carbondale, IL: Southern Illinois University Press.

Rösler, D. (2006). Foreign language learning with the new media: Between the sanctuary of the classroom and the open terrain of natural language acquisition. *German as a Foreign Language*, 1, 16-31.

Rost, M. (2013). *Teaching and research listening* (2nd ed.). New York, NY: Routledge.

Rüschoff, B. (1999). Construction of knowledge as the basis of foreign language learning. In B. Mißler & U. Multhaup (Eds.), *The construction of knowledge, learner autonomy and related issues in foreign language learning* (pp. 79-88). Tübingen: Stauffenburg.

Rüschoff, B. (2009). Output-oriented language learning with digital media. In M. Thomas (Ed.), *Handbook of research on Web 2.0 and second language learning* (pp. 42-59). London: IGI Global.

Rüschoff, B. (2010). Authenticity in language learning revisited: Materials, processes, aims. In B. O'Rourke & L. Carson (Eds.), *Language learner autonomy: Policy, curriculum, classroom* (pp. 121-134). Bern: Peter Lang.

Rüschoff, B., & Wolff, D. (1998). *Fremdsprachenlernen in der Wissensgesellschaft. Zum Einsatz der neuen Technologien in Schule und Unterricht* [Foreign language learning in an information-based society. The use of new technologies at school and in the lesson]. Ismaning: Hueber.

Ryan, K., Cooper, J. M., & Tauer, S. (2011). *Teaching for student learning: Becoming a master teacher.* Belmont, CA: Wadsworth Cengage Learning.

Sampath, K., Panneerselvam, A., & Santhanam, S. (2007). *Introduction to educational technology* (5th ed.). New Delhi: Sterling Publishers Private Limited.

Samuda, V., & Bygate, M. (2008). *Tasks in second language learning.* Basingstoke: Palgrave.

Sarré, C. (2011). Computer-mediated negotiated interaction: How is meaning negotiated in discussion boards, text chat and videoconferencing? In S. Thouësny & L. Bradley (Eds.), *Second language teaching and learning with technology: Views of emergent researchers* (pp. 189-210). Dublin: Research-Publishing.net.

Savery, J. R. (1998). Fostering ownership for learning with computer supported collaborative writing in an undergraduate Business Communication course. In C. J. Bonk & K. S. King (Eds.), *Electronic collaborators: Learner-centered technologies for literacy, apprenticeship, and discourse* (pp. 103-127). Mahwah, NJ: Lawrence Erlbaum Associates.

Saville-Troike, M. (2006). *Introducing second language acquisition.* New York, NY: Cambridge University Press.

Schärer, R. (2003). Sprachenportfolio [Language portfolio]. In K-R. Bausch, H. Christ, & H-J. Krumm (Eds.), *Handbuch Fremdsprachenunterricht* [Coursebook - foreign language learning] (pp. 387-390). Tübingen: Francke.

Scharle, A., & Szabo, A. (2000). *Learner autonomy: A guide to developing learner responsibility.* Cambridge: Cambridge University Press.

Schlepphege, J. (2009). *Creative poetry writing in the EFL classroom.* Norderstedt: GRIN Verlag.

Schmidt, R. (1990). The role of consciousness in second language learning. *Applied Linguistics,* 11, 129–158.

Schmidt, R. (1994). Implicit learning and the cognitive unconscious: Of artificial grammars and SLA. In N. Ellis (Ed.), *Implicit and explicit learning of languages* (pp. 165–209). London: Academic Press.

Schmidt-Schönbein, G. (2005). Teacher talk: Scaffolding. *Primary English,* 3, 6.

Schmitt, N. (2000). *Vocabulary in language teaching.* Cambridge: Cambridge University Press.

Schmitt, N. (Ed.). (2004). *Formulaic sequences: Acquisition, processing, and use.* Amsterdam: Benjamins.

Schmitt-Egner, D. (2012). "Raise your voice!" An autonomous learning concept to improve oral proficiency in the EFL classroom. In P. Lennon (Ed.), *Learner autonomy in the English classroom. Empirical studies and ideas for teachers* (pp. 235–271). Frankfurt: Peter Lang.

Schouten-van Parreren, C. (1989). Vocabulary learning through reading: Which conditions should be met when presenting words in texts? *Vocabulary Acquisition AILA Review,* 24(6), 75–85.

Schwienhorst, K. (2008). *Learner autonomy and CALL environments.* London: Routledge.

Schwienhorst, K. (2011). CALL and autonomy: Settings and context variables in technology-enhanced language environments. In C. J. Everhard, J. Mynard, & R. Smith (Eds.), *Autonomy in language learning: Opening a can of worms* (pp. 29–32). Canterbury: IATEFL.

Scornavacca, E., Huff, S., & Marshall, S. (2009). Mobile phones in the classroom: If you can't beat them, join them. *Communications of the ACM,* 52(4), 142–146.

Scott, W., & Gough, S. (2003). *Sustainable development and learning. Framing the issues.* New York, NY: RoutledgeFalmer.

Segumpan, R. G., & Bahari, F. B. (2006). Teachers' job stress and human resources development. The Malaysian experience. In R. Lambert & C. McCarthy (Eds.), *Understanding teacher stress in an age of accountability* (pp. 163–178). Greenwich, CT: IAP-Information Age Publishing.

Seidlhofer, B. (2011). *Understanding English as a lingua franca.* Oxford: Oxford University Press.
Sepúlveda, M. T. (2009). The importance of affect in teaching and coursebooks for young learners in Chile. *Humanising Language Teaching,* 6. Retrieved from http://www.hltmag.co. uk/dec09/mart01.htm
Sert, O. (2005). Comparative analysis of pairwork and individual assignments in two ELT classes. *Journal of Language and Learning,* 3(2), 219-232.
Sheerin, S. (1997). An exploration of the relationship between self-access and independent learning. In P. Benson & P. Voller (Eds.), *Autonomy & independence in language learning* (pp. 54-65). London and New York: Longman.
Sherman, J. (2003). *Using authentic video in the language classroom.* Cambridge: Cambridge University Press.
Shield, L., & Weininger, M. (1999). Collaboration in a virtual world: Group work and the distance language learner. In R. Debski & M. Levy (Eds.), *World CALL: Global perspectives on computer assisted language learning* (pp. 99-116). Lisse: Swets & Zeitlinger.
Shintani, N. (2012). Input-based tasks and the acquisition of vocabulary and grammar: A process-product study. *Language Teaching Research,* 16(2), 253-279.
Short, K. G. (2004). Researching intertextuality within collaborative classroom learning environments. In N. Shuart-Faris & D. Bloome (Eds.), *Uses of intertextuality in classroom and educational research* (pp. 373-386). Greenwich, CO: Information Age Publishing.
Siegel, M. (2006). Rearing the signs: Multimodal transformations in the field of Literacy Education. *Language Arts,* 84(1), 65-77.
Siek-Piskozub, T. (1995). *Gry, zabawy i symulacje w procesie glottodydaktycznym* [Games, play and simulations in the glottodidactic process]. Poznań: Uniwersytet im. Adama Mickiewicza.
Siek-Piskozub, T. (2004). Social constructivism in language didactics. *Acta Nicolai Copernici: English Studies,* 13, 11-25.
Siek-Piskozub, T. (2006). Constructivism in language education. In E. Lorek-Jezińska, T. Siek-Piskozub, & K. Więckowska (Eds.), *Worlds in the making. Constructivism and postmodern knowledge* (pp. 159-172). Toruń: Wydawnictwo Uniwersytetu Mikołaja Kopernika.

Sinclair, B. (2000). Learner autonomy: The next phase? In B. Sinclair, I. McGrath, & T. Lamb (Eds.), *Learner autonomy, Teacher autonomy: Future directions* (pp. 4-14). Harlow: Addison Wesley Longman.

Skehan, P. (1998). Task-based instruction. *Annual Review of Applied Linguistics*, 18, 268-286.

Skehan, P., & Foster, P. (2001). Cognition and tasks. In P. Robinson (Ed.), *Cognition and second language instruction* (pp. 183-205). Cambridge: Cambridge University Press.

Skinner, B. F. (1957). *Verbal behavior*. Acton, MA: Copley Publishing Group.

Slimani-Rolls, A. (2005). Rethinking task-based language learning: What we can learn from the learners. *Language Teaching Research*, 9(2), 195-218.

Smith, R. C. (2003). Teacher education for teacher-learner autonomy. In J. Gollin, G. Ferguson, & H. Trappes-Lomax (Eds.), *Symposium for language teacher educators: Papers from three IALS symposia* (CD-ROM). Edinburgh: IALS, University of Edinburgh.

Smythe, S., & Neufeld, P. (2010). "Podcast time": Negotiating digital literacies and communities of learning in a middle years ELL classroom. *Journal of Adolescent and Adult Literacy*, 53(6), 488-496.

Solvie, P. A. (2004). The digital whiteboard: A tool in early literacy instruction. *The Reading Teacher*, 57(5), 484-487.

Sperber, D. (1994). Understanding verbal understanding. In J. Khalfa (Ed.), *What is intelligence?* (pp. 179-198). Cambridge: Cambridge University Press.

Stefanou, C., Perencevich, K. C., DiCintio, M., & Turner, J. (2004). Supporting autonomy in the classroom: Ways teachers encourage student decision-making and ownership. *Educational Psychologist*, 39, 97-110.

Sturtridge, G. (1997). Teaching and language learning in self-access centres: Changing roles? In P. Benson & P. Voller (Eds.), *Autonomy & independence in language learning* (pp. 66-78). London and New York: Longman.

Styles, D. (2001). *Class meetings. Building leadership, problem-solving and decision-making skills in the respectful classroom*. Markham, ON: Pembroke Publishers.

Sueyoshi, A., & Hardison, D. (2005). The role of gestures and facial cues in second language listening comprehension. *Language Learning*, 55(4), 661-699.

Suskie, L. (2009). *Assessing student learning: A common sense guide.* San Francisco, CA: John Wiley & Sons.

Swaffar, J. K. (1985). Reading authentic texts in a foreign language: A cognitive model. *The Modern Language Journal, 69*(1), 15-34.

Swain, M. (1985). Communicative competence: Some roles of comprehensible input and comprehensible output in its development. In S. Gass & C. Madden (Eds.), *Input in second language acquisition* (pp. 235-253). Rowley, MA: Newbury House.

Swain, M. (1995). Three functions of output in second language learning. In G. Cook & B. Seidlhofer (Eds.), *For H. G. Widdowson: Principles and practice in the study of language* (pp. 125-144). Oxford: Oxford University Press.

Swain, M., Kinnear, P., & Steinman, L. (2015). *Sociocultural theory in second language education: An introduction through narratives.* Bristol: Multilingual Matters.

Sydorenko, T. (2010). Modality of input and vocabulary acquisition. *Language Learning & Technology, 14*(2), 50-73.

Taggart, G., & Wilson, A. (2005). *Promoting reflective thinking in teachers: 44 action strategies.* Thousand Oaks, CA: Corwin Press.

Tan, B. T. (2006). Student-teacher-made language teaching materials: A developmental approach to materials development. In J. Mukundan (Ed.), *Focus on ELT materials* (pp. 207-227). Petaling Jaya: Pearson Malaysia.

Tan, K. (2008). Academics' and academic developers' views of student self-assessment. In A. Havnes & L. McDowell (Eds.), *Balancing dilemmas in assessment and learning in contemporary education* (pp. 225-236). New York, NY: Routledge.

Taplin, M. (2002). A framework to facilitate professional growth in Mathematics teaching through action research. In Y. C. Cheng, K. T. Tsui, K. W. Chow, & M. M. C. Mok (Eds.), *Subject teaching and teacher education in the new century. Research and innovation* (pp. 167-191). Hong Kong: The Hong Kong Institute of Education.

Tharp, R., & Gallimore, R. (1991). A theory of teaching as assisted performance. In P. Light, S. Sheldon, & M. Woodhead (Eds.), *Learning to think: Child development in social context, Vol. 2* (pp. 42-61). Routledge: London.

The New London Group. (2000). A pedagogy of multiliteracies. Designing social features. In B. Cope & M. Kalantzis (Eds.), *Multiliteracies. Literacy learning and the design of social features* (pp. 9-37). London: Routledge.

Thomas, A. J., & Lowe, J. (2002). *Educating your child at home*. London: Continuum.

Thomas, K., & Orthober, C. (2011). Using text messaging in the secondary classroom. *American Secondary Education, 39*(2), 55–76.

Thomas, M., & Cutrim Schmid, E. (Eds). (2010). *Interactive whiteboards: Theory, research and practice*. Hershey, PA: IGI Global.

Thomas, M., & Reinders, T. (Eds.). (2010). *Task-based language learning and teaching with technology*. London: Continuum.

Thompson, S. M. (1996). Peer mediation: A peaceful solution. *The School Counsellor, 44*, 151–155.

Thomson, R., & Mabey, C. (2011). *Developing human resources*. New York, NY: Buttersworth-Heinemann.

Tindell, D. R., & Bohlander, R. W. (2012). The use and abuse of cell phones and text messaging in the classroom: A survey of college students. *College Teaching, 60*(1), 1–9.

Tinker Sachs, G., & Ho, B. (2007). *ESL/EFL cases. Contexts for teacher professional discussions*. Hong Kong: City University of Hong Kong.

Tomlinson, B. (1994). Pragmatic awareness activities. *Language Awareness, 3 & 4*, 119–129.

Tomlinson, B. (1999). Developing criteria for evaluating L2 materials. *IATEFL Issues*, (Feb/Mar), 10–13.

Tomlinson, B. (2003b). Humanizing the coursebook. In B. Tomlinson (Ed.), *Developing materials for language teaching* (pp. 162–173). London and New York: Continuum.

Tomlinson, B. (2003c). Materials evaluation. In B. Tomlinson (Ed.), *Developing materials for language teaching* (pp. 15–36). London and New York: Continuum.

Tomlinson, B. (2010). Principles of effective materials development. In N. Harwood (Ed.), *English language teaching materials* (pp. 81–108). Cambridge: Cambridge University Press.

Tomlinson, B. (2011a). Access-self materials. In B. Tomlinson (Ed.), *Materials development in language teaching* (pp. 414–432). Cambridge: Cambridge University Press.

Tomlinson, B. (2013a). Innovation in materials development. In K. Hyland & L. L. C. Wong (Eds.), *Innovation and change in English language education* (pp. 203–217). New York, NY: Routledge.

Tomlinson, B. (2014). Teacher growth through materials development. *The European Journal of Applied Linguistics and TEFL*, 3(2), 89–106.

Tomlinson, B. (Ed.). (2003a). *Developing materials for language teaching*. London: Continuum.

Tomlinson, B. (Ed.). (2011b). *Materials development in language teaching* (2nd ed.). Cambridge: Cambridge University Press.

Tomlinson, B. (Ed.). (2013b). *Developing materials for language teaching* (2nd ed.). London: Bloomsbury Academic.

Tomlinson, B. (Ed.). (2013c). *Applied Linguistics and materials development*. London and New York: Bloomsbury Academic.

Tomlinson, B., & Masuhara, H. (2004). *Developing language course materials*. Singapore: RELC Portfolio Series.

Tomlinson, B., Dat, B., Masuhara, H., & Rubdy, R. (2001). Survey review: ESL courses for adults. *ELT Journal*, 55(1), 80–101.

Tomlinson, C. A., & Allan, S. D. (2000). *Leadership for differentiating schools and classrooms*. Alexandria, VA: ASCD.

Toohey, K., & Norton, B. (2003). Learner autonomy as agency in sociocultural settings. In D. Palfreyman & R. C. Smith (Eds.), *Learner autonomy across cultures: Language education perspectives* (pp. 58–72). Basingstoke: Palgrave Macmillan.

Trajtemberg, C., & Yiakonmetti, A. (2011). Weblogs: A tool for EFL instruction, expression, and self-evaluation. *ELTJ*, 65(4), 437–445.

Trebbi, T. (Ed.). (1990). *Third Nordic workshop on developing autonomous learning in the FL classroom*. Bergen: University of Bergen.

Tsobanoglou, S. (2008). What can we learn by researching the use of textbooks and other support materials by teachers and learners (Unpublished master's dissertation). University of Nottingham, Nottingham, UK.

Tsui, A. B. M. (2003). *Understanding experience in teaching. Case studies of ESL teachers*. Cambridge: Cambridge University Press.

Tudor, I. (1993). Teacher roles in the learner-centred classroom. *ELT Journal*, 47(1), 22–31.

Tuttle, D. W., & Tuttle, N. R. (2004). *Self-esteem and adjusting with blindness* (3rd ed.). Springfield, IL: Charles C. Thomas.

Tuttle, H. G. (2009). *Formative assessment: Responding to your students*. New York, NY: Eye on Education.

Tzuriel, D. (2001). *Dynamic assessment of young children*. New York, NY: Kluwer Academic/Plenum Publishers.

Ur, P. (1996). *A course in language teaching. Practice and theory*. Cambridge: Cambridge University Press.

Ur, P. (2012). *A course in English language teaching* (2nd ed.). Cambridge: Cambridge University Press.

Ur, P. (2015). Using the course book: A teacher's perspective. *The European Journal of Applied Linguistics and TEFL*, 4(2), 5-17.

Ushioda, E. (2001). Language learning at university: Exploring the role of motivational thinking. In Z. Dörnyei & R. Schmidt (Eds.), *Motivation and second language acquisition* (pp. 93-126). Manoa: National Foreign Language Resource Center.

Usuki, M. (2007). *Autonomy in language learning: Japanese students' exploratory analysis*. Nagoya: Sankeisha.

van Avermaet, P., Colpin, M., van Gorp, K., Bogaert, N., & van den Branden, K. (2006). The role of the teacher in task-based language teaching. In K. van den Branden (Ed.), *Task-based language education: From theory to practice* (pp. 175-196). Cambridge: Cambridge University Press.

van den Branden, K. (2006). Training teachers: Task-based as well? In K. van den Branden (Ed.), *Task-based language education: From theory to practice* (pp. 217-248). Cambridge: Cambridge University Press.

Vandergrift, L. (2008). Learning strategies for listening comprehension. In S. Hurd & T. Lewis (Eds.), *Language learning strategies in independent settings* (pp. 84-102). Bristol: Multilingual Matters.

Vanderplank, R. (1988). The value of teletext sub-titles in language learning. *English Language Teaching Journal*, 42(4), 272-281.

van Lier, L. (1996). *Interaction in the language curriculum: Awareness, autonomy and authenticity*. London and New York: Longman.

van Lier, L. (2004). *The ecology and semiotics of language learning: A sociocultural perspective*. Dordrecht: Kluwer Academic Publishers.

van Lier, L. (2008). Agency in the classroom. In J. P. Lantolf & M. E. Poehner (Eds.), *Sociocultural theory and the teaching of second languages* (pp. 163-188). London: Equinox.

Villa, R. A., Thousand, J. S., & Nevin, A. I. (2008). *A guide to co-teaching: Practical tips for facilitating student learning.* Thousand Oaks, CA: Corwin Press.

Villa, R. A., Thousand, J. S., & Nevin, A. I. (2010). *Collaborating with students in instruction and decision making. The untapped resource.* Thousand Oaks, CA: Corwin Press.

Vilmi, R. (1994). Global communication through Email: An ongoing experiment at Helsinki University of Technology. Paper presented at EUROCALL 1994 conference, Karlsruhe.

Vygotsky, L. S. (1962). *Thought and language.* Cambridge, MA: MIT Press.

Vygotsky, L. S. (1978). *Mind in society.* Cambridge, MA: Harvard University Press.

Vygotsky, L. S. (1987). *The collected works of L. S. Vygotsky. Volume 1. Thinking and speaking.* New York, NY: Plenum Press.

Waldron, J. (1993). *Liberal rights: Collected papers 1981-1991.* New York, NY: Cambridge University Press.

Wall, S. (2003). Freedom as a political ideal. *Social Philosophy and Policy, 20*(2), 307-334.

Wallace, C. (1992). *Reading.* Oxford: Oxford University Press.

Walstad, W. B. (2006). Assessment of student learning in economics. In W. E. Becker, M. Watts, & S. R. Becker (Eds.), *Teaching economics. More alternatives to chalk and talk* (pp. 193-212). Cheltenham: Edward Elgar Publishing Limited.

Wang, M., Shen, R., Novak, D., & Pan, X. (2009). The impact of mobile learning on students' learning behaviours and performance: Report from a large blended classroom. *British Journal of Educational Technology, 40*(4), 673-695.

Waring, R. (2009). The inescapable case for extensive reading. In A. Cirocki (Ed.), *Extensive reading in English language teaching* (pp. 93-111). München: Lincom.

Warschauer, M. (1995). *Email for English teaching.* Alexandria, VA: TESOL Publications.

Warschauer, M. (2000). On-line learning in second language classrooms: An ethnographic study. In M. Warschauer & R. Kern (Eds.), *Network-based language teaching: Concepts and practice* (pp. 41-58). Cambridge: Cambridge University Press.

Waschk, K. (2004). Stationenlauf zum Thema Fruit. Eine ganzheitliche Erfahrung [Teaching the topic of fruits through the stations method: A holistic experience]. *Primary English*, 4, 8–11.

Wąsik, Z. (2006). Investigative perspectives in the construction of scientific reality: An epistemological outlook on the foundations of linguistic semiotics. In E. Lorek-Jezińska, T. Siek-Piskozub, & K. Więckowska, *Worlds in the making: Constructivism and postmodern knowledge* (pp. 21–35). Toruń: Wydawnictwo Uniwersytetu Mikołaja Kopernika.

Watanabe, Y., & Swain, M. (2007). Effects of proficiency differences and patterns of pair interaction on second language learning: Collaborative dialogue between adult ESL learners. *Language Teaching Research*, 11, 121–142.

Weathington, B. L., Cunningham, C. J. L., & Pittenger, D. J. (2010). *Research methods for the behavioural and social sciences*. Hoboken, NJ: John Wiley and Sons.

Weaver, C. (2002). *Reading process and practice* (3rd ed.). Portsmouth, NH: Heinemann.

Wells, C. G. (1994). *Changing schools from within: Creating communities of inquiry*. Portsmouth, NH: Heinemann.

Wells, G. (1990). Talk about text: Where literacy is learned and taught. *Curriculum Inquiry*, 20, 369–405.

Wendt, M. (Ed.). (2000). *Konstruktion statt Instruktion. Neue Zugänge zu Sprache und Kultur im Fremdsprachenunterricht* [Construction instead of instruction: New opportunities to access language and culture in a foreign language lesson]. Frankfurt: Peter Lang.

Wenger, E., McDermott, R. A., & Snyder, W. (2002). *Cultivating communities of practice: A guide to managing knowledge*. Cambridge, MA: Harvard University.

White, C. (2003). *Language learning in distance education*. Cambridge: Cambridge University Press.

Widdowson, H. G. (1978). *Teaching language as communication*. Oxford: Oxford University Press.

Widdowson, H. G. (1987). The roles of teacher and learner. *ELT Journal*, 41(2), 83–88.

Widdowson, H. G. (1998). Context, community, and authentic language. *TESOL Quarterly*, 32(4), 705–16.

Widodo, H. P., & Cirocki, A. (2015). Video-based listening tasks in the EFL classroom: A sociopragmatic perspective. *Asian EFL Journal, 81,* 62-90.

Wigglesworth, G., & Storch, N. (2009). Pairs versus individual writing: Effects on fluency, complexity and accuracy. *Language Testing, 26,* 445-466.

Wilczyńska, W. (1999). *Uczyć się czy być nauczanym?* [To learn or to be taught.] Warszawa: PWN.

Wilczyńska, W. (2002). *Autonomizacja w dydaktyce języków obcych. Doskonalenie się w komunikacji ustnej* [Autonomisation in foreign language didactics. Perfecting oral communication]. Poznań: Wydawnictwo Naukowe UAM.

Wilkins, D. A. (1972). *Linguistics and language teaching.* London: Edward Arnold.

Williams, M., & Burden, R. L. (1997). *Psychology for language teachers: A social constructivist approach.* Cambridge: Cambridge University Press.

Willing, K. (1988). *Learning styles in adult migrant education.* Adelaide: National Curriculum Resource Centre.

Willis, D. (1990). *The lexical syllabus. A new approach to language teaching.* London: HarperCollins.

Willis, D., & Willis, J. (2007). *Doing task-based teaching.* Oxford: Oxford University Press.

Willis, J. (1996). *A framework for task-based learning.* Harlow: Longman.

Willis, J. (2009). The TBL framework. The task cycle. In K. Van den Branden, M. Bygate, & J. M. Norris (Eds.), *Task-based language teaching. A reader.* (pp. 227-247). Amsterdam: John Benjamins.

Wolff, D. (1994). Der Konstruktivismus: Ein neues Paradigma in der Fremdsprachendidaktik [Constructivism: A new paradigm in foreign language teaching]. *Die Neueren Sprachen, 93,* 407-29.

Wolff, D. (1999). Zu den Beziehungen zwischen Theorie und Praxis in der Entwicklung von Lernerautonomie [Relationships between theory and practice in learner autonomy development]. In C. Edelhoff & R. Weskamp (Eds.), *Autonomes Fremdsprachenlernen* [Autonomous learning of foreign languages] (pp. 37-48). Ismaning: Hueber.

Wolff, D. (2002a). *Fremdsprachenlernen als Konstruktion. Grundlagen für eine konstruktivistische Fremdsprachendidaktik* [Foreign language learning as construction: The foundations of constructivist teaching]. Frankfurt: Peter Lang.

Wolff, D. (2002b). Methodological success factors. In D. Marsh, A. Ontero, & T. Shikongo (Eds.), *Content and language integrated learning in Namibia* (pp. 13-15). Jyväskylä: University of Jyväskylä.

Wolff, D. (2003). Integrating language and content in the language classroom: Are transfer of knowledge and of language ensured? *Proceedings of the Groupe d'Etude et de Recherche en Anglais de Spécialité*. Retrieved from http://asp.revues.org/1154

Wolff, D. (2011). CLIL and learner autonomy: Relating two educational concepts. *Education et Sociétés Plurilingues, 30*, 69-80.

Wong, J., & Waring, H. Z. (2010). *Conversation analysis and second language pedagogy. A guide for ESL/EFL teachers*. New York, NY: Routledge.

Wood, D. J., Bruner, J. S., & Ross, G. (1976). The role of tutoring in problem solving. *Journal of Child Psychiatry and Psychology, 17*(2), 89-100.

Wu, Y. (2009). Engaging advanced-level ESL students to read young adult literature in extensive reading settings. In A. Cirocki (Ed.), *Extensive reading in English language teaching* (pp. 349-374). München: Lincom.

Xiaoqiong, Y., Guoqing, Y., & Zeng, Z. (2013). Personalized teaching model based on moodle platform. In Z. Zhong (Ed.), *Proceedings of the International Conference on Information Engineering and Applications (IEA) 2012* (pp. 27-36). London: Springer-Verlag.

Yalden, J. (1987). *Principles of course design for language teaching*. Cambridge: Cambridge University Press.

Yan, C. (2007). Investigating English teachers' materials adaptation. *Humanizing Language Teaching, 9*(4). Retrieved from www.hltmag.co.uk/Jul07/mart01.htm

Young, R. (1986). *Personal autonomy: Beyond negative and positive freedom*. New York, NY: St. Martin's Press.

Zargar, S. S., & Ganai, M. Y. (2014). *Self-concept, learning styles, study habits and academic achievement of adolescents in Kashmir. A study on psychological variables and academic achievement of adolescents in Kashmir*. Hamburg: Anchor Academic Publishing.

Zaslavsky, O., & Sullivan, P. (Eds.). (2011). Setting the stage: A conceptual framework for examining and developing tasks for Mathematics teacher education. In O. Zaslavsky & P. Sullivan (Eds.), *Constructing*

knowledge for teaching secondary Mathematics. Tasks to enhance prospective and practicing teacher learning (pp. 1-22). New York, NY: Springer.

Zawadowska-Kittel, E. (2013). *Nowa matura z języków obcych: Szanse i zagrożenia* [The new Matura examination in foreign languages: Opportunities and risks]. Piaseczno: Lexem.

Zhao, Y. (2005). *Research in technology and second language education. Developments and directions.* Greenwich, CT: Information Age Publishing.

Zhong, Y. (2008). A study of autonomy English learning on the Internet. *English Language Teaching,* 1(2). Retrieved from http://www.ccsenet.org/journal.html

Zhou, Y. (2008). *Success of all. A comprehensive educational reform for improving at-risk students in an urban school in China.* Charlotte, NC: Information Age Publishing.

APPENDIX A

**LEARNER AUTONOMY
EFL TEACHER QUESTIONNAIRE
CONSENT TO PARTICIPATE IN RESEARCH**

You are being invited to take part in a learner autonomy research project. The aim of this project is to estimate the extent to which learner autonomy is developed in the Polish secondary school EFL classroom.

You will now be asked to complete a 25-minute questionnaire. Please note that all the data collected from you:

1. will be treated as confidential, and in no case will they be identified as you are not required to provide any personal information;
2. will be kept for six months and protected by password on the principal researcher's computer;
3. will be accessible only to the researcher conducting this project;
4. will be published in the form of an academic text and a conference presentation.

If you freely consent to participate in this study, please sign below. Your signature confirms that you understand what participation in this research project will involve. It also confirms that you are aware that taking part in this study is voluntary and that you are free to withdraw at any time before the data analysis stage has been finalised, without giving any reason.

Should you require further information on this project or your involvement in it, please contact Andrzej Cirocki.

....
Participant's signature date

RESEARCHER'S DETAILS
Dr Andrzej Cirocki
Anglia Ruskin University
East Road, Cambridge
CB1 1PT
UK

Email: Andrzej.Cirocki@anglia.ac.uk

I. Questions

1. Is developing learner autonomy in the EFL classroom important? (Please circle one letter from **a** to **e** and provide comments if need be.)
   a) Very unimportant
   b) Unimportant
   c) Neither important nor unimportant
   d) Important
   e) Very important
   ....

2. On average, what percentage of your classroom time do you devote to promoting learner autonomy? (Please circle one letter from **a** to **e** and provide comments if need be.)
   a) 0-20%
   b) 21-40%
   c) 41-60%
   d) 61-80%
   e) 81-100%
   ....

3. On average, what percentage of your classroom time would you like to devote to promoting learner autonomy? (Please circle one letter from **a** to **e** and provide comments if need be.)
   a) 0-20%
   b) 21-40%
   c) 41-60%
   d) 61-80%
   e) 81-100%
   ....

4. What methods and techniques do you employ to foster learner autonomy in your classroom? (Please circle the appropriate letters below and provide comments if need be.)
   a) Pair work/Group work
   b) Extensive reading
   c) Extensive listening
   d) Project work
   e) Learner portfolios/learner journals/learner self-reports/learner diaries
   f) Self-assessment sessions
   g) Learning strategy instruction
   h) Reflecting on learning sessions
   i) Self-access centre

j) Syllabus and course content negotiation
k) Technology-assisted teaching/learning
l) Dialogues/role-plays/simulations
m) Drama/skits/plays
n) Literature club/discussion club
o) Presentations (PowerPoint, Prezi, poster, etc.)
p) Homework tasks
q) Other ....
....

5. What kind of teaching resources do you use to foster learner autonomy?
(Please circle the appropriate letters below and provide comments if need be.)

a) Course books
b) Resource packs
c) Graded readers
d) Audio books
e) Real-life texts (prose, poems, newspaper articles, recorded interviews, etc.)
f) Self-assessment questionnaires/sheets
g) Technology-assisted language learning resources
h) Other ....
....

6. What criteria do you use to choose the Year One course book? (Please choose up to five criteria that are important for you. Provide comments if need be.)

a) Reasonable price
b) Well-prepared teacher's book and test book
c) Suitable language and content
d) Clearly presented grammar
e) A balance of all four skills
f) Learner autonomy
g) Attractive activities and tasks (games, songs, quizzes, real-life texts, etc.)
h) Matura examination practice
i) Other ....
....

7. What criteria do you use to choose the Year Three course book? (Please choose up to five criteria that are important for you. Provide comments if need be.)

a) Reasonable price
b) Well-prepared teacher's book and test book
c) Suitable language and content
d) Clearly presented grammar
e) A balance of all four skills
f) Learner autonomy

g) Attractive activities and tasks (games, songs, quizzes, real-life texts, etc.)
h) Matura examination practice
i) Other ....
....

8. To what extent do you agree that the course book you use with Year One students encourages them to: (Please circle one letter from **a** to **e** and provide comments if need be.)

A) work cooperatively?
   a) Strongly disagree
   b) Disagree
   c) Undecided
   d) Agree
   e) Strongly agree

B) choose a variety of learning strategies?
   a) Strongly disagree
   b) Disagree
   c) Undecided
   d) Agree
   e) Strongly agree

C) develop critical thinking through problem-solving tasks?
   a) Strongly disagree
   b) Disagree
   c) Undecided
   d) Agree
   e) Strongly agree

D) assess themselves?
   a) Strongly disagree
   b) Disagree
   c) Undecided
   d) Agree
   e) Strongly agree

E) integrate educational technology into the teaching-learning process?
   a) Strongly disagree
   b) Disagree
   c) Undecided
   d) Agree
   e) Strongly agree

F) integrate language skills for in- and out-of-class projects?
   a) Strongly disagree
   b) Disagree
   c) Undecided

d) Agree
   e) Strongly agree

G) perform relevant and meaningful learner autonomy tasks?

   a) Strongly disagree
   b) Disagree
   c) Undecided
   d) Agree
   e) Strongly agree

....
Please provide the title of the course book below
....

9. To what extent do you agree that the course book you use with Year Three students encourages them to: (Please circle one letter from **a** to **e** and provide comments if need be.)

A) work cooperatively?

   a) Strongly disagree
   b) Disagree
   c) Undecided
   d) Agree
   e) Strongly agree

B) choose a variety of learning strategies?

   a) Strongly disagree
   b) Disagree
   c) Undecided
   d) Agree
   e) Strongly agree

C) develop critical thinking through problem-solving tasks?

   a) Strongly disagree
   b) Disagree
   c) Undecided
   d) Agree
   e) Strongly agree

D) assess themselves?

   a) Strongly disagree
   b) Disagree
   c) Undecided
   d) Agree
   e) Strongly agree

E) integrate educational technology into the teaching-learning process?

   a) Strongly disagree
   a) Disagree

b) Undecided
c) Agree
d) Strongly agree

F) integrate language skills for in- and out-of-class projects?
a) Strongly disagree
b) Disagree
c) Undecided
d) Agree
e) Strongly agree

G) perform relevant and meaningful learner autonomy tasks?
a) Strongly disagree
a) Disagree
b) Undecided
c) Agree
d) Strongly agree

....
Please provide the title of the course book below
....

10. What type of tasks do you think should be included in course books to help EFL students to become independent learners? (Please circle the appropriate letters below. Provide comments if need be.)
a) Self-assessment tasks based on questionnaires
b) Mini-project tasks with the use of educational technology
c) Projects integrating all language skills
d) Real-life texts with tasks which aim to develop all language skills
e) Tasks connected with reflecting on learning sheets
f) Tasks based on learning strategy identification sheets
g) Video/film-based tasks
h) Other ....
....

11. How often do you develop pedagogical tasks for your students? (Please circle one letter from **a** to **e** and provide comments if need be.)
a) Never
b) Rarely
c) From time to time
d) Usually
e) Always
....

12. How often do you design tasks aimed at fostering your students' autonomy? (Please circle one letter from **a** to **e**. Provide comments if need be.)

a) Never
b) Rarely
c) From time to time
d) Usually
e) Always

....

13. Can you think of any problems that prevent you from fostering learner autonomy in your classroom? (Please write your opinion below.)

....
....
....
....

II. Profile of the Respondent

1. **What is your gender?** (Please circle one letter below.)
   a) male b) female

2. **How old are you?** (Please put the number in the space provided below.)

3. **What teaching qualification(s) do you have?** (Please provide the name e.g. *MA in TEFL* in the space provided below.)

4. **How many years have you been working as a teacher?** (Please put the number in the space provided below.)

5. **What's your employment status as a teacher?** (Please circle one letter from **a** to **c**.)
   a) full time
   b) part time (less than 50% of full time hours)
   c) part time (more than 50% of full time hours)

LEARNER AUTONOMY
IN THE SECONDARY SCHOOL EFL CLASSROOM
YEAR 2 STUDENT QUESTIONNAIRE
CONSENT TO PARTICIPATE IN RESEARCH

You are being invited to take part in a learner autonomy research project. The aim of this project is to estimate the extent to which learner autonomy is developed in the Polish secondary school EFL classroom.

You will now be asked to complete a 20-minute questionnaire. Please note that all the data collected from you:
1. will be treated as confidential, and in no case will they be identified as you are not required to provide any personal information;
2. will be kept for six months and protected by password on the principal researcher's computer;
3. will be accessible only to the researcher conducting this project;
4. will be published in the form of an academic text and a conference presentation.

If you freely consent to participate in this study, please sign below. Your signature confirms that you understand what participation in this research project will involve. It also confirms that you are aware that taking part in this study is voluntary and that you are free to withdraw at any time before the data analysis stage has been finalised, without giving any reason.

Should you require further information on this project or your involvement in it, please contact Andrzej Cirocki.

....
Participant's signature   date

RESEARCHER'S DETAILS
Dr Andrzej Cirocki
Anglia Ruskin University
East Road, Cambridge
CB1 1PT
UK

Email: Andrzej.Cirocki@anglia.ac.uk

I. Questions

1. Do you agree that developing learner autonomy is important? (Please circle one letter from **a** to **e**. Provide comments if need be.)
- a) Strongly disagree
- b) Disagree
- c) Undecided
- d) Agree
- e) Strongly agree

....

2. To what extent do you agree that your teacher gives you enough tasks to develop your autonomy? (Please circle one letter from **a** to **e**. Provide comments if need be.)
- a) Strongly disagree
- b) Disagree
- c) Undecided
- d) Agree
- e) Strongly agree

....

3. To what extent do you agree that your Year One course book encouraged you to: (Please circle one letter from **a** to **e** and provide comments if need be.)

A) work cooperatively?
- a) Strongly disagree
- b) Disagree
- c) Undecided
- d) Agree
- e) Strongly agree

B) choose a variety of learning strategies?
- a) Strongly disagree
- b) Disagree
- c) Undecided
- d) Agree
- e) Strongly agree

C) develop critical thinking through problem-solving tasks?
- a) Strongly disagree
- b) Disagree
- c) Undecided
- d) Agree
- e) Strongly agree

D) assess yourself?
   a) Strongly disagree
   b) Disagree
   c) Undecided
   d) Agree
   e) Strongly agree

E) integrate educational technology into the learning process?
   a) Strongly disagree
   b) Disagree
   c) Undecided
   d) Agree
   e) Strongly agree

F) integrate language skills for in- and out-of-class projects?
   a) Strongly disagree
   b) Disagree
   c) Undecided
   d) Agree
   e) Strongly agree

G) perform relevant and meaningful learner autonomy tasks?
   a) Strongly disagree
   b) Disagree
   c) Undecided
   d) Agree
   e) Strongly agree

....
Please provide the title of the course book
....

4. How often does your teacher provide you with non-course-book-based tasks? (Please circle one letter from **a** to **e**. Provide comments if need be.)
   a) Never
   a) Rarely
   b) From time to time
   c) Usually
   d) Always

....

5. To what extent do you agree that the non-course-book-based tasks help you to become an independent learner? (Please circle one letter from **a** to **e**. Provide comments if need be.)
   a) Strongly disagree
   b) Disagree
   c) Undecided

d) gree
e) Strongly agree
....

6. Can you think of any problems that prevent the fostering of learner autonomy in your EFL classroom? (Please write your opinion below.)
....
....
....
....
....

II. Profile of the Respondent

1. **What is your gender?** (Please circle one letter below.)
    a) male   b) female

2. **How many years have you been learning English?** (Please put the number in the space provided below.)
....

3. **Do you attend any extra-curricular English classes such as private tutoring, FCE or CAE examination courses?** (Please provide details in the space provided below.)
....

4. **Which level of the Matura examination are you planning to take?** (Please circle one letter below.)
    a) basic   b) advanced   c) undecided

5. **What are the reasons why you learn English?** (Please provide details in the space provided below.)
....

LEARNER AUTONOMY
IN THE SECONDARY SCHOOL EFL CLASSROOM
YEAR 3 STUDENT QUESTIONNAIRE
CONSENT TO PARTICIPATE IN RESEARCH

You are being invited to take part in a learner autonomy research project. The aim of this project is to estimate the extent to which learner autonomy is developed in the Polish secondary school EFL classroom.

You will now be asked to complete a 20-minute questionnaire. Please note that all the data collected from you:
1. will be treated as confidential, and in no case will they be identified as you are not required to provide any personal information;
2. will be kept for six months and protected by password on the principal researcher's computer;
3. will be accessible only to the researcher conducting this project;
4. will be published in the form of an academic text and a conference presentation.

If you freely consent to participate in this study, please sign below. Your signature confirms that you understand what participation in this research project will involve. It also confirms that you are aware that taking part in this study is voluntary and that you are free to withdraw at any time before the data analysis stage has been finalised, without giving any reason.

Should you require further information on this project or your involvement in it, please contact Andrzej Cirocki.

....
  Participant's signature   *date*

RESEARCHER'S DETAILS
Dr Andrzej Cirocki
Anglia Ruskin University
East Road, Cambridge
CB1 1PT
UK
Email: Andrzej.Cirocki@anglia.ac.uk

I. Questions

1. Do you agree that developing learner autonomy is important? (Please circle one letter from **a** to **e**. Provide comments if need be.)
- a) Strongly disagree
- b) Disagree
- c) Undecided
- d) Agree
- e) Strongly agree

You can add extra information or justify your opinion below.
....

2. To what extent do you agree that your teacher gives you enough tasks to develop your autonomy? (Please circle one letter from **a** to **e**. Provide comments if need be.)
- a) Strongly disagree
- b) Disagree
- c) Undecided
- d) Agree
- e) Strongly agree

3. To what extent do you agree that your Year Three course book encouraged you to: (Please circle one letter from **a** to **e** and provide comments if need be.)

A) work cooperatively?
- a) Strongly disagree
- b) Disagree
- c) Undecided
- d) Agree
- e) Strongly agree

B) choose a variety of learning strategies?
- a) Strongly disagree
- b) Disagree
- c) Undecided
- d) Agree
- e) Strongly agree

C) develop critical thinking through problem-solving tasks?
- a) Strongly disagree
- b) Disagree
- c) Undecided
- d) Agree
- e) Strongly agree

D) assess yourself?
   a) Strongly disagree
   b) Disagree
   c) Undecided
   d) Agree
   e) Strongly agree

E) integrate educational technology into the learning process?
   a) Strongly disagree
   b) Disagree
   c) Undecided
   d) Agree
   e) Strongly agree

F) integrate language skills for in- and out-of-class projects?
   a) Strongly disagree
   b) Disagree
   c) Undecided
   d) Agree
   e) Strongly agree

G) perform relevant and meaningful learner autonomy tasks?
   f) Strongly disagree
   a) Disagree
   b) Undecided
   c) Agree
   d) Strongly agree

Please provide the title of the course book
....

4. How often does your teacher provide you with non-course-book-based tasks? (Please circle one letter from **a** to **e**. Provide comments if need be.)
   a) Never
   b) Rarely
   c) From time to time
   d) Usually
   e) Always

5. To what extent do you agree that the non-course-book-based tasks help you to become an independent learner? (Please circle one letter from **a** to **e**. Provide comments if need be.)
   a) Strongly disagree
   b) Disagree
   c) Undecided
   d) Agree
   e) Strongly agree

6. Can you think of any problems that prevent the fostering of learner autonomy in your EFL classroom? (Please write your opinion below.)

....
....
....
....

II. Profile of the Respondent

1. **What is your gender?** (Please circle one letter below.)
    a) male b) female

2. **How many years have you been learning English?** (Please put the number in the space provided below.)
....

3. **Do you attend any extra-curricular English classes such as private tutoring, FCE or CAE examination courses?** (Please provide details in the space provided below.)
....

4. **Which level of the Matura examination are you planning to take?** (Please circle one letter below.)
    a) basic   b) advanced   c) undecided

5. **What are the reasons why you learn English?** (Please provide details in the space provided below.)
....

APPENDIX B

CONSENT TO PARTICIPATE IN RESEARCH
FORM FOR THE SCHOOL PRINCIPAL

Title of Research Project: Learner Autonomy in the Polish Secondary School EFL Classroom

Declaration of Consent

1. I agree that the research project named above has been explained to me to my satisfaction.
2. I confirm that I have the authority to give permission for my school to take part.
3. I understand that my school's participation is voluntary and that we are free to withdraw at any time without penalty.
4. I grant permission to the researcher to conduct the above named research in my school.

```
..........................................                    ..........................................
            Name                                                         Signed


..........................................                    ..........................................
           School                                                         Date
```

City: **Gdańsk**

Once signed, please return this form to the researcher:

Andrzej Cirocki
Anglia Ruskin University
East Road, Cambridge
CB1 1PT
UK

Email: Andrzej.Cirocki@anglia.ac.uk

CONSENT TO PARTICIPATE IN RESEARCH FORM FOR THE SCHOOL PRINCIPAL

Title of Research Project: Learner Autonomy in the Polish Secondary School EFL Classroom

Declaration of Consent

1. I agree that the research project named above has been explained to me to my satisfaction.
2. I confirm that I have the authority to give permission for my school to take part.
3. I understand that my school's participation is voluntary and that we are free to withdraw at any time without penalty.
4. I grant permission to the researcher to conduct the above named research in my school.

....	....
Name	*Signed*
....	....
School	*Date*

City: **Sopot**

Once signed, please return this form to the researcher:

Andrzej Cirocki
Anglia Ruskin University
East Road, Cambridge
CB1 1PT
UK

Email: Andrzej.Cirocki@anglia.ac.uk

APPENDIX C

LEARNER AUTONOMY
EFL TEACHER QUESTIONNAIRE
CONSENT TO PARTICIPATE IN RESEARCH

You are being invited to take part in a learner autonomy research project. The aim of this project is to estimate the extent to which learner autonomy is developed in the Polish secondary school EFL classroom.

You will now be asked to complete a 20-minute questionnaire. Please note that all the data collected from you:
1. will be treated as confidential, and in no case will they be identified as you are not required to provide any personal information;
2. will be kept for six months and protected by password on the principal researcher's computer;
3. will be accessible only to the researcher conducting this project;
4. will be published in the form of an academic text and a conference presentation.

If you freely consent to participate in this study, please sign below. Your signature confirms that you understand what participation in this research project will involve. It also confirms that you are aware that taking part in this study is voluntary and that you are free to withdraw at any time before the data analysis stage has been finalised, without giving any reason.

Should you require further information on this project or your involvement in it, please contact Andrzej Cirocki.

....
Participant's signature   date

RESEARCHER'S DETAILS
Dr Andrzej Cirocki
Anglia Ruskin University
East Road, Cambridge
CB1 1PT
UK

Email: Andrzej.Cirocki@anglia.ac.uk

I. Questions

1. Is developing learner autonomy in the EFL classroom important? (Please circle one letter from **a** to **e** and provide comments if need be.)
- a) Very unimportant
- a) Unimportant
- b) Neither important nor unimportant
- c) Important
- d) Very important

....

2. On average, what percentage of your classroom time do you devote to promoting learner autonomy? (Please circle one letter from **a** to **e** and provide comments if need be.)
- a) 0-20%
- b) 21-40%
- c) 41-60%
- d) 61-80%
- e) 81-100%

....

3. On average, what percentage of your classroom time would you like to devote to promoting learner autonomy? (Please circle one letter from **a** to **e** and provide comments if need be.)
- a) 0-20%
- b) 21-40%
- c) 41-60%
- d) 61-80%
- e) 81-100%

....

4. How do you go about fostering learner autonomy in your classroom? (Please circle the appropriate letters below and provide comments if need be.)
- a) Pair work/group work
- b) Extensive reading
- c) Extensive listening
- d) Project work
- e) Learner portfolios/learner journals/learner self-reports/learner diaries
- f) Self-assessment sessions
- g) Learning strategy instruction
- h) Reflecting on learning sessions
- i) Self-access centre

j) Syllabus and course content negotiation
k) Technology-assisted teaching/learning
l) Dialogues/role-plays/simulations
m) Drama/skits/plays
n) Literature club/discussion club
o) Presentations (PowerPoint, Prezi, poster, etc.)
p) Homework tasks
q) Other ....
....

5. What kind of teaching resources do you use to foster learner autonomy? (Please circle the appropriate letters below and provide comments if need be.)
a) Course books
b) Resource packs
c) Graded readers
d) Audio books
e) Real-life texts (prose, poems, newspaper articles, recorded interviews, etc.)
f) Self-assessment questionnaires/sheets
g) Technology-assisted language learning resources
h) Other ....
....

6. What criteria do you use to choose the Year One course book? (Please choose up to five criteria that are important for you. Provide comments if need be.)
a) Reasonable price
b) Well-prepared teacher's book and test book
c) Suitable language and content
d) Clearly presented grammar
e) A balance of all four skills
f) Learner autonomy
g) Attractive activities and tasks (games, songs, quizzes, real-life texts, etc.)
h) Matura examination practice
i) Other ....
....

7. What criteria do you use to choose the Year Three course book? (Please choose up to five criteria that are important for you. Provide comments if need be.)
a) Reasonable price
b) Well-prepared teacher's book and test book
c) Suitable language and content
d) Clearly presented grammar
e) A balance of all four skills

f) Learner autonomy
g) Attractive activities and tasks (games, songs, quizzes, real-life texts, etc.)
h) Matura examination practice
i) Other ....
....

8. To what extent do you agree that the course book you use with Year One students encourages them to: (Please circle one letter from **a** to **e** and provide comments if need be.)

A) work cooperatively?
a) Strongly disagree
b) Disagree
c) Undecided
d) Agree
e) Strongly agree

B) choose a variety of learning strategies?
a) Strongly disagree
b) Disagree
c) Undecided
d) Agree
e) Strongly agree

C) develop critical thinking through problem-solving tasks?
a) Strongly disagree
b) Disagree
c) Undecided
d) Agree
e) Strongly agree

D) assess themselves?
a) Strongly disagree
b) Disagree
c) Undecided
d) Agree
e) Strongly agree

E) integrate educational technology into the teaching-learning process?
a) Strongly disagree
b) Disagree
c) Undecided
d) Agree
e) Strongly agree

F) integrate language skills for in- and out-of-class projects?
a) Strongly disagree
b) Disagree

c) Undecided
   d) Agree
   e) Strongly agree

G) perform relevant and meaningful learner autonomy tasks?
   a) Strongly disagree
   b) Disagree
   c) Undecided
   d) Agree
   e) Strongly agree

....
Please provide the title of the course book below
....

9. To what extent do you agree that the course book you use with Year Three students encourages them to: (Please circle one letter from **a** to **e** and provide comments if need be.)

A) work cooperatively?
   a) Strongly disagree
   b) Disagree
   c) Undecided
   d) Agree
   e) Strongly agree

B) choose a variety of learning strategies?
   a) Strongly disagree
   b) Disagree
   c) Undecided
   d) Agree
   e) Strongly agree

C) develop critical thinking through problem-solving tasks?
   a) Strongly disagree
   b) Disagree
   c) Undecided
   d) Agree
   e) Strongly agree

D) assess themselves?
   a) Strongly disagree
   b) Disagree
   c) Undecided
   d) Agree
   e) Strongly agree

E) integrate educational technology into the teaching-learning process?
   a) Strongly disagree

b) Disagree
c) Undecided
d) Agree
e) Strongly agree

F) integrate language skills for in- and out-of-class projects?
a) Strongly disagree
b) Disagree
c) Undecided
d) Agree
e) Strongly agree

G) perform relevant and meaningful learner autonomy tasks?
a) Strongly disagree
b) Disagree
c) Undecided
d) Agree
e) Strongly agree

....
Please provide the title of the course book below
....

10. What type of tasks do you think should be included in course books to help EFL students to become independent learners? (Please circle the appropriate letters below. Provide comments if need be.)
a) Self-assessment tasks based on questionnaires
b) Mini-project tasks with the use of educational technology
c) Projects integrating all language skills
d) Real-life texts with tasks which aim to develop all language skills
e) Tasks connected with reflecting on learning sheets
f) Tasks based on learning strategy identification sheets
g) Video/film-based tasks
h) Other ....
....

11. How often do you develop pedagogical tasks for your students? (Please circle one letter from **a** to **e** and provide comments if need be.)
a) Never
b) Rarely
c) From time to time
d) Usually
e) Always
....

12. How often do you design tasks aimed at fostering your students' autonomy? (Please circle one letter from **a** to **e**. Provide comments if need be.)

a) Never
b) Rarely
c) From time to time
d) Usually
e) Always

....

13. Can you think of any problems that prevent you from fostering learner autonomy in your classroom? (Please write your opinion below.)

....
....
....

II. Profile of the Respondent

1. **What is your gender?** (Please circle one letter below.)
   a) male   b) female

2. **How old are you?** (Please put the number in the space provided below.)
....

3. **What teaching qualification(s) do you have?** (Please provide the name e.g. *MA in TEFL* in the space provided below.)
....

4. **How many years have you been working as a teacher?** (Please put the number in the space provided below.)
....

5. **What's your employment status as a teacher?** (Please circle one letter from **a** to **c**.)
   a) full time
   b) part time (less than 50% of full time hours)
   c) part time (more than 50% of full time hours)

APPENDIX D

ELT Course Book Evaluation Sheet

General Appearance, Layout and Design
(Is the course book attractive and suitable for secondary school students?)

Methodology
(Is the methodology appropriate for young adult learners? Does the course book promote learner-centred instruction? Does the course book promote communicative methodology? Does the course book promote task-based instruction?)

Language Content and Skills
(Does the course book help to develop communicative competence? Is there a balance of skills?)

Topics
(Are the topics realistic, appealing, relevant, challenging and controversial?)

Activities and Tasks
(Are the activities/tasks interesting, varied, engaging, challenging and sufficient? Do they promote meaningful communication, skills integration, problem-solving, creativity and different types of classroom work? Are they conducive to the internalisation of newly introduced language? Are the tasks authentic, complex and purposeful?)

The Matura Examination
(Does the book help students to be prepared for the Matura examination? How?)

Learner Autonomy Development
(Does the course book promote learner autonomy development? Does the course book encourage students to choose a variety of learning strategies, develop critical thinking, assess themselves, integrate educational technology into the teaching-learning process and integrate language skills for in- and out-of-class projects?)

Other Comments

SUBJECT INDEX

A
accommodation 85, 93
approach
   classroom-related 22, 55-62
   communicative 48-49, 71, 109
   focus-on-form 87-88
   genre-based 100-101
   learner-related 51-55
   modular 103
   resource-related 22, 62-71
   technology-related 22, 71-76
   unit 103
assessment
   formative 60, 61, 103
   interactive formative 60
   peer 61
   planned formative 60
   self- 58-62
   summative 61
assimilation 93, 111
assisted performance 41, 42
authenticity
   task 109-113
autonomy
   learner 18, 19, 27-29
   personal 46-47
   teacher 202-203

B
backwash effect 79, 120
behaviourism 31, 48

C
centres
   controlled-access 64
   drop-in 64
   open-access 64
   programmed learning 48, 64
   self-access learning 63-65
   study 64
classroom
   management 203-204, 225
   metaphors 225-227
   setting 224-227
collaboration 21, 35, 43-45, 49, 62, 78, 105, 116, 144, 196, 217, 225, 229
collectivism 56
communities of practice 209, 210, 211, 212, 217, 231, 251, 250, 251
competence
   communicative 86-87
   grammatical 86
   illocutionary 86, 87
   sociolinguistic 86
   textual 86
connectivity 84-86
constructivism
   endogenous 33
   exogenous 33
   progressive 32
   psychological, 33
   social 21-22, 33, 70
convenience sampling 141, 142, 143
cooperation 36, 42, 43, 52, 113, 143, 144
co-teaching 57
course books
   adaptation 122-124, 212, 230
   evaluation 228-229, 231
creativity 73, 224

D
decision-making 18, 27, 43, 53, 55, 56-58, 61, 73, 107, 188, 204, 217, 232
deschooling 45, 46
development
   cognitive 35-37, 93
   psychosocial 34

developmental psychology 34-45
differentiation 94, 95
discourse 87, 225

E
empowerment 56-58
engagement 55, 56, 58, 66, 91, 97, 111, 112-113, 115, 135, 149, 198, 223
    modes of 112-113
equilibration 93
European language portfolio 60-61
examination-orientated language education 127-128
exploitability 96-100

F
feedback 41, 53, 57, 61, 70, 75, 103, 196, 212, 222, 224, 227-228, 229, 230, 232

G
graded readers 25, 68, 153, 154, 155

I
inclusion 94, 95
individualisation 48, 94-95
input
    comprehensible 39, 71, 234
    finely-tuned 216
    roughly-tuned 216
instruction
    examination-orientated language 127-128, 198-199
    student-centred 55
    task-based language 107
    task-supported language 107
intention
    communicative 110
    informative 110
interaction
    interpersonal 38-39
    intrapersonal 38
    social 37-40

interlanguage 39, 215
internalisation 38
intertextuality 80, 101

J
journals 131, 142-144

K
knowledge
    declarative 43, 65
    explicit 65
    implicit 65
    procedural 43, 65

L
language
    acquisition 32, 39, 40, 53, 67, 92, 102, 111, 124, 217, 249, 250
leadership 43, 44, 205, 209
learner
    autonomous 29-31
    centeredness 31, 55
    identity 37, 56
    needs 127, 213
learning
    blended 72, 75, 76
    collaborative 21, 43, 44, 75, 193, 225, 232, 250
    computer-assisted language 71
    experiential 34, 72
    lifelong 19, 26, 189
    self-directed 24, 63
    transformative 45
learning styles 55
learning community 19, 56
literacy 73, 74, 75, 82, 113, 191

M
materials
    ELT 24, 122
    instructional 15, 22, 25, 78, 79, 103, 104, 199, 200, 206, 207, 210, 217, 232

self-access, 65-71
technology-based 75, 76, 193, 194
Matura examination 14, 79, 119, 120, 121, 126, 127, 140, 155, 156, 157, 158, 159, 165, 190, 192, 193, 203, 249
mediation 35, 40-41, 42, 49, 78
metacognition 28
methods
   qualitative 126, 130-133, 144, 147, 148, 171, 247
   quantitative, 126, 130-133, 141, 142, 144, 147, 148, 167, 171, 194, 247
modalities 81, 82, 217
motivation
   extrinsic 116
   intrinsic 45, 50, 55, 85, 113, 116
multiword units 89

N
needs
   objective 213
   subjective 213
   target 213
negotiation
   interactive 38-39
   meaning 35, 40, 49, 78, 103, 223
   personal 38, 205
   procedural 38-39, 205

O
output hypothesis 39-40

P
personal growth 45
personalisation 23, 84, 94-96, 122, 192, 230
pilot study 23, 126, 133-138, 141, 142, 143, 181, 188, 192, 194, 251
plurilingualism 60
power distance 56

problem-solving 22, 35, 42, 43-45, 49, 52, 53, 78, 98, 106, 107, 109, 161, 168, 175, 178, 191, 222, 231
processing
   semantic 39
   syntactic 40
professional development 200, 201, 209, 212, 248, 249
project method 45
purposefulness 23, 116, 123

R
rationalism 32
reciprocity 41
reflection
   critical 18, 26, 27, 59, 129, 188
   self- 21, 242

S
scaffolding
   game-like 41
   sequential 41
   vertical 41
schemata 85, 111, 112
self-concept 44, 189
self-esteem 44, 55, 76, 188, 189, 196, 221
self-instruction 18, 50
social constructionism 32
social semiotics 81
strategies
   affective 52, 54
   cognitive 28, 54
   communication 112
   metacognitive 52, 54
   social 52, 54
structural cognitive modifiability 210
suitability
   content 23, 84, 91-93
   language 23, 84, 86-90
   personalisation 23, 84, 94-96

syllabus
   negotiation 57-58
   proportional 127

T

Task
   complexity 113-115
   demands 114-115
   goals 212, 213-215
   procedures 212, 221-222
   support 114
tasks
   complex 20, 22, 24, 40, 44, 65, 82, 104, 108, 113- 115, 121, 124, 129, 162, 195, 198, 207, 209, 224, 246
   content-related 216-217, 234
   learning-related 216-217, 234
   pedagogical 20, 21, 22, 23, 24, 79, 80, 84, 96, 103, 106, 108, 114, 123, 124, 125, 128, 165, 193, 194, 195, 199, 206
teacher roles 212, 222-224
technology
   computer 13, 71, 113, 155, 179
   educational 22, 71-76, 73, 78, 91, 119, 121, 123, 137, 160, 161, 162, 163, 164, 165, 167, 168, 174, 175, 176, 177, 178, 179, 190, 193, 196, 214, 222, 226
texts
   authentic 21, 65-68, 80, 193, 225
   expository 100, 102
   multimodal 23, 82-83, 85, 92, 99, 104
   narrative 86, 100, 102
textuality 80, 101
thematic coding 131
thinking
   critical 40, 61, 74, 97, 102, 137, 154, 160, 161, 162, 163, 164, 168, 174, 175, 176, 177, 178, 179, 193, 196, 217

   reflective 210, 211
thinking routines 97-99
topicality 91-92, 101
transaction 38, 68
triangulation 130

V

variety 84, 100-103
vocabulary
   active 89
   passive 89

Z

zone of proximal development 35-37, 43, 94, 96

www.ingramcontent.com/pod-product-compliance
Lightning Source LLC
Chambersburg PA
CBHW072022240426
43667CB00044B/2047